TECHNIQUE IN CHESS

BY

GERALD ABRAHAMS, M.A. (Oxon.)
Barrister at Law

Author of
Teach Yourself Chess
The Chess Mind, etc., etc.

Dover Publications, Inc.
New York

Published in Canada by General Publishing Company, Ltd., 30 Lesmill Road, Don Mills, Toronto, Ontario.
Published in the United Kingdom by Constable and Company, Ltd., 10 Orange Street, London WC 2.

This Dover edition, first published in 1973, is an unabridged and corrected republication of the work originally published by G. Bell and Sons, Ltd., in 1961. This edition is published by special arrangement with G. Bell and Sons, Ltd.

International Standard Book Number: 0-486-22953-X
Library of Congress Catalog Card Number: 73-77379

Manufactured in the United States of America
Dover Publications, Inc.
180 Varick Street
New York, N. Y. 10014

CONTENTS

A WORD ON NOTATION

I have normally used the Staunton (or English) notation, but in order to avoid ambiguities have made occasional use of the algebraic (or continental). The important difference between the two systems is that the user of the continental one is always looking at the board from White's side. From White's left the files are abcdefgh and from White's side to Black's side the ranks are 12345678. Thus White's K1 is e1. Black's K1 (even when Black is recording his move) is e8.

The Forsyth notation, which I have also used, is a great economy in the presentation of positions. One looks at the board from White's side and reads it as one reads a book, from left to right and down the page: *starting at Black's back row*, and treating each line as a collection of spaces, or pieces and spaces. White pieces are indicated by capitals, Black by small letters, spaces by the number of consecutive empty squares as they occur on each line.

Thus if Black's King is on Black's King's square, stalemated by a White pawn at White's K7 and White King at K6, the Forsyth description is 4k3, 4P3, 4K3, 8, 8, 8, 8, 8, (or, for the last five lines, 40). Let the reader try the following:

32, 5p2, 6RB, 1K2p3, 3k4

If he gets it right he will find that he has Diagram 1 in this book.

PART ONE: INTRODUCTORY

CHAPTER I
DESCRIPTION OF TECHNIQUE

FREQUENTLY an annotator of Chess concludes his review of a game, or a line of play, with the expression 'the rest is a matter of technique'. I have also seen such comments as 'X demonstrated the superiority of his technique'. On occasion I have failed to understand what a writer had in mind when he used this language, if, indeed, he had anything in mind. On other occasions (quite rare ones) I have seen the term 'technique' (as I thought) usefully employed. But it is never easy to use, whether inside or outside Chess.

The semantic difficulty of the word, as well as the importance of the features of Chess that it connotes, encouraged me to give some talks, over the air, on Points of Technique. A not unfavourable response has made me feel the desirability of a book on the subject; not a definitive treatise, which would be a difficult undertaking even for the best equipped, but an essay in the presentation of some specific methods of play, and some particular pieces of knowledge and advice, that should be useful to a student of the game at many stages and levels of study.

I have had difficulty in the isolation of what may properly be called technical activity in Chess from those processes of direct seeing and thinking that are the essential operations of the Chess mind in action. But at least I have satisfied myself that some processes are nearer to the technical than others. A brilliant study by Réti (Diagram 1) may serve to illustrate what I mean.

This problem is solved by the perception of a possibility that is not easy to see on the part of any one obsessed by the conventional values of the pieces.

1 R—Q3 ch   K—K8   2 R—KB3!

Study by Réti
1   (Corrected by Chéron)

White to play and win

If now

2 ....   K—Q8   3 B—Kt4 wins

Hidden in the marble is a mate (R—Q3) if the pawn is promoted.
If instead

2 ....   K—Q7   3 B—B1 wins

because if 3 .... P—K8 = Q, 4 R—Q3 mate.

But, instead of P—K8, let Black play

3 ....   P × B (= Q)

then

4 R × Q   K—K6   5 K—B2   P—B6

and we are concerned with the perception of moves very different
in quality or richness from the imaginative idea involved in the
earlier moves.

At this point White must not play 6 K—Q1 because then 6 ....
P—B7 draws (e.g. 7 R—R1, K—B6; 8 R—B1, K—K6 and White
can do nothing).   Correct at move 6 is R—K1 ch.

There could follow

6 ....   K—B7   8 K—K3   P—B7
7 K—Q2   K—Kt7   9 R—K2 wins

Alternatively

6 ....   K—B5   8 R—KB1   K—B6
7 K—Q2   P—B7   9 K—Q3

a typical *zugzwang*; compulsion of the defender to move and lose.

That set of variations is something that can be seen by the naked eye. But it can also be classified as a typical method of play, and included among the pieces of knowledge that have accumulated around the promotion of pawns.

It may, or may not, be technique; but, at least, the difference between this play and the early play indicates the direction in which we should look for technique; viz. in familiar purposive methods of play without speculation; in the knowledge of the functions and resources of pieces and pawns that a player acquires in play, and which, being acquired, save some efforts of concentration, releasing the energy of the player for coping with more difficult problems. So applied, the word 'technique' will at least be useful to describe some phases of play (early and late) and some instances of error. In the following pages it may well be that the reader will benefit a little bit by a heightened awareness of aspects of the game that he knows but insufficiently values.[1]

Primarily this collection of examples of methods of play is designed to help the novice. That is why many of the examples and analyses are elementary. But I have yet to meet the good player who cannot benefit from dwelling on the relatively elementary. Indeed, good players are capable, especially in middle game complications, of losing sight of the technical signposts.

[1] The reader may have seen the Réti study with the Rook at a3—not g3. Having seen Chéron's correction I find that the original is 'cooked' (i.e. has an alternative solution—evidently a flaw). Chéron has cleverly eliminated this.

The reader can learn something from the cook. Place the Rook on a3 and try the following:

1	B—Kt4	K moves	3 K—B1	P—B6
2	B×P	K×B	4 R—R2 ch	

If

4	....	K—K6	6 R—R3 ch wins.	
5	K—Q1	P—B7		

If

4	....	K—K8	8 R—Kt8 ch	K—B8
5	R—R8	P—B7	9 R—KB8	K—Kt7
6	R—K8 ch	K—B8	10 K—K2 wins.	
7	K—Q2	K—Kt7		

Technically (or tactically) interesting is the need to draw the Black King (by moves 3 and 4) to the first rank. If e.g. 3 R—R8, P—B6; 4 K—B2, P—B7; 5 R—K8 ch, K—B6, draws. In this variation 4 R—K8 ch would be met by 4 .... K—Q7.

This analysis does not diminish the relevance of Réti's study to the text.

2

White to play

In point is Diagram 2 showing a position from a tournament game between good players.

White played P—KKt4 and, though he eventually won, he was playing badly in doing so: for after 1 .... P—KKt3; 2 P × P, R × R; 3 K × R, P × P; 4 B × P, Q—B8 ch; 5 K—R2, Q—B5 ch; 6 Q × Q, P × Q; and Black has all the technical resources that are available to a Knight among pawns. White was insufficiently 'technique-conscious'. Had he thought, he would have found some such move as 1 R—KB1. If 1 .... R × P; 2 B—R3 (not 2 B × P, R—R7 ch); 2 .... Q—K1; 3 P—KKt4, R—R5; 4 Q—B2! Good tactics, but also good technique: a fairly elementary precaution against a

3   Marshall—Schlechter
(San Sebastian 1911)

Black to play

fairly obvious danger. This study demonstrates, if nothing else, that good players can afford to think about open lines, etc. It also carries a general technical lesson. Don't liquidate advantages unless you can see a clear winning endgame.

A different error is a surprising one on the part of the great Schlechter, whose play, from the Diagram 3 position, suggests that at that moment he was not 'technique-conscious', nor aware of a quite familiar winning process available to him.

The actual play was: 1 .... K—K5; 2 K—B2, K—Q6; 3 K—B3, P—Kt4; 4 K—B2, K—K5; 5 K—K2, K—B5; 6 K—B2, K—Kt5; 7 K—Kt2, P—R5; 8 P—R3 ch, and the game was drawn.

Correct, and unanswerable, is: 1 .... K—Kt5; 2 K—B1, K—R6; 3 K—Kt1, P—R5; 4 K—R1, P—Kt4; 5 K—Kt1, P—Kt5; 6 K—R1, P—Kt6; 7 P × P, P × P; 8 K—Kt1, P—Kt7, wins.

The error may be described as a failure to see. It may also be said that a player with technical experience, even with a fraction of Schlechter's technical experience, would be aware that King and two pawns in that type of position can defeat King and one pawn. Given that awareness, the calculation would be easy.

In this book, without attempting any dogmatic definition, I have accumulated a number of examples that are calculated to make the reader 'technique-conscious'. I add the warning that sign-posts are not useful to anyone unless he can see his own way with some clarity.

Many of the studies are from the endgames: not because there is no technique elsewhere, but because many of the simple methods of exploitation of the functions of pieces are only isolated in the endgame. I also deal with some points from the earlier game, i.e. before advantages have crystallised. But these are fewer because the earlier game is usually too dynamic for technical valuations.

In neither field have I attempted any exhaustive treatment. For endgames, there are great manuals in existence, such as Fine's *Basic Chess Endings* and Chéron's inestimable and brilliant compilation, *Lehr- und Handbuch der Endspiele*. For the earlier game, Capablanca, Euwe, Znosko-Borovski, Tarrasch, Tartakover and Nimzovitch (to name but a few) have provided a magnificent library.

The name of Nimzovitch is particularly important because that name embodies a danger. The greatness of that master consists, of course, in those imaginative powers that made him the Crown Prince of Chess, even when Alekhine was its Kaiser. In his theoretical writings, however, he overestimated the utility of many classifications he had made, of types of attacking and defensive manœuvres. In this he was following the great, but misleading, example of Lasker, who also sought to find a mathematical logic for Chess, but who, when asked how he found a certain winning move, confessed 'I just saw it. That's all.' How else can one account for such a piece of play as Nimzovitch's brilliant stroke in the position shown in Diagram 4 (1 P—B3, Q × P; 2 Kt—Q7!).

4   Nimzovitch (White)

White wins

You may say that 1 P—B3 'cuts-off' a line of action, or 'interferes', and that the capture creates a 'battery' in White's favour. But what talk of batteries and interferences would help any player to see what a Chess genius saw?

The important criticism of Nimzovitch and Lasker is that a 'vocabulary' is not necessarily helpful. Certain phrases like 'blockade', 'over-protection', 'cut-off King', 'opposition', 'backward pawn', 'hanging pawns', '*zugzwang*', are useful because they help to draw the attention of the player to important methods of play. Such a word as 'outpost' may or may not be useful (they are not all good). But many other expressions are evidently useless. A phrase like 'restricted advance' does not offer any guide to the selection of a move by way of 'restricted advance' in preference to 'full expansion', or whatever expression describes the longer move. Again, the pawn's 'lust to expand' (a rare instance of 'pathetic fallacy' in Chess) does not help in the decision whether or not to advance. At best these phrases describe moves in the way that classifications in rhetoric describe verbal effects. But the man who has to give an order to other men is not assisted by being told to speak in the imperative. The situation makes him aware how he should behave. The description is an unnecessary self-consciousness.

In this book, then, I have avoided terms which merely describe movements without isolating any useful, recurring, method of play. Indeed, I have concentrated on the exposition of methods without concerning the reader overmuch with terminology.

For me it follows that, while agreeing that Chess can be played methodically, I must strenuously deny that there is any 'system' for Chess. Common sense, to a degree; logic within limits; but everything subordinate to the task of seeing what can be done. For this reason, and also in order to emphasise the limits of my own purpose, I call this book, not 'The Technique of Chess', but *Technique in Chess*. The selection of examples has been arbitrary, even accidental. I only claim, for all and each of them, that they may prove useful in the way that good work, being seen and studied, inspires students to good efforts.

Tentatively, in order to assist myself in the isolation of examples, I have adopted an heuristic description of technique—awareness of the functions of the pieces and of their peculiar resources in the geometry of the Chess board: and methods of exploiting these things in recurring situations.

Thus the first thing a player learns is the powers of the pieces as stated in the rules of the game. But when he has learned the powers, he requires to be shown (unless he be gifted with genius) some special things that pieces can do: e.g. the fork, the pin, etc. This is very elementary technique. Less elementary are some mating processes, processes of pawn promotion, etc. More advanced are, in the early game, the importance of open files, and open lines generally, and examples of their exploitation; in the later game, the importance of having a move to lose, etc.

Technique includes both the simple attacking of a pawn or piece, or the defending of it, and the recognition, without effort, that an immediate recapture is not necessary, an apparent attack not effective, or that an apparent defence is not adequate. If I play

   1 P—Q4   P—Q4   2 P—QB4

and am aware that 2 .... P × P does not really win a pawn, I am possessed of technical knowledge. (Also the thing is clearly visible: 2 .... P × P. If I want it back, 3 Q—R4 ch, Kt—B3. And now, not immediately 4 Q × P, Q × P; but 4 P—K3 and the Black pawn must fall.)

More advanced is such knowledge as the following:

| 1 P—Q4 | P—Q4 | 3 Kt—QB3 | Kt—KB3 |
| 2 P—QB4 | P—K3 | 4 B—Kt5 | QKt—Q2 |

Can I win a pawn now because the Knight is pinned?

| 5 P×P | P×P | 6 Kt×P |

The answer is 6 .... Kt×Kt, and 7 B×Q is avenged gorily with
7 .... B—Kt5 ch.

This is something 'visible' to the good Chess eye. It is also
learnable, a piece of useful knowledge, a part of one's equipment:
technique in fact.

Technique may be described epigrammatically as what you do
not need to think about. Just as the good pianist does not fumble
for keys, so the equipped Chess player does not laboriously work
out the obvious sequences of capture and recapture: pawn advance
—King move, etc.

In this connection it is obviously necessary to take into account
the factor of 'distance'. A move may be 'technical' at the moment
when it is made. Yet to the player seeing it at the end of a sequence
it may have involved an imaginative effort, it may be an idea.
Interesting is the following position (Diagram 5):

Tieplov—Balkin
5   (Moscow, 1959)

Black has played

15 ....   Kt—B5
There followed:

16 Q—K3   Q × P   17 Q—B5
This is a failure to see something.
Correct is

17 B × Kt   B × Kt   19 R × Q   P × B
18 Q × B   Q × Q   20 B—Q5 winning.
Black takes advantage prettily:

17 Q—B5   B × Kt   19 K—R1   Q × Kt!
18 QR—Q1   Kt—R6 ch
Now this nineteenth move, at short range, is familiar enough
to be called a technical move. At a distance it is a clever 'idea'.

A simpler illustration is from a game between the author (White)
and R. J. Broadbent:

8, 6p1, 16, 2pbk3, B5P1, rP3P1P, 1K1R4.

This position is, incidentally, of technical interest, because the
situation of the Black Rook is the result of an indirect guarding of
a pawn. When White played B × P at a7, Black, with R—R1, regained a pawn at a2. But meanwhile B—B5 enabled that Rook
to be imprisoned.

However, the feature in present point is the play that took place,
many moves later, in the Forsyth position:

36 ....   R × B   38 P × R   K—B6
37 R × B ch   K × R
And this is a threat to win by K—Q7, which must be countered
by 39 K—B1 (which wins). That K—B1 is 'technical', yet it had
to be seen ahead, in conjunction with Black's threat; at the latest
when White moved to attack the Black Rook.

This kind of apprehension is of ideas: but it is also a manifestation of a 'latent technique': an awareness of the resources of the
pieces. If that awareness is, so to speak, awake, the task of seeing
lines of play is easier, and errors are less likely.

Yet the frequent occurrence of elementary oversights shows that
one's technique is not always in action; or always adequate. Here
are a few examples. From the first World Championship match
between Botvinnik and Tal, the position in Diagram 6 arose after
Tal had played 25 Kt—R5. In this position there are many technical matters of which no one would be better aware than Botvinnik.
The pressure on the Queen's file is intense; and Black's Knight at
f6 is tied to the defence of the Knight at d7. Some relief of pressure could be obtained if the Kt from h5 exchanged itself at f6.

That is why Botvinnik played 25 .... B—Kt3. In doing so he made a bad error. He had overlooked an elementary manœuvre which is so familiar as almost to be technical. 26 R × Kt ch, Kt × R; 27 R × Kt ch, K × R; 28 Kt—B6 ch, K—Q3. 29 Kt × R.

White has won two minor pieces for a Rook.[1]

6   Tal—Botvinnik

The continuation is not without technical interest: 29 .... R—QB4; 30 Kt—R6, P—B3; 31 Kt—Kt4, B × P; 32 Kt × BP, B × B.

Now here a bad player might play 33 Kt—K4 ch, K—Q4; 34 Kt × R, expecting K × R, after which he would recapture the Bishop. This is rendered impossible by the *zwischenzug* (or 'intervening move') 34 .... B—B5 ch, of which the result is that Black has now won two minor pieces for a Rook.

These things are seen by good players—overlooked by inferior (or tired) players. Awareness of possibilities of this type is part of technique. The technically well-equipped player knows where to look and what kind of phenomenon to look for.

When he is playing 'technically' he is, to that extent, relying on experience rather than intellect: he is exercising his habit system, not his vision. This reliance can be misplaced unless the habit system is marvellous indeed.

So, in a recent simultaneous exhibition at the B.B.C., that fine player Gligoric, playing Black against a strong British amateur (Littlewood), made the technically probable move and incurred serious disadvantage.

---

[1] An oversight of an elementary technical point is called a 'blunder'; but many players accuse themselves of blundering when they miss quite difficult points.

Littlewood—Gligoric

(From a Simultaneous
7   Display, January 1960)

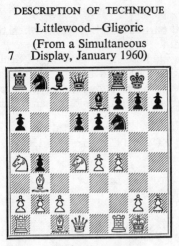

White to move

At the position in Diagram 7, White played 11 P—K5, P × P;
12 P × P; and Black who, had he been thinking, would have played
Kt—K5, actually made the normal-appearing move, 12 .... Kt—
Q4, which was met by the very effective 13 Kt—B5, threatening to
get rid of Black's useful Bishop. There followed: 13 .... P × Kt;
14 B × Kt, R—R2; 15 B—K3, R—Q2; 16 Kt—Kt6, R—B2; and
White had gained a splendid initiative, and some strategic advantages making for victory. (A later error by White reduced the game
to a draw.) Another way of looking at the position is to say that
'technically' the square f5 was a weak one; or that the pawn at e6
was called upon to exercise a double function. That kind of treatment is a strain on the notion of technique; those things are tactical
possibilities to be seen with the mind's eye.[1]

The essence of technique is that it is a labour saver. Knowledge
of elementary methods and basic strategic truths saves a player
from working through long sequences of moves. Let him 'know'
what is technically good or technically bad: 'know' what is technically possible and technically impossible.

[1] It may interest the reader to compare this diagram with Diagram
No. 168 on p. 165, which shows an experience of the author's against
a great master, who also overlooked (under the conditions of simultaneous play) the weakness of an empty square. Psychologically, empty
squares are harder to attend to than are occupied squares. A general
awareness of this truth is necessary to all players. The notion is, perhaps,
too vague to be called technical.

These things are particularly important when transition is being made to the endgame.

From a high level, here is Tal making a decision that can be called technically bad, because he exchanges a piece that would be very strong in the pawn endgame for a piece that happens to be tactically embarrassing in the middle game (Diagram 8).

8   Botvinnik—Tal
(World Championship 1960)

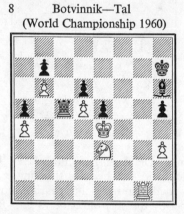

The play is of great interest:

42 Kt—B5	R—B5 ch	45 K—K2	R × P
43 K—Q3	R × P	46 Kt—K4	
44 Kt × P	R—Q5ch	(threatening a fork)	
46 .... K—R1		47 Kt—B6	
		(threatening mate)	

47	R—Q7 ch	49 R—Kt6	P—QR5
48 K—B3	R—Q1		

(This is the technical error. It were better to preserve the Bishop. This is one instance of the 'critical moment' in endgame play, or in transition to an endgame: the moment when one has to be aware of the methods of winning and the material necessary for victory, to say nothing of the resources of the opponent.)

50 R × B ch	K—Kt2	54 R—QR7	P—R6
51 R—R7 ch	K × Kt	55 P—Kt7	K—B4
52 R × KtP	R—Q6 ch	56 R × P	R × P
53 K—Kt2	R—QKt6		

and the endgame cannot be won by Black.

The above examples show, inter alia, the variety of situations in which specific methods or principles are learnable and useful. Anyone who has progressed in any degree will realise what the author means in saying that technique (whatever it is) is inexhaustible. To the searcher for examples the problem is one of selection from great quantities of Chess situations. Chess literature—new or old—offers a range of examples in which many classes of Chess player can find some some assistance appropriate to their needs. Many of the examples are very easy, some quite hard, some both hard and easy! There are thoughts that were 'ideas' and are now technical. These are very illuminating! But to some player or other, any example can be useful.

I add the following illustration of this thesis:

16, 4p3, 4p3, 4P3, 4Rpk1, 2K5, 8. This study by Peckover presents what looks like a loss. When White's Rook goes, technique indicates that White must be squeezed out of the defence. But to anyone who has seen endings with middle board stalemates, there occurs: 1 R—Q3, K—Kt7; 2 R—Q2 ch, P—B7; 3 K—Q3, K—Kt8; 4 R—Q1 ch, P—B8 (= Q) ch; 5 K—K3!, K—Kt7!; 6 R × Q, K × R; 7 K—B3 draws. This shows, as clearly as the first Réti study, the distinction between technique and idea. It also shows how ideas, being absorbed, can enlarge technique.

In conclusion, I would reiterate that (by reason of the richness of Chess) there is no unified body of doctrine that can be called Chess Technique. And there is no function of unity that can make the selection of examples other than arbitrary. Accordingly, whatever planning is attempted, the result can only be an aggregate of points of Technique. Whoever attempts any collection, it must remain a question, for the reader, of acquiring a large number of bits of knowledge. The better the Chess vision, the less necessary the learning. But the acquiring of ideas is a valuable experience at all stages of Chess, because in Chess we see the recurring miracle of intellectual experience, that, through being shown even old and familiar things, the talented ones are inspired to find new ideas of their own.

CHAPTER II

THE SCOPE AND USES OF TECHNIQUE: SOME INSTANCES OF METHOD

Most readers will be acquainted with Molière's Monsieur Jourdain who, when they began to teach him prose, discovered that he had been talking prose all his life without knowing it. Similarly, many Chess players have been using some Chess technique all their playing lives without being aware of the process. But that is not the end of the parallel. Just as good prose (a good technique of language) is recognisable but indefinable, so are the techniques of many Arts and Sciences, including Chess.

Who can isolate, in the speech of an orator, his ideas, his feelings, his method? Is his lambent clarity a feature of the thought that he utters and creates? Or is it the effect of some special device, or architectonic, that he (consciously or unconsciously) employs? Lord Macaulay, himself one of the greatest masters of prose that ever lived, said that grammarians and rhetoricians derive their rules from the great performances, and that one cannot criticise the great performances as instances of the application of rules.

Something like this assessment can be made of the smooth Chess performances of such players as Capablanca or Rubinstein. Not here an application of technique, but here a source of technique. In that analysis lies the refutation of the claim, suggested (rather than definitely made) by no less than Emanuel Lasker, that fine combinative movements can be deduced from rules. That matter is illustrated in the text. Suffice it here to say that for Chess technique more modest claims should be made. But first let us find it.

In Chess there are no formulae corresponding to the calculation by which the Draughts player can work out whether or not he has the last move.[1]

At a lower level, in card games and crossword puzzles for example, one discerns the technical equipment readily. The crossword

---

[1] Interesting are those 'match' games in which the player has to capture last or avoid capturing last. A use of binary numeration solves the problem. (See Northrop: *Riddles in Mathematics*, for the analysis.)

solver, when he sees the expression 'large number', is ready with his M or D; the Bridge player knows about finessing, leading to weakness, cross-ruffing, squeezing, etc., and he does arithmetic. In activities involving the body—athletics and the manual aspects of music—devices are learned and taught. But where the essence of activity is the play of ideas, then one cannot easily distinguish between the intuition of the Scientist or Artist and those ancillaries that facilitate his task.

Nevertheless, in all the mental activities some rules are discernible. In the case of Chess the difficulty is to discern any rules that are, at once, additional to the basic laws of the game, and distinguishable from ideas in the game. To the average good player—indeed to any player who makes Chess into more than a game of chance —the effort, and the process, is one of seeing—*vision*. Given the formal powers of the pieces, one looks to see what one can achieve with them. One enters, as it were, into an argument with oneself (the Chess player's only opponent) about the effects of moves— the intention, or threat, the refutation of this, the reply to the refutation, other approaches to the question, and so on. To the operational activities that are, in play, worked out in such series of consequences, with all the perceptible variations, one applies the term *tactics*. But frequently the board is too opaque, the position insufficiently translucent, for clear decisive analysis— or for definitely effective operations. Then other aspects of mind undertake control. To this, more general, planning about the future of the game—the thoughts that are dominant when there is nothing immediate to think about—we give the name *strategy*. Do not these two functions, it may be asked, exhaust the Chess activity? What room is left for anything called Technique?

Yet good players use the term frequently. At Bad Gastein in 1948, that excellent master Canal described his error in the annexed position (Diagram 9) as a 'technical error', because it had to do with 'pinning'. Not all masters would agree that Lundin's move, which took advantage of Canal's error, was merely, or essentially, technical.

From the same tournament a possibility that occurred to the author, and which possesses technical features, was described (by the same master Canal) as essentially tactical (Diagram 10).

The technical aspect is the relief of a pin by the removal of the major piece with an attack on some pawn or piece. Cognate is a position (Diagram 11) in which that very strong Israeli player,

Point of Technique
Lundin—Canal
9   (Bad Gastein, 1948)

Tactical Point, or
10   *Technical?*

Black plays 15 .... R—K1;
allowing 16 Q—B4, creating a
pin.   Correct is 15 .... Kt—Q4.

Black can unpin with 1 ....
QR—K1. If 2 P×P, Q×P;
3 Q×Q, R×Q; 4 P—B7, R—B1;
5 R—Q1, K—B1!

Extrication from Pin
Persitz—Czerniak
11   (Tel-Aviv, 1956)

22 Q—B2, R—QB1; 23 Kt×B, Q×Kt; 24 Q—Q3, Q×Q;
25 R×Q, Kt×Kt; 26 B×Kt, P—Q5; 27 R—B4, with
superiority.

Persitz, unpinned a Knight by removing, with threats, the major
piece against which the minor piece was pinned.[1]

[1] Here is a similar idea at an early stage of the game (from a Queen's
Gambit Accepted) 1 P—Q4, P—Q4; 2 P—QB4, P—QB3; 3 Kt—QB3,
Kt—KB3; 4 Kt—KB3, P×P; 5 P—KKt3, B—B4; 6 B—Kt2, P—K3;
7 0—0, QKt—Q2; 8 B—Kt5, P—KR3; 9 B×Kt, Kt×B; 10 Kt—K5,

These moves can be described as instances of *zwischenzug*—intervening move—but that is only an aesthetic classification. This type of move is usually seen as a variation in a tactical line of play. Occurrences like this are frequent. The simple form occurs whenever it is desirable to delay a recapture in order to impede the opponent or safeguard oneself. However, without affirming or denying Signor Canal's terminology, I mention it in order to show the semantic difficulties. No harm is done if, in seeking technique, the student enjoys the contemplation of some clever tactical ideas.

The next diagram shows the difficulty of distinguishing between Technique and Strategy (Diagram 12).

12   *Technique or Strategy?*

By 5 P—Q4 (met by P—K3) White has prepared to attack the diagonal with 6 P—B4!

The opening moves were:

1 Kt—KB3	P—Q4	4 0—0	Kt—QB3
2 P—KKt3	B—B4	5 P—Q4	P—K3
3 B—Kt2	P—B4	6 P—B4	

Black's third move is over-ambitious and shows a failure to appreciate the weakness of his long diagonal. White's 5th and 6th moves are technically right, as well as tactically and strategically good. That is to say, they express an appreciation of the right method of working against a weak centre. P—Q4 fixes Black's QP, blockades it, and P—QB4 directly attacks the diagonal.

Q—B2; 11 Q—R4, Kt—Q2; 12 Kt×QBP. This is possible because if 12 .... P—QKt4, White has (inter alia) 13 Q—R5.

Compare also the position: 4rk2,6kt1,3p4,8,4Kt3,8,2RK4,8. White can play 1 Kt×P, because in answer to R—Q1, there is 2 R—B8, meeting a pin with a counter-pin.

To revert to the question, how to distinguish Technique from Tactics and Strategy, I would suggest that one should seek something analogous to equipment with syntax in language, to equipment with the scales in music, i.e. to those equipments which save concentration, as the very use of familiar words saves thinking.

In Chess also there are mental economies. There is a certain scope for method, involving less thought than the planning of a particular game, and less effort than the perception of a tactical process. This method is not a rule, but an aggregate of bits of knowledge and equipment, and a skill with the pieces in the execution of specific processes.

Included in the equipment are some general statements derived from general experience. 'Let pawns capture towards the centre' —'Develop towards the centre'—'Don't move the same piece or pawn twice before development is complete'. (That is very good advice, though it is subject to overriding strategic considerations.) 'Bring out Knights before Bishops.' (The Bishop requires less development.) Again, 'Put your Rook on the line of his Queen, no matter how many other pieces intervene.' That doggerel jingle incorporates some experience. As a tactical or strategic decision it may be wrong because you may be bringing your Rook under a masked battery, or you may be placing it where it has less scope than elsewhere. A quite frequent error is the following. With R—K1 one pins a Knight (on e5) against a Queen (on e7). Comes Kt—B6 ch and the exchange is lost. But the awareness of whatever advantage there may be in the pinning of minor pieces, even remotely, against the Queen, is (for what it is worth) part of technique. Other empirical statements may be mentioned. 'Don't pin your opponent's KKt before he has castled King's side.' This again, is not to be treated as a dogmatic principle. In a specific position the pinning may be very good, even if he hasn't castled. (In some openings, e.g. Caro Kahn, it is Black's solution to the problem of developing the QB.) On the other hand, the move may be bad even if the opponent has castled. (One possibility is that he may play Kt × KP with a mating threat.) Another dictum is: 'Don't pursue Queen's side pawns, especially with the Queen'. (The idea is that an important piece is taken too far from the scene of central or King's side action.) Examples are numerous of the relevance, and irrelevance, of this proposition. Again, the late F. D. Yates, a great ornament of British Chess, used to describe P—KB4 as 'a move that is always too early'. That did not prevent him from playing it often enough. On occasion he played it too early for his opponent!

Maxims can be multiplied. Steinitz said: 'Make your King a fighting piece'; and very often King moves towards the centre are essential.

One dangerous thought is: 'Don't miss a check: it might be mate.' This is worth mentioning because it is at least equally wise to reserve checks. Diagram 13 shows a position from which Bobby Fischer failed to defeat Tal precisely because he checked.

Fischer—Tal
(From the Candidates'
13   Tournament, 1959)

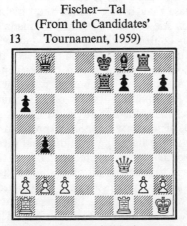

White to play his 22nd move

After 1 Q—B6 ch, R—Q2 Black got a defence mobilised. Instead, 1 QR—K1 (pinning a Rook!) wins. If in answer, 1 .... K—Q1; 2 Q—QB6; and now R—Q2 is unplayable because of R × BP. So much for maxims.

Little bits of learning like the above, therefore, are useful only in conjunction with a good knowledge of the functions of the pieces; nor could any collection of maxims be useful unless overloaded with qualifications. The maxims are distillations from the vague activity that players call Judgment—a certain appreciation of the tensions of a position, a sense of balance, a feeling for tempo. This is not a describable technique. But the player of good judgment can, at times, formulate useful general technical advice.

In this category I would include one piece of wisdom that many novices seem slow to appreciate, namely, the undesirability of leaving any set of squares that is relevant in the undisputed control of the opponent. Thus if your Black squares are vacant at d4, e3, f2, etc., and an opponent's Bishop or Queen or Knight can control them, then clearly it is undesirable to rid yourself of that piece of yours, the Black-squared Bishop, that might be mobilised to operate on those squares. This may be a point of strategy rather than technique. But it is valuable as an aspect of the general assessment to be made when one is considering the exchange of pieces. With experience there should develop an awareness of what pieces are most useful in specific pawn configurations. Too much guidance cannot be expected in the form of rules.

In the same class may be mentioned the obvious undesirability of having an open file (Rooks' files are frequent instances) which the opponent can control with his Rook, but which you cannot control with a Rook because his Bishop covers the square at the base. This kind of development can occur from Fianchetto developments after a Bishop has been exchanged for a Knight.

There are many comparable lessons of experience.

For his purposes the student is advised to think of technique as a bundle of methods of coping with practical problems that are frequent in play: methods in the handling of individual pieces, or groups of pieces, for purposes that are always recurring: from the mere guarding of an attacked piece, to the exploitation of slight endgame advantages.

Indeed, many tactical processes can be analysed into series of short technical processes. That is not to say that technical equipment will produce great ability in tactical play. The factors of concentration and ability to see slightly ahead are unteachable. But, given a modicum of ability, the mere knowledge of pins, etc., will take a player some small distance into the tactical field.

Diagram 14 illustrates this. The position was observed in a junior competition. (The virtue of Chess is that its beauties are not secluded in the enclaves of the mighty.) Black is in difficulties as great as anyone would encounter in the World Championship. His best move is probably R—Q1, after which P—QKt4 would embarrass him. However, he played 1 .... Kt—K1, and White replied 2 R—K6 ch compelling K—Q2. Now White has available moves that should be clear to anyone possessed of a little experience in the handling of the pieces.

3 R—B6 forcing R—QB1   5 B—Kt6
4 R—R6 forcing R—QR1

taking advantage of the pin and winning a pawn. Very, very little more than elementary technique was necessary for apprehension of this. But the clouds of futurity darkened the counsel of White, who played 3 K—B2 allowing Kt—Q3 and some defence.

Black is still under great pressure; and the Diagram is incidentally useful as illustrating what I call 'penetration'. This word is not in general use as a technical term in Chess, but it describes

14

what is happening when, through some wedge of pawns, or establishment of pieces, one player is operating aggressively inside the field that should be space available to his opponent. Not all penetrations are fatal. They can paralyse without killing. Indeed, the victim may recover. However, the notion is one to be borne in mind, and a player is wise who asks himself from time to time—'Where can my opponent penetrate?' E.g. 'In certain circumstances can he establish Rooks or Knights in my half of the board, or can he, with his control of lines (ranks, files or diagonals), limit my movements with threats and demonstrations of force?' The notion is the more important for the reason that, in every opening, a player who is trying to develop his own forces always leaves some avenue open to his opponent. If, for example, he presses his pawns to K4 and QB4, he concedes a good square for a Knight at the opponent's Q5. This only becomes serious if there is no compensation, e.g. if one player is left with an established piece that can only be shifted by its translation into a supported passed pawn, and the other player has no corresponding position of strength.

When such advantages are gained, victory from them can often be obtained by play that can be called technical, e.g. the obvious sweeping up of pawns. But as we saw in the example, a scintilla of vision is also required: and that makes processes hard to classify. Let it be said then, that technique can teach very elementary

tactics: but not everybody who is taught the functions of the pieces
(as distinct from their mere powers) is learning the ability to exploit his knowledge of them.

Technique is 'know-how' with various degrees of difficulty.

Here is a fairly elementary example. The beginner knows how
a King moves, and he knows how a Rook moves, and he knows
the meaning of Mate. But can he force mate with a King and
Rook against a lone King? Let the beginner place the Black King
on White's K8 (its own K1), White King on K6, White Rook on
K1. The method is: 1 R—QB1. If Black plays K—Q1, then
2 R—QB2 (or 3, 4, 5, 6). The Black King must return to K1, and
3 R—B8 is mate. That elementary manœuvre is one instance of
the principle of *zugzwang* (move compulsion) which is a feature of
Chess, especially of the endgame. The thing is also apprehensible
as a simple tactical process. But, in practice, this bit of method
becomes, as it were, a part of one's knowledge of the moves of the
pieces, part of an awareness of their functions, in addition to their
formal powers. The player whose knowledge of the Rook move
is adequate to the mating process above described will, with application, be able to force the opposing King from anywhere to the
back row, through the repetition of the *zugzwang* processs. Thereafter he will not, in assessing any position, have any doubt at all
as to the outcome of the game if it is reducible to King and Rook
against King. To that extent he has acquired technique.

Also part of technique are such processes as the laborious (though
not difficult) mate with Bishop and Knight, and the fact that two
Knights cannot force mate.[1] Differences of degree of difficulty
are illustrated by the fact that two Knights can force mate in some
situations where the defender has a pawn. This process, worked
out (but not invented) by Troitzki, can be called technical; but for
most players it requires all the concentration of difficult tactical play.

Technique, then, is characterised by degree of difficulty. At the
lower level we have seen elementary mating processes. But though
all losses are 'notional' mates (in the way that every death is a
heart-failure), the majority of lost games end before mate; particularly many where the advantage of one pawn is turned into
the advantage of a Queen. Here, in the processes of promoting
and defence against promotion, there is a good deal of undifficult,
but very important, technique. In point is appreciation of the

---

[1] The 'technique' of K, B and Knight *v.* King is to 'muster' the King
to a corner controlled by the Bishop. If one bears that in mind the
process becomes easier.

opposition, of the limitations of Bishops of opposite colour; and such pieces of knowledge as that two pawns on the 6th can defeat a Rook, and (as we shall see) that there are exceptions to this. Similarly the strange power of a BP to thwart a Queen.   Also in this category may be included the rule of the King within the square (I am inclined to agree with my lamented friend and pupil, Gordon Crown, that nobody relies on this: one 'sees' whether or not the King is within reach).   More important than an abstract rule such as this are studies in the capacities of minor (and major) pieces to cope with pawns that are advancing to promotion.

Many of these processes are easy, and some are hard.   Sometimes a brilliant idea (such as Réti's, diagrammed in the later text, p. 59) being apprehended, becomes part of technique.   Few of these ideas are as hard as the play of King and two Knights against King and pawn, and can be readily absorbed.   Indeed, they save labour.

Very interesting is a position reached by Botvinnik in a simultaneous exhibition, in which he appreciated the need for an unusual 'side-step'.   (Diagram 15.)

Botvinnik
(From a Simultaneous
15   Display, Moscow, 1945)

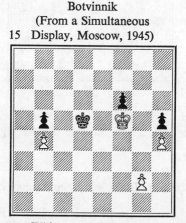

White to move and win

He thought, at the time of the game, that, with best defence, Black could draw.   Thus:

1 P—Kt4	P × P	5 P—R6	P—B5 ch
2 K × P	K—K5	6 K—Kt2	K—K7
3 P—R5	P—B4 ch	7 P—R7	P—B6 ch
4 K—Kt3	K—K6		

and Black promotes as quickly as White. Then he realised that, on move 4, he need not play his King to Kt3, but can play it to R3. If the Black pawn advances he can stop it when it reaches B7 by K—Kt2. If Black moves his King, White's pawn wins the promotion race because White uses at least one move less with his King than in the line first presented.

That point, and that manœuvre, being apprehended, they become part of learning, part of technique, part of the player's latent power of using his pieces.

A simple statement of the theme is presented in Diagram 16.

16

White to play and win

Here, obviously, a simple pawn race does not win. But White can turn the race into a winning one by altering the condition at the finish.

1 K—B2   K—R7
(otherwise K—Kt3 puts Black's King and pawn out of action).

2 K—B3   K—R6   3 K—B4   K—R5
Now 4 P—B4, P—K.4 ch, and 5 — not K—B3, but Botvinnik's 'side-step' — K—K3.
Now it is evident that Black's pawn advance will stop at Kt7 when White plays K—B2. Indeed, K—B2 followed by K—Kt1 is an immediate threat. Therefore,

5	K—R6	8 P—B7	P—Kt7
6 P—B5	P—Kt5	9 P—B8	=Q ch wins.
7 P—B6	P—Kt6		

The reader may work out for himself that this method would be valid if the White pawn in the diagram were at QKt2, but not if it were at QR2, Q2 or K2.

So ideas are absorbed into Chess and become 'method'. There is no limit to the difficulty of the processes that can become technical, so long as, being absorbed, they prove easier. Perhaps the essence of the 'technical device'—as distinct from general technical skill (which is really a judgment acquired in experience)—is its learnability. And many points of technique are sufficiently hard to see 'by the light of nature' to justify learning. Thus the player with King and Rook against King, Rook and Rook's pawn, in the next diagram (Diagram 17) may require to be told what the best square is for his King; far from the pawn or very near to it, but not on any middle squares. (So if, in the diagram position, the White King were at g5 and the Black pawn at a4, White must run for g2 in order to be safe.) The point is that if the King is at, say, f2 when the Black pawn is at a2, Black will win with R—R8: if R × P, R—R7 ch wins the Rook.

17

White to move and draw

1 K—Kt2.   Not 1 K—B2 (or Q2), R—R8;
2 R × P, R—R7 ch, wins

In this class are many studies, in the text, showing duels between pieces, especially those in which success is the promotion of a pawn or the prevention of promotion.

Some of these methods, having been shown in master play, or by analysts, become part of 'stock'. By way of contrast, there are ideas which are hard, and do not become part of ordinary equipment, though they operate to inspire other ideas. Many very great endgame compositions remain outside technique because of their individualities and difficulty. On this principle, one must also be chary of applying the term Technique to anything exceedingly difficult, however elemental it may appear. When Alekhine saved a game against Reshevsky in an ending of Rooks when he was two pawns down, the commentators said, '*Mit einer grossartigen technik gespielt*' (Diagram 18).

Reshevsky—Alekhine
18   (Avro, 1938)

Black to make his 42nd move

But I would rather say that he found resources with his great vision. The play is of great interest:

42	R—R7	45 R × P	P—R5
43 K—B3	R—R6 ch	46 P—Q5	
44 K—B2	R—Q6		

It may have been better to let this pawn fall, with R—QR5, and get the King side pawns moving.

46	P—R6	49 R—R5	R—Q7 ch
47 R—R7 ch	K—B3	50 K—B3	R—Q6 ch
48 R—R7	K—K4	51 K—K2	

Better is 51 K—Kt4. If then R—Q7; 52 P—Kt3 seems to win.

51	R—QKt6	52 K—B2

(P—R4 seems better, but Black with Rook and pawn on the seventh and able to attack the advancing pawns from the rear would not be helpless. In this variation, which is very difficult, the Black King can come forward, but the QP advances.)

52	R—Kt7 ch	55 K—R3	P—R7
53 K—Kt3	R—Kt6 ch	56 P—Q6 dis ch	
54 K—R4	R—Kt7		

(White judged that he could do nothing with the King side pawns in the present position. If e.g. 56 P—Kt4, K—B5; 57 P—Q6, R—Q7, and White is in *zugzwang*.)

| 56 .... | K × P | 57 P—Kt4 | K—B3! |

bringing it very cleverly to the aid of the QRP.

| 58 K—Kt3 | K—Kt3 | 60 P—R3 |
| 59 R—R8 | K—Kt4 | |

(Note—not 60 P—R4, R—Kt6 ch; 61 K—B4, R—Kt5 ch; 62 K—Kt5, R—R5 wins for Black!)

| 60 .... | K—Kt5 | 61 K—B4 | R—QB7! |

and now the threat to cut off the Rook is overwhelming. White cannot sacrifice with R × P because his pawns are insufficiently advanced.

| 62 R—Kt8 ch | K—B6 | 63 R—QR8 | K—Kt5 Drawn. |

To this ending there is more than technique, there is keen insight. Chéron points out that had White arranged his King at KR4 with pawns at KKt4 and KR3, he could have had a position similar to that won by Tarrasch against Tchigorin in 1893. In other words, 'learning' might have helped Reshevsky to win.

Similarly, many a piece of play by a master with elemental forces, winning, for example, with Rook and pawn against Bishop and pawn, is, perhaps, too hard to be called technical, though much may be learned from such efforts. So, too, if a position occurs with a very narrow margin of victory, for example, two Knights and pawn against Bishop or Knight, people speak of the 'technique' involved in preventing the minor piece from sacrificing itself for the pawn. But it seems more realistic to say that that process is exceedingly difficult tactics, beyond the scope of any stateable 'method'.

Of problems that present themselves, whether through a composer, or in a game (the source is immaterial), and which require great tactical insight for their solution, typical is the following composition by Kasparian (Diagram 19).

19 Study by Kasparian	20 Study by Rinck
	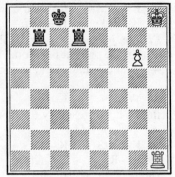
White to play and win	White to play and draw

The solution is

1 B—Kt5	P—Kt6 (best)	4 P—B8 (=Q)	R—Kt8 ch
2 R—Q2 ch	K—R8	5 R—Q1	R—Kt7
3 P—B7	R × B	(threatening mate)	

6 Q—R3 ch	R—R7	8 R—QKt2	R—R7
7 R—Q2!	R × Q	9 R—Kt1 mate	

That composition fully deserved the first prize that it won in a Russian competition in 1939.

By way of contrast, here (Diagram 20) is a pretty study by Rinck, which can be called practical because it involves resources that a player can find useful and should be aware of. Such a study is a contribution to technique.

The solution is

1 R—B1 ch	K—Kt1	4 R—R8 ch	K—Kt3
2 P—Kt7	R × P	5 R—R6 ch, etc.	
3 R—B8 ch	K—R2		

That perpetual check is of a kind not infrequent. Some elegant compositions have been created in which the position of Rooks enables the King to escape the perpetual, but the Rinck study expresses the normal inescapable perpetual check when the Rooks are 'engaged'.

Pursuant to that line of thought, many compositions by distinguished experts are included in this book—exhibiting ideas which may, or may not, be absorbable as technique. In any event they cannot fail to 'amuse and instruct'.

Relevant are many studies which, while not teaching a method, do serve to demonstrate that certain operations can be done.

Thus here is a study by Kopaev (Diagram 21) showing that in a proper setting Queen and Bishop can defeat Queen.

21	Study by Kopaev	22	Study by Keres

White to play and win	White to play and draw

1 Q—Q6	Q—R7 ch	5 B—K3 ch	K—Kt1
2 K—B8	K—Kt2	6 Q—Kt5 ch	K—B1
3 Q—B7 ch	K—R3	7 K—K7	Q—R7
4 Q—B6 ch	K—R2	(Q—R6 comes to nothing after B—B5.)	

8 Q—R6 ch	K—Kt1	11 Q—R7 ch	K—B1
9 B—R7 ch	K—B2	12 Q—R8 ch	Q—Kt1
10 B—Kt6 ch	K—Kt1	13 Q—B6 ch	

The variations in this study are immense, but it constitutes an object lesson (rather than a statement of method) and is near to the practicalities of Chess.

Also useful are studies showing unexpected features that can occur, such as the domination of major pieces (e.g. the Queen) by minor pieces; which will be illustrated.

At the most practical level some great players have shown the resources of the board in their compositions as well as in their play. Thus Diagram 22 is a study by Keres.

The instructive point is that White must not play the 'obvious' K—B4. This loses:

| 1 K—B4 | R—Kt7 | 3 R moves R—B7 ch |
| 2 R × P ch | K—R5 | |

then takes the RP with a standard winning position.

The draw is as follows:

1 K—B5. If now 1 .... R—Kt7; 2 R × P ch. If then 2 .... K—R5; 3 R—K4 guards the RP indirectly.

Therefore

| 2 .... | K × P | 4 K—R4 | R—Kt8 |
| 3 K—Kt5 | P—Kt6 | 5 R—R3 | |

and Black must return the Rook to Kt7.

Normally in Master Chess the element of technique is taken for granted; and what determines the play is the idea, the refinement or subtlety, whether learnable or merely to be enjoyed.

The following position (Diagram 23) is from actual play (between two Russian women). The technical aspect of the position is that King and Rook's pawn can draw against King and Rook if properly placed. Thus, if Black's King were at h1, and pawn at h2, clearly R × P for Black would draw. But that piece of knowledge is not enough. What move to make now? Good is K—R8! Rubtsova played 68 .... P—R6, and White with R—Kt3 created *zugzwang* and won.

Bikova—Rubtsova
23   (Moscow, 1958)

Black to play

If

69	R × P	71 K—Kt3
70 R × R	K—R8	(technique this) followed by

72 R—QR8

and Black is in a mating net.

In playing through the games of the best players, one becomes aware that a strong technical equipment is implicit in their play. In Diagram 24, giving the position reached between Gligoric and Keres in the Candidates' Tournament of 1959, the player of the

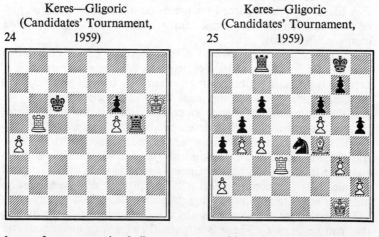

Keres—Gligoric
(Candidates' Tournament,
24   1959)

Keres—Gligoric
(Candidates' Tournament,
25   1959)

lesser forces contrived (it was not accidental) to liquidate dangerous pieces at the cost of a pawn and to retain some counterbalance to his opponent's advantage, and to be mobilised in the best way to ward off loss. He holds the KBP as a gauge. There followed: 62 R—K5, K—Kt2; 63 P—R5, K—R2; 64 P—R6, K—R1; 65 R—Kt5, K—R2; 66 R—R5, R—Kt8. Draw.

From earlier in the same game Diagram 25 shows play gaining a good square for a Knight at the cost of broken pawns.

30 K—Kt2	P × P	32 R × P	Kt—Kt4
31 R—Q4	Kt—B6		

A technical feature is that the Knight is here inferior to the Bishop and so cannot win a pawn in the variation played. If 33 .... Kt × P; 33 B—Q2 leaves the Knight without a move.

The literature of master Chess is rich in exploitations that are instructive. But most of them are characterised by more than technique. That is another way of saying that technique is not enough. To start with a simple example. Imagine play ending with the gain of a piece by one player on one side of the board among pawns, leaving the opponent's King loose among pawns on the other side of the board. If the remaining piece (say a Knight) can sacrifice itself for a dangerous pawn, the thing may reduce to a rival study in promotions. But there may be such a range of variations (e.g. in the order of pawn captures) that technique is postponed until the precise working out of sequences of moves has been carried out.

A player may have placed his pieces on all the best squares, and be in a position to win pawns. But which pawn to win? or What happens afterwards?

In one of the 1958 World Championship games (the 14th) Botvinnik refused the chance of winning a King's side pawn, but kept up a pressure on both wings, eventually breaking through on the Queen side, while his opponent won the King side pawn.

If there is technique in such an ending, it lies in the early awareness of the possibilities that developed, the clear appreciation that White's ultimate pawn position would be more effective than Black's. But the endings of this type—and all the difficult transitions to the endgame that occur in master Chess—are too subtle to be classified technically. The common factor is an effort to do two things: to preserve advantages, and to liquidate advantage into victory.

The variety of the examples already cited suggests a distinction that can be drawn. There is a 'patent' element in technique, and a 'latent'. Patent is, be it said, any explicit method, for instance of forcing the promotion of a pawn, winning with Rook and Bishop against Bishop, etc., etc. Latent is all that awareness of method and functions of pieces that is involved in the player's insight. Occasionally this can be isolated instructively.

Thus, place a White Queen at KR6, White Bishop at Q3; Black has King at KKt1, Rook at KB1, pawns at KB2 and KR2. This shows a threat of mate in one move by the Queen. Move the Rook to K1 and it is a threat of a mating process by B × P ch, B—Kt6 dis ch, Q—R7 ch and Q × P mate. In the next diagram (26) thought of this kind is latent.

The position is from a game between Capablanca and Nimzovitch. Here Nimzovitch played B × Kt. Why did he not play K—R1 with a view to R—Kt1, etc.? Because he saw (and how hard it is to see all an opponent's resources!) that if 1 .... K—R1; 2 Kt—K4, B—K2; 3 KKt—Kt5, P×Kt; 4 Kt—B6, B×Kt; 5 B—K4, and mate is inescapable. He did not have to 'see' 5 .... K—Kt1; 6 Q×P mate.

26 Capablanca—Nimzovitch   27

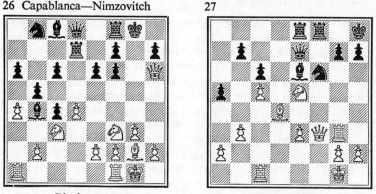

Black to move   Black to move

You can experiment with this position and make it harder. Take Black's Rook from Q2 and put a Bishop there, and consider for first move 1 .... R—K1.

The same series of moves is now available, and Black has to realise that 5 .... K—Kt1 will not escape mate (the more elaborate one); but in either case the distinction is clear. The end mating process is familiar: the familiarity is in an awareness of the functions of the pieces. What required vision was the perception of a series of forcing moves to the mating situation. A minimal technique—an awareness of mating powers by Queen and Bishop—is latent; is indeed basic. Without that awareness, the tactical thinking does not commence.

A less frequent mating configuration, following a shorter tactical process, is shown in Diagram 27 from a position reached by the author in a simultaneous display. The opponent played

1 ....   B—Q4
thinking that

2 Q—B4
could be met by 2 .... Kt—R4.

What he had not seen was:
3 Q—R6

This is playable because of
3 ....   P × Q   5 Kt—R6 mate.
4 Kt—B7 dbl ch K—Kt1

That particular mating process should be known to players, whether they are equal to seeing it 'with the naked eye' or not. It is frequent enough to be 'technical', an important feature of the life of Kings in corners, and comparable to smothered mate.

One must be able to see such a thing, or one must know it. Having been shown it, a player may become capable of seeing it. Let it be classified as a tactical percept that can be learned; can be in the latent technique of the well-equipped player.

In master Chess, and generally, there are innumerable examples of the relevance of technique (latent and patent) to practical play. In this position (Diagram 28) (for which I am indebted to a Russian article by Grand Master Auerbach) it looks as if Black should win. But he allowed a liquidation of material in ignorance of some resources of a Knight.

Sheftz—Kholmov
28   (Dresden, 1956)

Black to play

The play was as follows:

69 ....   Q—K2 ch   70 K—B2   Q—R2 ch
                               (Q—B4 ch is better)

71 K—B1   B—R6 ch   72 K—K2   B—Kt5 ch

73 K—B1   P—B6   74 Q—B2

(a move that would not have been playable had Black's Queen stood at c5)

74	Q—R8 ch	79 Q—K3	Q×Q ch
75 Q—K1	Q—R3 ch	80 K×Q	B×P
76 K—B2	Q—Q3	81 Kt—K4	B—B4
77 Q—K4 ch	P—Kt3	82 Kt—Kt5 ch	
78 P—R3	Q—B4 ch		

(he dare not allow this exchange)

82 ....   K—R3   83 Kt×P   B×P

And here in Forsyth notation is the resultant remarkable position

16, 6pk, 7p, 8,4KKt2, 5kt2, 2b5, 8,

in which, apparently, Bishop and two joined passed pawns cannot beat a Knight.

After 84 K—B4 there is some very interesting play available. Thus Black can lose a move, throwing the onus, as it were, 84 .... B—B4; 85 Kt—Kt5, P—R5; 86 Kt—B3, K—R4; 87 Kt—Kt5, B—Q2; 88 Kt—K4, B—B1; 89 Kt—B6 ch, K—R3; 90 Kt—K4, B—B4; 91 Kt—Kt5, K—R4; 92 Kt—R7 (inter alia) draws.

The play shows the consequences of failure to appreciate something that might be called technical, if the word be widely enough applied.

Apropos of this ending, let it be mentioned that there are frequent positions in Chess when the few hold their own against the many. Technically valuable is the following, where Rook and

29   Study by Del Rio

White to play, can only draw

pawn fail to defeat a Bishop (Diagram 29). If 1 P—B7, K—Kt2

holds the position. If 1 R—Q7, B—Kt6 (not B—B2) is adequate. This is exceptional. Not only has the pawn gone too far, but the Rook cannot exploit the position of the Bishop. How delicate the matter is we see in the companion Diagram 30, in which the Bishop fails to hold the major force. The basic difference is that the Bishop has here no central squares. The method is seen in the simplest variation. 1 R—Kt4, B—Kt6; 2 R—Kt4, B—R7; 3 R—Kt8 ch, K—Q2; 4 R—Kt7 ch, K—Q1; 5 P—Q7, K—K2; 6 R—Kt2. Now B—K3 is unplayable. So White gets in R—Q2 and K—Q6, winning. But, obviously, the Bishop's moves need not be so obliging. Variations are numerous and subtle. This is a particularly hard study.

Study by
30 von Guretzki-Cornitz

White wins

Such a position is semi-technical only, because many tactical variations are involved in the liquidation. There are technical advantages, of which the exploitation is merely technical: for example—King and pawn against King. But very many technical advantages—indeed the vast majority of the interesting advantages —require tactical exploitation. Fairly elementary is the following position reached by the author some years ago in a tournament:

8,p7,r3pk2,1p1p1pp1,2bP3p,P1P1P3,2B3PP,R1K5.

Here Black has a pawn to the good and more control of the board than his opponent. (Of casual interest is the fact that the position of the Black pawn at a7, rather than a6, is very convenient—an example of the wisdom of not moving pawns unnecessarily.) The liquidation of this advantage is not easy. The important feature that can be exploited is the restraint exercised by Black's Bishop on the scope of White's Rook. But this restraint is only actualised when the attack is moved over to the King's side. Black played P—K4 in order to make this possible, and the position that resulted some moves later was:

8, p7, 5k1r, 1p1p1p2, 2b3pp, P1P1P1P1, 2B2KRP, 8.

Black now wins tactically, sacrificially: but it requires to be said that this kind of sacrifice is familiar enough to be semi-technical. 44 .... P×P ch; 45 P×P, P—Q5!; 46 BP×P, B—Q4; 47 P—K4 (Blockade); 47 .... P×P; 48 K—K3, K—Kt4; and White is helpless against the threat of R—R3. Of course, the p at e4 is guarded by the potential pin.

Apropos of this pawn sacrifice, let it be borne in mind as a feature of Chess that a mobile pawn can frequently make itself useful by vacating its square. Also as well as clearing lines, the pawn sacrifice may also create a blockade.

Of the vacation of a square quite a good example is from a position reached between the author (White) and C. H. O'D. Alexander in 1946 at Nottingham:

3k2r1, R3bp2, 2b1pp1p, 8, 1pBP4, 5Kt2, 1P3PPP, 5K2.

With 25 P—Q5, which Black confessed to not having anticipated, White can get, if the pawn be taken, a most valuable square for the Knight.

Black replied 25 .... R—Kt5! and White, had he not been attracted by the *ignis fatuus* of possible victory, would have drawn by 26 P×B, R×B; 27 R—R8 ch, K—B2; 28 R—R7 ch, K—Q1— Perpetual check.

Coincidentally, from the author's experience of Chess at Nottingham (ten years later), is the sacrificial use of a pawn in order to restrict the opponent's scope.

After the moves 1 Kt—KB3, Kt—KB3; 2 P—B4, P—KKt3; 3 Kt—B3, B—Kt2; 4 P—K4, P—Q3; 5 P—Q4, 0—0; 6 P—KR3, P—B4; 7 P—Q5, P—K3; 8 P×P, P×P; 9 B—Kt5, Kt—B3; the author obtained, with 10 P—K5, a very healthy position against that strong player, L. Barden.

After 10 P—K5, P×P; 11 B—Q3, Q—Kt3; 12 0—0, White was able to give the game the kind of shape he likes.

From the same tournament, indeed played the next day, is a position which shows how technical advantages develop from tactical-strategic efforts: and how a tactical line of play takes on a shape which can be classified. Yet the technical forms are relatively accidental. In the position:

3r1rk1, 1p2q1pp, 2p1pkt1kt, 2Pp1p1b, 1p3Q2,
1P1P1KtPP, P1R1PPB1, 3KtR1K1,

the author (Black) had planned on the assumption that White's capture of the pawn at b4 involved loss of tempo that could be exploited. Therefore:

21 ....   B × Kt
(for tactical purposes, the Bishop can do nothing better than rid the board of a defender)

22 B × B   P—K4
gaining tempo.

23 Q × KtP   P—K5
with great control of space.

24 B—Kt2	P—KKt4	26 P—Q4	Kt—R4
25 Q—Q2	Q—Kt2	27 R—B3	P—Kt5

(Here the 'technical move' seems to be P—B5, but tactically that comes to nothing, because of 28 P—Kt4.)

28 P—KR4	P—B5	29 P × P	Kt—B4

Blockade and attack.

30 Kt—K3	Kt × RP	34 R—KB1	Q—B3
31 P—B5	Kt × P	35 Q—K3	Q—R5
32 Kt × Kt	R × Kt	36 P—R4	Kt—B5
33 P—Kt4	R(Q1)—KB1	37 R—B2	

to make Q—KKt3 possible.

37	Kt × B	39 R—B3	P—Kt6 wins.
38 K × Kt	R—B6		

Move 38 .... R—B6 is of a familiar type, yet is fresh in the context. Moves like this, which are technically describable, are yet not technique, because no rule can be laid down for them. I have seen moves like R—B6 fail. Their importance is that they illustrate how, at certain moments, formal values count for nothing. They enter into technique in the same way that many combinative movements do: viz. they enhance awareness of what the pieces can do.

As for rules, add this grain of salt: that rules are subordinate to situations. Evidence of this truth is easily adduced. Thus suppose one is playing Ruy Lopez, and one is aware of an endgame feature, that three pawns can hold an opposite four, if two of the four are doubled: viz. pawns on QB3, QKt2, QR3, can hold off four pawns, if the doubled pawns are on the Bishop's or Rook's file. (The pawn that arrives at Kt5 is ignored.)

On that basis, it must not be supposed that exchanges are good. (I am not saying, dogmatically, that they are bad!) Thus:

1 P—K4	P—K4	3 B—Kt5	P—QR3
2 Kt—KB3	KtQB3	4 B × Kt	QP × B

leaves White with a technical advantage, but at the technical cost of a minor exchange; and the strategical-tactical chances available to Black (e.g. 5 P—Q4, B—KKt5! is promising). Perhaps it hardly needed saying that technique is not enough. Let it be added, then, that even in technical positions, technique is not enough.

This is true at late as well as early stages.

I saw a good player (admittedly playing very rapidly) miss the win in the following position: 16, 6p1, 5p1p, 7k, 4B3, 2K2P2, 8. He played K—Kt5(?). The technical indication is to oppose the hostile King. But what is needed is a King movement via R6 to Kt7, because the White King is very fast in the approach to f1. If 1 .... K—R6; 2 B—Kt5, K—Kt5 loses no tempo because White has lost tempo and the pawn path is free. The essence of this position is to keep separate things separate. But perhaps clarity cannot be taught.

What, then, can be taught? Some methods, involving awareness of the full functions of the pieces; some precautions, based on an awareness of the dangers that arise from opportunities given to pieces. Add to these 'ceaseless vigilance'. To train that vigilance, let the reader absorb subtleties from games and studies. I conclude this chapter with a study which is an education in itself.

From this one can learn: (a) Something about the speed of Kings. (b) A familiar endgame fact—that a promotion may be rendered useless by a mating net. (c) A resource available to a 'promoter' (this is the cleverness latent in the key). And (d), when that is appreciated, a nice piece of learning about duels between Rook and Knight. Here is the solution: 1 K—R7!, P—R5; 2 K—Kt6, P—R6; 3 K—Kt5, P—R7; 4 K—Kt4, P—R8 (=Q); 5 K—Kt3 wins. Now see why the first move was not K × P!

However, the board is not exhausted. Try 4 .... P—Kt4!; 5 K—Kt3, P—R8 (=Kt) ch—a 'subpromotion'. Now win. The variations are many. Suffice here one main line. 6 K—B3, P—Kt5 ch; 7 K × P, Kt—B7 ch; 8 K—B3, Kt—Q6; 9 R—R5!, Kt—K8 ch;

31   Study by Moravec

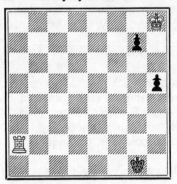

White to play and win

10 K—K2, Kt—Kt7; 11 R—R1 ch, K—R7; 12 K—B3, Kt—R5 ch; 13 K—Kt4, Kt—Kt7; 14 R—R2, K—Kt8; 15 K—Kt3, Kt—K6; 16 K—B3, Kt—Q4; 17 R—Kt2 ch, K—R8; 18 R—Q2, Kt—B3; 19 R—Q6, Kt—K1; 20 R—K6, Kt—B2; 21 R—QB6, Kt—Q4; 22 K—Kt3 or B2 forces mate.

PART TWO: THE EXPLOITATION OF MATERIAL ADVANTAGES

CHAPTER III

KINGS AND ASCENDING PAWNS

Chess may be inexactly, but usefully, divided into two phases—the struggle for advantage, and the attempt to liquidate acquired advantages into victory. This second phase, the exploitation, may terminate the play, at a relatively early period; or the game may end in a phase that we call endgame, or ending. (By a paradox of usage 'end of the game' is not equivalent to 'endgame' or 'ending'.)

If there is a phase of Chess in which technique makes itself evident, patent rather than latent, that phase is the endgame, because it is there that the idiosyncrasies of pieces and groups of pieces, and features of the geometry of the board (such as the special features of Rook's files, Bishop's files, etc.) become uniquely relevant and perceptible in isolation. Some of these features we shall study first. For the purposes of players who do not early annihilate, or become annihilated, the most frequent margin of clear advantage is the solitary pawn in King and pawn against King. Ability to handle this advantage is vital, because most play is controlled by the assumption that the eventual possession of a 'pawn plus' is the justification of all planning. The resultant advantage is not always sufficient for victory. But ability to handle the position is often a decisive factor.

First let it be said that King and two pawns against King and one pawn is frequently a solider foundation for victory than King and one against a lone King. Indeed it may be hazarded that, generally, in the dynamics of Chess, clear advantages seem to lessen with the diminution of pieces. (That is on the assumption that the lesser force is less active than the greater force.)

The relative advantage of King and two against King and one, as contrasted with King and one against King, is clear in Diagram

32. If there were no King's pawns, Black would draw. As the
position is, White is about to win the Black pawn. A bit harder
is Diagram 33. If there were no Queen's pawns in this diagram
the position would be drawn. As it stands White wins, whichever
player has the move.

32   33

White wins, whoever has the
move

White wins, whoever has the
move

White to move does not play

1 P—K4 ch	P × P
2 P × P ch	K—K4

3 K—K3

because this only draws—viz.:

3	K—K3
4 K—Q4	K—Q3
5 P—K5 ch	K—K3

6 K—K4	K—K2
7 K—Q5	K—Q2
8 P—K6 ch	

and now, this is technically vital,

8	*K—K1*
9 K—Q6	K—Q1

10 P—K7 ch	K—K1
11 K—K6	Stalemate.

It is very important for the beginner to observe that setting.
If your King is at K2, the opposing pawn at your K3, his King at
your K4 or Q4 or B4, you must move back on the file, to K1, so
as to meet K—Q6 with K—Q1, and K—B6 with K—B1. If you
play, wrongly, K—Q1 and he plays K—Q6, you must then move
K—K1, and now P—K7 forces you to B7 and your opponent,
with K—Q7, forces promotion. (Incidentally, it may occur to the
reader that this situation is one where a 'doubled pawn' can be

useful. The pawn lagging behind on the same file can make a move instead of the King, and Black is forced to go to the wrong square!)

In the diagram position, White to move may play

1 P—Q4

This puts Black into a difficulty. If he plays 1 .... K—K3, there follows 2 K—Kt4 (opposition play, explained later).

2	K—B3	6 K—B6	K—Q2
3 K—B4	K—K3	7 K—K5	K—B3
4 K—Kt5	K—K2	8 K—K6	*zugzwang.*
5 K—B5	K—Q3		

The King is squeezed and Black must abandon the pawn. But note that White still needs the two pawns in order to win. Suppose at this moment a jackdaw hopped away with White's KP.

Black plays

8	K—B2	11 P—Q5	K—Q2
9 K × P	K—Q2	12 P—Q6	K—Q1
10 K—K5	K—K2		

and we have the draw already seen. If instead of 1 .... K—K3 he plays 1 .... K—Kt4, then 2 P—K4. Now either he will get this to K5 (better than × P) with a squeeze position as above, or else Black captures.

In this case

| 1 P—Q4 | K—Kt4 | 3 K × P |
| 2 P—K4 | P × P | |

White has achieved the winning type of position (Diagram 34).

34

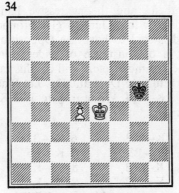

Black to play: White wins

3	K—B3	5 K—B6
4 K—Q5	K—K2	

If now

5	K—Q1

White wins directly with the pawn advance, because the pawn will arrive at Q7 when the King is at Q1 (forced to move). Or, lazily, with

6 K—Q6	K—B1	8 P—Q5, etc.
7 K—B7	K—K2	

While considering this point, make the following experiment:

Place King on K1, pawn on K2 and Black King at K8. How do you force a win?

If you try, you will find that pawn moves fail. White's method is: 1 K—B2 or K—Q2 followed by King advance. Thus:

1 K—Q2	K—Q2	3 K—K4	K—K4
2 K—K3	K—K3	4 P—K3	

A very good example, this, of the frequent need, in endgame Chess, of losing a move in order to create *zugzwang*. Then follows: 5 .... K—K2; 6 K—K5, K—K1; 7 K—K6, K—Q1; 8 P—K4, K—K1; 9 P—K5, K—Q1; 10 K—B7, wins.

Other variations are not difficult to work out. Observe that, from the original position Black to move draws. He occupies e5 as the White King reaches e3 and holds the position. An important technical term is worth mentioning here. When, after such manœuvring for position, King eventually faces King with one square between them, and the aggressive King cannot by-pass the defending King or force him to give ground, the player who holds the ground is said to have the Opposition. This term, or principle, which is one instance of wider principles (*zugzwang*, ability to play the last move, etc.), will be illustrated later.

Meanwhile we return to Diagram 33. Let Black have the move. If he plays 1 .... K—K4, White may reply 2 K—Kt4 and a possible sequence is:

2	K—K3	6 K—B5	K—Q3
3 K—B4	K—B3	7 K—B6	K—Q2
4 P—Q4	K—K3	8 K—K5	K—B3
5 K—Kt5	K—K2	9 K—K6	*zugzwang*.

The Black King is squeezed because White's pawns are controlling plenty of space—one reason against reducing the force by exchanges. Black's best first move is evidently 1 .... K—Kt4. White can easily go wrong here. 2 P—K4 is tempting because, if P × P ch, 3 K × P gives the 'King in front of pawn' advantage.

But in answer to

2 P—K4

Black plays

| 2 .... | K—B3! |

If then,

| 3 P × P | K—K4 |

achieves a drawn position.

If, instead,

| 3 K—B4 | P × P | 5 K—Q4 | K—Q3 |
| 4 K × P | K—K3 | | |

—also drawn. The King is ahead of his pawn, but, by reason of opposition, cannot gain control.

It follows that, in answer to 1 .... K—Kt4, White must not move the KP. 2 P—Q4 is also not very clever. Best is 2 K—Kt3, and develop a squeeze on the Black King.

Thus:

1	K—Kt4	3 K—R4	
2 K—Kt3	K—B4	and gently pushes itself	
		round to B6.	

At this point (move 3) Black is helpless. He cannot play 3 .... P—Q5 because of 4 P—K4 ch, and if the Black King then moves via B5 to K6, the White pawn becomes uncatchable, promotes itself, and can stop the Black pawn.

The resultant position from that line of play would be similar to one set out in Diagram 35.

The winning process is an important part of technique.

1 Q—K2

(one may also start with check)

| 1 .... | K—B8 | 3 Q—Q3 ch | K—B8 |
| 2 Q—B4 ch | K—Kt8 | 4 Q—B3 ch | |

This is the key to the solution. Black must block the pawn for a move, giving White a tempo.

4	K—Q8	5 K—B3

and clearly Black has lost (K—K8; 6 K—K3, etc.).

Incidentally, it doesn't matter how far away the White King is, because every few moves White gains a tempo for the King's approach.

Now observe one of the eccentricities of the board. Move the position in Diagram 35 one square to the left (see Diagram 36).

35

White to move and win

36

White to move, can only draw

1 Q—Q2	K—Kt8	3 Q—B3 ch	K—Kt8
2 Q—Kt4 ch	K—R8	4 Q—Kt3 ch	K—R8

and Q × P produces stalemate. This is a peculiarity of the Bishop's file. To add a little complexity, note that if in Diagram 36 the White King were at K3, K2 or K1, White could still win. A series of checks would end with Queen at R3 and Black King at Kt8. Then K—Q2 is decisive.

The reader will readily appreciate that the Rook file also has its stalemate feature.

If the King is at QKt8 and pawn at QR7 the Queen checking on the Knight's file drives the King into R8 but gains no useful tempo.

For Queen against pawn, then, those files are peculiar.

In other endings Knight files have their peculiarities, which will be mentioned. Suffice it here to ask the reader to put White pawns on g6 and f7, Black pawn g7, White King on e6, Black King on f8. White can do nothing. But if the position be moved one to the left he wins, because he can work round to the other side of the Black pawn. To revert to the promotion theme, move the pieces in Diagram 33 one square to the left (Diagram 37).

37

Black to play.   What result?

38   Study by Troitski

White to play.   What result?

There is a subtle difference from the position in Diagram 33—
the Black pawn is a Bishop's pawn! Let us try:

1	K—B4	6 P—Q5	K × P
2 K—B3	K—K4	7 P—Q6	K—Kt7
3 K—Kt4	P—B5!	8 P—Q7	P—B6
4 P—Q4 ch	K—K5	9 P = Q	P—B7
5 K—Kt3	K—Q6	which is like Diagram 36 (drawn).	

Before the reader moves from this topic, here is an example
(Diagram 38) of the significance of the BP in a situation where
its relevance is very hard to see. The study is fascinating and
has recently been made more so by the discovery of a 'cook'.

White's first manœuvre is fairly obvious to anyone who has ever
'sacrificed'. (This does not mean everyone who has ever played,
because novices exist at the level of fair prices and 'nothing for
nothing'.)

1 P—K6	P—B5	2 B—B3 ch

deflecting the Black Bishop.

2	B × B	3 P—K7

and it looks as if White has achieved Queen against Bishop and
pawn. But the resources of Chess are not easily exhausted.

3	B—B3 ch	5 P—K8 = Q ch
4 K × B	P—B6	

and, remarkably, cannot win. It reduces to a case of Queen against Bishop's pawn. There is added difficulty here, that for the moment the BP is only at the 6th and the King is on the wrong side of it. However, owing to the fact that the White King interferes with one line of check, Black can correct these defects. For long this solution was unchallenged—and it remains a fine piece of Chess. But recently a Scottish amateur (L. J. Stirling) discovered the following line of play: 1 B—K7, B—R4; 2 B × P, B—Q1 ch; 3 K—Kt6, K—K7; 4 P—K6, K—Q6; 5 B—B8! 4 K—K5; 6 B—Kt7, B—K2; 7 K—B7, B—Kt5; 8 B—B8 wins. Other answers to 1 B—K7 lose more easily. (The experts had explored 1 B—K7, B—R4 but had missed the gain of tempo achieved by 5 B—B8! See *B.C.M.*, April 1962, and *Chéron* Vol. 2., Diag. 1194.)

Let us return, however, to the stage before Queens appear on the board. The reader must not infer, from my proposition about King and two pawns against King and pawn, that these positions are normally easy. Far from it!

Diagram 39 shows a favourable appearance, but the win is not simple.

39

White to move and win

If White seeks to work round to QKt6, he will find that the
Black King can keep him away, while still within reach of the
QP. Thus:

1 K—Q4	K—Q1	3 K—Kt4	K—Kt1
2 K—B4	K—B1	4 K—R4	K—B1
			(not K—Kt2)

5 K—R5	K—Kt2

and White must retreat. The play on three squares (by White on
QKt4, QR4, QR5, by Black on QB1, QKt1, QKt2) is called Triangulation (a process which will be further illustrated later).

Now try on the other wing:

1 K—B6	K—Q1	2 K—B7	K—Q2

If 2 K—K6, K—K1, and there is no entry—3 P—Q7 ch leads to
stalemate.

Yet White can win! The method is sacrificial.

1 K—B6	K—Q1	3 K—B7	
2 P—Q7!	K × P		

and White has the opposition, and a useful vacant square.

3	K—Q1	8 K × P	K—B1
4 K—K6	K—B2	9 K—Q6	K—Q1
5 K—K7	K—B1	10 P—B6	K—B1
6 K—Q6	K—Kt2	11 P—B7 wins.	
7 K—Q7	K—Kt1		

Incidentally, sacrifices are often necessary in order to gain ground
or lose a move as the case may be.

Thus Tarrasch, having pawns on QR2 and QR3 adjacent to
opponent's pawn on the latter's QKt4, wanted the 'opposition', for
play on the opposite side of the board.

He played 1 P—QR4, P × P; 2 P—QR3, forcing the opponent
to move—a neat exploitation of an apparently worthless feature,
a 'backward doubled pawn'. A simple statement of the theme is
Diagram 40 (1 .... P—R4; 2 P × P, P—R3, etc.).

Diagram 41, however, shows something harder, actually not
soluble by sacrifice.

1 P—B6 ch is very good, if Black accepts it.

Black to play and win

White to move and win

Thus:

| 1 P—B6 ch | P × P ch | 3 K × P | K—Kt1 |
| 2 K—B5 | K—B1 | 4 P—Kt7, etc. | |

If instead,

| 2 .... | K—Q1 | 3 K—Q6 | |
| | | (threatening P—Kt7) | |

| 3 .... | K—B1 | 4 K × P | |

as in the previous variation.

But the sacrifice is thwarted, as sacrifices often are, by refusal.

| 1 P—B6 ch | K—B1 | 3 K—Q7 |
| 2 K—Q6 | K—Kt1 | |

(not 3 P—B7 ch, K—B1 and the King is immovable)

| 3 .... | P × P | 4 K × P | K—B1 |

with the simple draw already seen. But there is a subtler approach.

| 1 K—K5 | K—B3 |

(if 1 .... K—Q1; 2 K—Q6, and eventually gains Q7 so that he
can play P—B6 when the Black King is at R1)

| 2 K—Q4 | K—Q2 | 3 K—Q5 |

and we are back at the diagram position with Black to move.
3 .... K—K2 is unplayable because P—B6 then wins easily. So
he must give ground and White reaches Q7 in time to see Black
go to R1.

It should be observed that, though King and two pawns against King and pawn is not easy, it is clear that the side with the majority has plenty of scope, more scope than when the only capital asset is a single pawn.

In the conflicts that take place on the relatively empty board, before Queens reappear, considerable subtlety and perfect accuracy are more in evidence (and demand) than is the speculative imagination that creates combinations to win material.

A fine piece of endgame play by Marshall (Diagram 42) exhibits subtlety, and illustrates a phenomenon in Master Chess, viz. that those who are recorded as great combinative players, men such as Marshall, Spielman, Blackburne, Mieses, were, all of them, precisians of the endgame.

Marshall—Leonhardt,
42   (Hamburg, 1911)

White to play and win

In the diagram position White obviously has more control than Black. Nevertheless, he must calculate exactly what happens when he lets the Black King emerge, and he must arrange to have his pawns in the relatively best position:

1 P—QR3   K—B1   2 P—QR4
(observe the 'losing of moves' technique)

2 ....   P—Kt4
Becoming committed. But if 2 .... K—Kt1; 3 P—Kt3, K—B1; 4 K—R7, K—B2; 5 P—Kt5, P×P; 6 P×P, P—Kt4; 7 P—Kt4, and Black must eventually make losing moves.

| 3 P—R3 | K—Kt1 | 5 P—R4 | P × P |
| 4 P—Kt3 | K—B1 | | |

(In Chess, unlike Draughts, simple exchanges do not always alter the expectation of last moves.)

5	P × P	8 K—Q5	K—Q2
6 P × P	K—Kt1	9 K—K5	K—B3
7 K—B5	K—B2		

If 9 .... K—K2 White will play P—QR5. If then K—B2 White plays K—Q6 and promotes in seven moves. If 9 .... K—Q2, K—B6 threatens a promotion in eight. Black can cope with neither.

10 P—KR5

Shortening his queening process.

| 10 .... | P—R4 |

A desperate try.

| 11 P × P | K—B4 | 13 K—B6, resigns. |
| 12 P—KR6 | K—Kt5 | |

White can Queen in five, Black needs seven moves.

On the open board, when forces are diminished, we find struggles of two types. Speed races, on the one hand: and on the other hand, a principle of *festina lente*—a reluctance to commit oneself and an effort to make the other commit himself first—efforts, in fact, to lose moves rather than to gain them.

When players are working out pawn sequences to promotion the necessities are accuracy and clarity. It may seem platitudinous to advise the student not to confuse his pawn movements, and to be careful to separate out the King moves from the pawn moves. But failure to achieve that quite elementary degree of clarity is a feature of the confusion of mind which is bad play. If you have pawns at c5 and h5 and the opposing King is at e5, the King is in a position to overhaul either of the pawns as they advance to c8 and h8 respectively, but it cannot overhaul both. Not every novice realises this. More sophisticated is the following situation. Pawn is racing against pawn, and one of the pawns is nearer to its objective. But there are King moves as possibilities. The normal technique required in this situation is to separate the King moves from the pawn moves in the perspective of moves that is contemplated.

The important distinction in types of position is that in some cases the King moves make a difference to the pawns' prospects —in other cases the King's moves can be disregarded; or countered, so as to be neutralised.

Diagram 43 shows a simple case. White to move only draws. Apparently he has a King move (K—Q4) which affects Black's pawn. But it is neutralised by Black's K—B7. Then the pawn race goes on unaffected. If White gets really confused and on his second move plays K—B4, then he loses: 2 .... P—Kt6; 3 P—Kt6, P—Kt7; 4 P—Kt7, P—Kt8 = Q; 5 P—Kt8 = Q, Q—R7 ch, wins the Queen!

43

White to move, can only draw

But a player contemplating in the distance a position like 24, 1p6, 4P2K, 2k5, 16, has to be sure whose move it will be. Black, to move, plays K—Q5; his pawn can wait. One line of play is:

| 1 .... | K—Q5 | 3 K—B2 | K—Q6 |
| 2 K—Kt3 | K × P | heading off the White King. | |

A very simple position is the following:
24, 3k4, 3p3P, 8, K7, 8—
One must bear in mind that for every White pawn move there is a defensive King move (the Black King is in 'The Square'). White to move must start with P—R5. Now, not P—Q6, because White promotes first and checks at Q8, winning the Queen (I call this threat, by Queen or Rook on the file, or by Bishop on the diagonal, 'a stab in the back'). So Black must play 1 .... K—Q4.

Consider also the following: 16, 6P1, 16, 4p2K, 1k6, 8. White to move gains nothing by the King move, because Black replies with

a King move. Thus K—Kt2, K—B7, K—B3, K—Q6, and the
pawn race is unaffected.

On the other hand, in the position 24,5P2,kp6,4K3,16, a King
move makes a difference. 1 K—Q2 threatens to stop the Black
pawn. Thus 1 .... P—Kt6; 2 K—B1.

So Black must play 1 .... K—R6. Now the pawn race is
affected because White promotes with check!

Note that White has no other way of winning. He cannot rely
on a 'stab in the back'. Thus 1 P—B6, P—Kt6; 2 P—B7, P—Kt7;
3 P=Q, P=Q; 4 Q—R8 ch, K—Kt6; 5 Q—Kt8, K—R7, guards
the Queen.

Slightly more difficult is Diagram 44. If the pawns race, with
White starting first, White wins, because of the 'stab in the back'
resource.

44

White to play.   What result?

When, on the fourth move he promotes and Black likewise promotes,
he plays Q—R8 ch, and next move, with Q—Kt8 ch, wins the Queen.

But Black's King is just near enough to the White pawn to be
able to alter the outlook.

If 1 P—K5, K—Kt2! Now if 2 P—K6, K—B1, and Black is
able to reach e8. White must mobilise his King: 3 K—Kt5, K—Q1;
4 K—B6, K—K1, and White, with K—K5, just gets a draw.

White, in the circumstances, may play 2 K—Kt5. But then
Black resumes the pawn race with P—Kt5. Now when both are
promoted, there is no stab in the back to Black's King, as in the
first variation.

But now alter the position very slightly (Diagram 45). The White
King is at R5, instead of R4.

45

White to play and win

1 P—K5	K—Kt2	3 K—Kt6
2 P—K6	K—B2	

If now

| 3 .... | K—Q1 or Q3 | 4 K—B7, wins. |

If, instead, the pawn race goes on, White promotes while Black is only on the sixth and, of course, wins.

In this situation, then Black's K—Kt2, being ineffective, amounts only to loss of tempo. If he does not try this move, he loses by the stab in the back.

A subtlety suggested by these studies is seen in Diagram 46. White has a clever resource.

46

White to play.   What result?

1 B × P ch

threatening B—Q3. Black, therefore, must capture. Now

2 P—B7	P—B7	3 P—B8 = Q

If

3	P—B8 = Q	4 Q—B8 ch, wins.

But Black need not lose. On move 3 he does not hurry but
plays K—Kt6 and draws because the unpromoted pawn is a
Bishop's pawn, whose value has already been seen.

Diagram 47 shows an idea used by Troitski in which the 'stab
in the back' win is beautifully prevented.

47 Study by Troitski	48

White to play. What result?   White to play and win

1 P—K6	R—Q6 ch	5 R—K4	R—K6
2 K—K5	P—K6	6 R × R	K × R
3 R × P	P—K7	7 P—K7	P = Q
4 R × P ch	K—B7	8 K—K6!, draws.	

Diagram 48 is easy, but not so easy as it appears.

White has a choice of pawn moves. Is it material which he
moves? The KRP is out of the Black King's reach. The QRP
can be reached—is 'within the Square'.

Yet the QRP has one advantage: it threatens to promote with
check. But there is more to it than that.

1 P—QR5

Black can deal with it. The pawn race QBP and KRP is unaffected by the duel of King with QRP. The movements seem to
be separate. Therefore

| 1 .... | K—Q4 | 3 P—R7 | K—Kt2 |
| 2 P—R6 | K—B3 | | |

Now the KRP starts.

| 4 P—R5 | P—B5 | 6 P—R7 | P—B7 |
| 5 P—R6 | P—B6 | | |

And here White cruelly reveals the point of his choice of 'first pawn'.

7 P—QR8 = Q ch K × Q   8 P = Q ch and wins.

The varieties of King and pawn endings cannot all be illustrated in a small book. But the advice that can be given is: look out for special features, especially checks posterior to promotion, and tempo-gainers.

Diagram 49 is tantalising. It looks as if the Black King is near enough to cope with the White pawns. But this is deceptive.

49

White to play and win

1 P—R5   K—K1

and now, not 2 P × P, K—B1; but

2 P—R6

This ties the Black King for ever, and White King has leisure to deal with Black's QRP and return to the King's side to force the win.

Diagram 50 shows a win facilitated by a checking threat.

50

White to play and win

1 P—KR4 cannot be met by P—QR4 because eventually P—R8 gives check. Therefore 1 .... P × P is necessary and 2 P—Kt5 puts White one move further ahead in the race.

Black's KRP is irrelevant, because every KRP move by Black is met by a King move on the part of White—a skirmish outside the battle.

Diagram 51, reprinted from the *Chess Amateur*, was played by the author in 1923.

51

Black to play and win

1	P—R4	2 K × P

P × P is useless because P—B4 allows the Black King to stop the RP and White can do nothing to impede the BP.

| 2 .... | P × P | 3 K—Kt4! |

Best, because at Kt6 or Kt5 he is exposed to check from a promoting pawn.

| 3 .... | P—B4 | 5 P—R5 | P—Kt6 |
| 4 P—R4 | P—B5 | 6 P × P | |

(if P—R6; 7 P × P and promotes, controlling h8)

6	P × P	9 P—R8 = Q	Q—K5 ch
7 P—R6	P—Kt7	10 K—Kt3	Q—K4 ch
8 P—R7	P—Kt8 = Q	(or 5)	

forces Queen exchanges leaving a win for Black.

An incidental feature of that position, something that beginners find hard to appreciate, is that proximity exists on diagonals as well as on ranks and files. A King, to stop a pawn at R5, has no need to be nearer than a Queen's or King's file (according to the side of the RP) provided that it is on the fifth rank. This fact explains the apparently surprising speed of the King in many endings. Perhaps the most spectacular, and certainly one of the most important, is a study by the late Richard Réti which may well be called 'The Rocket-propelled King'—Diagram 52.

52   Study by Réti

White to play and draw

The position in the diagram was actually reached, in 1921, in a game played in Berlin. White confidently resigned. It was left to the genius of Réti to discover the draw. The King is terribly far from the Black pawn, and is far too slow to catch it in the ordinary way; but there is something in this position that seems to accelerate it tremendously.

The point is that, if the King reaches K6, the QBP can be forced home. Therefore,

1 K—Kt7   P—R5   2 K—B6

with a threat of K—K6. So Black, in order to avert the promotion of White's QBP, plays

2 ....   K—Kt3

Now 3 K—K5! A further threat. If the King reaches Q6, the pawn can be forced home. So in desperation Black captures it!

3 ....   K × P

But now White has travelled far, and with K—B4 he overhauls the pawn that had so long a start.

This spectacular movement has been used by composers in other settings. Indeed, Diagram 53 shows Réti 'plagiarising' himself.

53   Study by Réti

White to play and draw

The solution of that study, with the difficult key-move (K—K7 obstructing his own pawn!), is good Chess. (1 K—K7, P—Kt4; 2 K—Q6, P—Kt5; 3 P—K7, B—Kt4; 4 K—B5, draws.) But the original simple statement of the idea is classic in its beauty, and perfect without need of embellishment.

The normality in Chess of a final battle between pawns, with Kings participating, is clear from the Chess vocabulary and some conventional Chess notions.

'Make your King a fighting piece,' says Steinitz. This is valuable advice in the middle game—and examples are frequent. But, particularly, it will be observed in good Chess that as the end of the middle game approaches, with the deforestation of the board —the removal of the heavy timber (*Abholzung*, as the Germans call it), players make every effort to centralise the King, or to bring it near to the pawn clusters that matter.

But even if the King is in an apparently unfavourable position, do not despair. As the Réti study shows, the King is a very fast mover. Quite striking is the following position: 8,6p1,5pPp,5P1P, 8,1k7,8,1K7. This study, by a strong British player, Hooper, shows a draw cleverly obtained. White's first move is retreat: K—R1. If now Black runs for the pawns, White follows, not nearly so far behind as one would expect. 1 K—R1, K—B6; 2 K—R2, K—Q5; 3 K—Kt3, K—K4; 4 K—B4, K × P; 5 K—Q5, and cannot be kept from KB7.

To hold back a King one needs a Rook.

A very serious defect in an endgame is a 'cut-off King'. Suppose White to be a pawn to the good. He has, say, a pawn at b5 with a King alongside at a5. Each side has a rook and the Black Rook is in a position to give check from such a square as a1. Now if the Black King at this moment is on a square like a7, b7 or c7, this game will be drawn. If the defending King is, however, away at h1 or h8, the attacking King can cope with the Rook and manœuvre its pawn forward (Diagram 54).

54   *Cut-off King*

Similar considerations apply if the diagram be altered so that the Black King is at h1 and the White Rook controls the second rank. These considerations hold good, too, if the Black King be nearer, say, at f5, cut-off by a Rook on the fourth file, or at f3, cut-off by a Rook on the fourth rank. The cutting-off can be horizontal or vertical. The important question is always, how near is the King? If near enough, rescue operations are possible. So, in Diagram 55, Black, to move, draws. 1 .... R—Q2 2 R—QB2, K—Q1; 3 K—Kt3, R—B2, and the King cannot be kept out of a good defensive position. Note, however, the importance of the handicap constituted by 'cutting-off'. If, in Diagram 55, the White King were at Kt3, instead of Kt2, White would win. Thus 1 .... R—Q2; 2 R × R, K × R; 3 K—R4, K—B3; 4 K—R5, K—B2; 5 K—R6 (note *not* K—Kt5, K—Kt2 draws), 5 .... K—Kt1; 6 K—Kt6, K—R1; 7 P—Kt5 (not 7 K—B7, K—R2; 8 P—Kt5, K—R1; 9 P—Kt6, stalemate), 7 .... K—Kt1; 8 K—B6, K—B1; 9 P—Kt6, K—Kt1; 10 P—Kt7, K—R2; 11 K—B7, wins.

55 *King being restored*	56 *Lucena technique*

To revert to the theme of Diagram 54. If the hostile King is cut-off or sufficiently far away, the King and pawn can manœuvre themselves to victory.

Thus from Diagram 54:

1 K—Kt6	R—Kt8	5 K—B7	R—B8 ch
2 K—B6	R—B8 ch	6 K—Kt8	R—Kt8
3 K—Kt7	R—Kt8	7 P—Kt7	
4 P—Kt6	K moves		

and now we arrive at a position, analogous to what is called the 'Lucena Position', where the win is clear. Diagram 56 is an example of the process. Here the Rook checks and moves up to the fifth rank. After R—B2 ch and K—Kt2, the play is:

1 R—R5

threatening K—B7 or K7; contemplating

2 K—B7	R—B8 ch	4 R—Q5, wins.	
3 K—Q6	R—Q8 ch		

If, in Diagram 56, the Black Rook were at d1, the White Rook might, for convenience, move only to the fourth rank. But even from there, it offers an umbrella to the King.

1 R—R4	R—K8	3 K—Q6	R—Q8 ch
2 K—B7	R—B8 ch	4 K—B6	

White is now threatening 5 R—QB4, followed by K—B7. Therefore,

4	R—B8 ch	5 K—Q5!

and R—Q4 protects it. Let it be added that, not only where Kings are concerned, it is always important to see whether a Rook's control of a file can be interfered with by an intervening piece. Thus, Diagram 57 is quite instructive. Black should not play 1 .... R—Kt8 ch, because of 2 K—R2. Then we have the familiar prevention by the pawn itself of access to the eighth rank. In any event, the desirable defence is from behind the pawn, not from in

57   *Cut-off Rook*   58

Black to play

front of it. So Black plays 1 .... R—KR8. But White, with 2 R—R4 ch and 3 R—R4, cuts the Black Rook off from the defence. This, incidentally, is one of a few tricks that can be played on a Rook. Diagram 58 shows an apparent defence. Not 1 .... R—Q1, because 2 K—B7 brings the King into action too quickly. But 1 .... R—B5 seems admirable. However, the reply is:

  2 R—K5 ch   K moves   3 R—K4 ch

deflecting the Rook or winning it. And suppose the White Rook were at KKt7, instead of K7, something similar happens, quieter but as deadly.

  1 ....   R—B5   3 R—Kt4!
  2 R—Kt5 ch   K moves   pinning the Rook.

This idea is beautifully presented in Diagram 59, a study by Emanuel Lasker.

59   Study by Lasker

White to play and win

In this position Black's disadvantage seems to be offset by his pawn at h2 which ties the White Rook.

But White cleverly demonstrates that the Black Rook's 'double function' (guarding h2 and covering c8) is more difficult to discharge.

  1 K—Kt7   R—Kt7 ch

(There is no option.)

  2 K—R6

(There is no Lucena cover on the other side because the White Rook is tied.)

  2 ....   R—QB7   3 K—Kt6
                                     (threatening R × P.)

  3 ....   R—Kt7 ch   5 R—R3 ch K—R7
  4 K—R5   R—QB7   6 R × P wins.

Another version of this study has the Black King at a4 and it can even be at a5 or 6. Then White's checks intervene to drive it back.

These sacrificial decoys and pins of the Rook, as practical devices in the endgame, are among those 'ideas' that become absorbed, and so technical.

Technique includes these as well as simpler geometrical truths about the occupied board.

From the elementary geometry of the board can be drawn the next handicap to the defence that we have to consider. This obtains in the situation where, other things being equal, one player has a 'remote passed pawn'.

All players are aware that a passed pawn, i.e. a pawn with no opposing pawn in front of it, or in either adjacent file, is an advantage. Strategians aiming at 'remote passed pawn' have something more in mind; namely, the consideration that when the pawn races start the pawn further from the defending King has the advantage, not necessarily of being uncatchable, for it may well be caught, but in that the effort it calls for from the defence will be fatal in other ways. A simple example is the following (Diagram 60).

60

Black to play

Material is numerically equal, but Black, to play, is faced with the threat of P—R4. If that happens while he is at his B7, he cannot catch it. Therefore he must play K—B6 (not K—Kt7). Then White has time to play K—B4, K—Kt5, K × P, K × P, K × P, before the Black King can return to the scene. Nor do the Black pawns constitute any threat to White.

However, observe, that if one alters the diagram position some-
what, giving White another pawn, on QKt3, and Black a pawn
on KKt3, then White cannot win. Thus 1 .... K—B6; 2 K—B4,
K—Kt5; 3 K—Kt5, K—R3; 4 K×P, P—R5; 5 P×P, P—Kt6;
6 P×P, P—B7, wins.

Therefore White has to stay on the squares KB4 and KKt5 or
KR4 and KKt5, and Black stays on QR6, QKt5. (If White gets in
P—R4, then Black has squares QR4 and QKt5).

Another easy, but quite pretty, example of the remote passed
pawn is afforded in Diagram 61.

Because the Black King is tied to the dangerous White QRP,
White has time to consume the two King's side Black pawns.

61   62

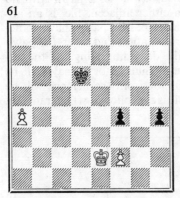

White to play and win   White wins, whoever has the
                                      move

But let not White play 1 K—B3. Then with 1 .... P—R6
Black would win! That is an amusing demonstration of the power
of broken pawns. In the diagram position the winning line is
1 K—B1 and round via Kt2 (if a pawn moves, Kt1 and R2).

Note, *en passant*, that two broken pawns can hold a King as
effectively as two joined pawns. Indeed, there are situations when
the broken pawns are superior. Thus in Diagram 62.

White to move can play K—Kt1. Then Black, to move, loses.
If K—R1 or R2, P—B7 wins. If K—B2 or B1, P—R7 wins. If
the pawns were lower down the board, e.g. at R5 and B5, the
game would be drawn. The Black King at Kt2 can play quite
simply, K—Kt1, and White cannot advance. Black can even play
K—B3 (or R3). If K—B3, 2 P—R6, Black cannot, of course,

capture, but must return to B2. From then on his play must
be K—B2, K—B3, K—B2, etc.

Diagram 63 is a simple endgame study exploiting the power of
broken pawns.

Black to play can take advantage of the technical feature, Bishops
of opposite colour.

63

White to play, wins.
Black to play, draws

Thus:

| 1 .... | K—R3 | 3 B—Kt2 | P—B3! |
| 2 B × P | K × P | 4 B × P | K—Kt5 |

winning the BP and eventually giving his Bishop for the RP.

But White to move wins by

1 B × P ch

If 1 .... K × B; 2 P—R6, tying the King for ever. White, then,
has time to travel to g8, win the Bishop and so create *Zugzwang*.
After B × P ch, if 1 .... K—R3; 2 B—Kt2, K × P; 3 P—B6,
K—Kt4; 4 K—B5, K—B4; 5 K—Q6, etc. (Observe that if the
White King started from R3 instead of Kt4 White would not win,
being unable to reach g8.)

Nor has Black time in which to sacrifice.

| 1 B × P ch | K—R3 | 3 B × P | K × P |
| 2 B—R1 | P—B3 | 4 B—Q7 wins | |

The possibilities latent in the last few diagrams bring into focus the power of the pawns as dynamic agents. We have already seen that they can break up pawn formations, and we shall be seeing other activities.

To revert to Diagram 60. If Kings were far away, the Black pawns would constitute a winning formation, and 1 .... P—R5 breaks through. If they were higher up the board this would not be effective. Then 1 .... P—R4; 2 P × P, P—Kt5; 3 P—R6 promotes first.

A useful example of pawn dynamics is afforded in Diagram 64.

64   Played 1922

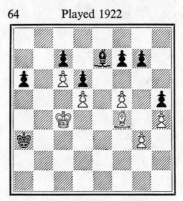

White to play and win

The endgame was tactically conceived, by the author, in actual play in 1922, but the technical feature is that pawns that have squares to move to, even protected squares, must be looked at as potential 'breakers-in'. In the diagram position Black had not had time to play P—B3. That would have been a typical 'blockade'. In its absence White, to move, plays 1 P—B6. The Bishop cannot capture because of White's B × P ch. Therefore,

| 1 .... | P × P | 2 P—Kt4 |
| | | a second act of breaking. |

| 2 .... | P × P | 4 P—R6 | K—R4 |
| 3 P—R5 | B—B1 | (there is nothing better) |

| 5 P—R7 | B—Kt2 | 6 B × P, wins. |

Observe, in the diagram position, a point of order. (Points of order are often vital in Chess.) White cannot alter the order of his breakings. If 1 P—Kt4, P—B3; 2 P × P is met by B—B1, and Black stands firm.

Also, if 2 P—Kt5, Black just ignores it.

Consequently, White must 'stand upon the order of his going' and play P—B6 before P—Kt4.

The position also illustrates other truths, e.g. that quantity of pawns (White has fewer) is less important than their dynamic quality.

Thus omit the Bishops from Diagram 64 and transfer White's BP to K4, and we have a type of threat frequent in Chess. P—K5 wins quite simply. That could be prevented by P—B3 on the part of Black, and that is an interesting example of over-protection. In practice this move would be played as a tactical necessity, but the technical description is useful for situations where there is no immediate tactical necessity.

Another truth, to be remarked before passing from this position, is that formulæ are unreliable. In Diagram 64 the pawn at g3 is a 'backward pawn', one of the 'untouchables' of Chess, precisely because it is so easily touched by the opponent. In this position, however, its dynamic potential is not less than that of the forward pawns.

The moral is that in Chess one judges not by forms but by functions.

Perhaps the most spectacular example of what pawns can do against pawns is Diagram 65.

65

White to play, wins.
Black to play, draws

The winning move is 1 P—Kt6. This threatens P × BP and P × RP. So the aggressor must be captured.

But if RP × P, White now advances P—B6. This pawn must be taken. Then P—R6 clearly wins.

If, on move one, Black plays BP × P, a corresponding process is available: 2 P—R6, P × P; 3 P—B6, wins.

(Note that a Black King nearer to the scene of action could make this line unplayable.)

If in the diagram position Black has the move he must play 1 .... P—Kt3. This draws; but not 1 .... P—R3, which is met by 2 P—B6! and not 1 .... P—B3; 2 P—R6!

The lesson of this diagram is the following. Although, from one point of view, pawns are at their best in line abreast, because they are uncommitted, yet if they are to be secure against pawns facing them the proper structure is triangular, with the centre pawn apex to the rear.

Thus pawns at QR3, QKt2, QB3 can hold any advance of three directly facing pawns. They wait for the opponent to make the capture. They are also safe if the opponent has four or five pawns on those three files, provided that the extra pawns are on the B or R file. But four pawns consisting of BP, RP and two KtP might, with appropriate handling, break the configuration, because there would be two spearheads.

As an incidental, the following artificial position is amusing:

4k3, 5 ppp, 32, PPP5, 3K4.

A player named Szen treated this as a game in itself, and analysed it copiously.

It has been suggested that whoever moves first wins, but I think this has not been demonstrated.

The suggestion is 1 K—K2, K—Q2; 2 K—B3, K—B3; 3 P—QR4, P—R4; 4 P—B4, P—B4; 5 P—Kt4, P—Kt4; 6 K—K3, K—Q3; 7 K—Q4, with opposition. This is not tendered here as a valid winning line.

Against dynamic pawns, a King can be surprisingly good and surprisingly weak.

Interesting is Diagram 66.

Looking at it arithmetically one expects Black to win. If it be Black's move, he does win with P—Kt6. But if one works out how he wins after that (it is not difficult) one realises the inner reality of the position, which is the possibility of *zugzwang*. Someone has to abandon a strong point. But White, with the move, has a resource that preserves all his options—K—Kt1. *Il recule pour mieux sauter.*

Now work out the sequences. The Black King, as we saw in a

previous example, cannot move. Only his pawns can move. If, then, he plays 1 .... P—Kt6, White plays 2 K—Kt2. If Black plays 1 .... P—B6, White replies 2 K—B2.

66

White to play and win.
Black to play and win

If 1 .... P—R6; 2 K—R2: in either case another pawn has to move, the BP or RP respectively, and White, with K—Kt3, holds everything.

Observe that White must not, on move one, play K—R1, B1, R2 or B2. One line of demonstration should suffice. 1 K—B1, P—R6; 2 K—B2, P—Kt6 ch; 3 K—B3, P—R7; 4 K—Kt2, P—B6 ch; 5 K—R1, P—B7; 6 K—Kt2, P—R8 = Q ch; 7 K × P, P—B8 = Q mate.

From this the reader will realise that, if the Black pawns were at f3, g3 and h3, the White King, whether at f1, g1 or h1, would be helpless. His position at g2, inside a triangle, is not comparable to his position at g3.

Again, if the diagram position be unaltered as to the King's side, but the Queen's side complex be placed one rank lower down the board (King at b7, pawns at a5 and c5), Black wins.

Thus 1 K—Kt1, K—Kt1. Now neither White pawn can advance. (If P—R6, K—R2; if P—B6, K—B2.) So White must move and lose.

The next diagram (67) is from a game by Edward Lasker (not to be confused with Emanuel Lasker) and shows a player making the wrong interpretation of the powers of pawns to hold off pawns. Perhaps technique was not enough.

67   Ed. Lasker—Moll

Black to move

Correct is

1	P—B3

If, then,

2 P—B4	P—R3

If instead,

2 P—R6	P×P	4 P—Kt5	P—R5 wins.
3 P—B4	P—R4!		

But the order of moves cannot be varied.

Black played 1 .... P—R3, and could have lost by the following process (had his opponent seen it):

2 P—B6	P×P	5 P×P	K—K4
3 P—B4	K—Q5	6 P×P	K—B3
4 P—Kt5	BP×P	into *zugzwang*!	

So far much of the discussion has been on the speed of pawns and Kings. But the last diagram reintroduces us to another important aspect of King and pawn contests. Here we are working on the assumption that the last shall be first; and we are trying to move last.

It may well be the case that, in Chess, as in Draughts, the second player has the ultimate advantage, since he is less committed. This is concealed by the fact that the first player, early, can occupy more space; and human beings do not like being crowded against their will. However that may be, certain it is that when, at the end of the game, the short range pieces are mainly concerned (Kings and pawns and, in some contexts, Knights) and some vital possibilities are irreversible moves, then the resemblance to Draughts (a game of short range pieces) is heightened, and the game is dominated by the reluctance of the player to commit his pieces irretrievably. So we have seen, in King and pawn against King, the operation of a principle of *zugzwang*. He wins or draws whose opponent commits himself.

This is the logic of the technical feature that is called 'opposition'.

Opposition, in its pure form, is seen on an open board where the only pieces are the two Kings. Place the Kings at e4 and e6. Now White at e4 wants to reach a square on the fifth or sixth rank. Having the move, he cannot achieve this. If he plays to d4, the adverse King opposes him at d6. On the other hand, were it the adversary's move, the latter would be forced to play to d6 or f6, and the King from e4 can reach the fifth, sixth, seventh or eighth.

Having achieved this, he can be prevented from returning.

Thus, the Black King moves to d6. Now 2 Kf5, Kd5, and Black has regained the opposition. White used his gain of opposition to reach the square he wanted. Had he been concerned only to restrict the Black King, he would have met Kd6 with Kd4, etc.

Opposition also exists on the diagonal. Thus place the Kings at d4 and f6, White, to move, can be prevented, at least, from reaching any place in the large square of which the sides are e5 to e8 and e5 to h5.

In practical Chess the principle usually applies to a contest between Kings in respect of some square adjoining pawns. In point is the very simple Diagram 68.

68

White to move, draws.
Black to move, loses

White, to move, achieves nothing.　Black, to move, loses.

1	K—Kt2	4 K—Q5	K—K2
2 K—Kt5	K—B2	5 K—K5	K—B2
3 K—B5	K—Q2	6 K—Q6	K—B1

(Note: here Black occupies an opposition square, but White has gained the field he wished to occupy, and the pawn configuration thereafter biases the play.　The pure mathematical opposition is distorted by pawns in the same way that pure space-time is warped by matter.)

7 K—K6	K—Kt2	11 K—B6	K—B1
8 K—K7	K—R2	12 P—Kt6	K—Kt1
9 K—B7	K—R1	13 P—Kt7 wins.	
10 K×P	K—Kt1		

Note that if at move eight the play were 8 K—B6, K—Kt1, White would win by 9 K×P, K—R1; 10 K—B7, etc.　If White is to move in the diagram position, he achieves nothing.

1 K—Kt5	K—Kt2	3 K—Q5	K—Q2
2 K—B5	K—B2	4 K—K5	K—K2

and his progress has ended.

5 K—Q5　　　　　K—Q2, etc.

If White were to retreat, he would be in trouble.　Thus: 1 K—Kt4, K—Kt3; 2 K—B4, K—B3; 3 K—Q4, K—Q3; 4 K—K4, K—K3; 5 K—B4, K—Q4; 6 K—B3, K—K4; 7 K—Kt4, K—K5; 8 K—R4, K—B5; 9 K—R3, K×P; 10 K—Kt3.

Now White has regained the opposition and this enables him to draw.　The position is different from Black's position as it was when White captured at Kt6.　There is a margin for manœuvre: 10 .... K—B4; 11 K—B3, P—Kt4; 12 K—Kt3, P—Kt5; 13 K—Kt2 (B2 is not fatal); 13 .... K—B5; 14 K—B2, P—Kt6 ch; 15 K—Kt2, K—Kt5; 16 K—Kt1.　(This is the only move.　He must be able to meet K—B6 with K—B1 and K—R6 with K—R1.)

Note here the general truth that a pawn at its fifth blocked by an opposing pawn is more dangerous than a pawn at its fourth similarly blocked, precisely because of the difference in scope for defensive manœuvres when the obstructing pawn falls.[1]

This is not pure opposition theory.　But the student is guided by

---

[1] Different considerations apply, of course, when Rooks are on the board.

the need to be in the standard opposition position, i.e. with one intervening square between the Kings on the same file.

The term 'opposition' is quite a useful one, but the truth of the matter is that opposition is, among the Chess men, one instance of *zugzwang*. The principle that an odd number of squares should exist between the two Kings for the second player to have the opposition is true enough. Among pawns the important thinking is more empirical.—Shall I be driven into a position from which I must retreat? In point is Diagram 69.

69

Either to play.   What result?

White, to move, must tread warily. If he leaps on the adverse pawn with K—B5, Black plays K—Q5 and Black wins! So White plays 1 K—Kt5. Black cannot play K—Q5 because of White's K—B5. So let him try 1 .... K—B5. Now 2 K—B6, K—Q5; 3 K—B5, wins.

Similarly, if it were Black's turn to move 1 .... not K—Q5; but K—B5 threatening K—Q6. Whatever White does is inadequate to the saving of the pawn.

2 K—Kt5   K—Q6   3 K—B5   K—Q5
or

2 K—Kt3   K—Q6   3 K—B3   K—Q5

Here, clearly, the pawns distort the field from the point of view of pure opposition theory. The requirement is: play so that your move creates the *zugzwang*. There are no laws or rules or formulæ

here, but the technique is characterised by a certain restraint. 'Beware
of making the threat too quickly. There may be a good answer.'

Incidentally, the position in Diagram 69 is worth working out
to the end. Certainly do not jump to the conclusion that whoever
has the move wins.

1 K—Kt5	K—B5	4 K × P	K—B3
2 K—B6	K—Q5	5 K—K6 wins.	
3 K—B5	K—B4		

But if Black is wise he will, on the first move, forget about
threatening White's pawn.

1 K—Kt5	K—Q3!	3 K × P	K—K2
2 K—B6	K—Q2		

and now he draws by the technique shown in previous diagrams.

At this point, it may be useful to refer to a word that has been
used in connection with earlier examples. The King has been
said to indulge in a process called Triangulation.

The word is harder than the idea. The basic fact is that the
King can move to an adjacent square in one move, two moves or
three moves, without returning to its point of origin. Thus it can
move from e2 to e3, or from e2 to d3 to e3, or from e2 to d2 to
e3 or from e2 via d2 and d3 to e3.

In positions where there is a frame of pawns, etc., preventing pure
opposition play, this side-stepping of the King is frequently seen.

The play from Diagram 70 illustrates the process. Let White's
first move be 1 K—K3. Now if Black plays K—K3 he is lost,

70

White to play

by reason of 2 K—K4. The mathematics of opposition give us that result. This King cannot occupy a square on the same file as the antagonist with an odd number of squares between. But it can keep on the same colour, diagonally adjacent to an opposition square, and that serves the same purpose. Ergo K—Q3. Now White, if he plays 2 K—K4, gains nothing because K—K3 opposes him. So he deviates to Q3 (or B3) en route for K4. That will complete a triangular movement, hence 'triangulation'. If Black plays 2 .... K—K3, then 3 K—K4 will win. Black is, therefore, compelled either to Q2, an opposition square, from which he can reach K3 (this is also a triangulation), or K2 (because strict opposition is not necessary before K—K4 is played; this fact is due to the pawn frame), or he can play K—K4, which looks compromising. But K—K4 is not fatal. In answer to 2 .... K—K4, White plays 3 K—K3, and now the situation is again critical. If 3 .... K—K3; 4 K—K4 wins. But 3 .... K—Q3 allows Black to meet 4 K—K4 with K—K3. Then, in turn, White dare not play 5 K—K3 because of 5 .... K—K4, penetrating, but must triangulate with K—Q3. From the diagram position, this dance can go on for ever.

71

White to play

This diagram (71) shows a position where the triangulation is vital. White to move would lose if he played K—K3. So he must play 1 K—Q2 (or B2). If Black plays K—Q3 (or B3) White must still keep out of K3. So he must play 2 K—K2 and reserve K—K3 as an answer to Black's K—K4, or to be made if Black tries other directions by K—QB3, and so gets out of touch with e5.

Sometimes the configuration is such that one side or the other has less triangulation-space than he needs.

Diagram 72 shows White winning a pawn because he can triangulate.

1 K—Q2

Clearly now K—Q4 is useless against 2 K—Q3. So Black plays subtly:

1	K—B2	3 K × P	K—K3
2 K—Q3	K—Q2		

White cannot, it seems, win the game after this:

4 P—B6	P × P	6 K—Kt6	K—Q3
5 K—B5	K—Q2	leads to loss.	

72

73

White wins the QP, whoever has the move

White to play and draw

It may be said, generally, that there are two types of King against King manœuvres, when pawn configurations are involved.

One type is resolved by opposition thinking, the other is made more empirical by the need to measure out the triangulation spaces that will be required for the manœuvring.

Of opposition play, Diagram 73 is a superb example.

White to play only has one move, K—R1! Pure opposition theory might suggest K—R3, but this seems to fail against K—K8.

In answer to K—R1, however, Black can make no progress.

1	K—K8	4 K—R3	K—Q5!
2 K—Kt1	K—K7	5 K—R2!	
3 K—Kt2	K—Q6		

If the Black King tries to work round, then White prepares to triangulate, so as to meet K—KB4 with K—Kt3.

But it can happen that the space problems of one side are exploitable.

Famous is Diagram 74, the Lasker–Reichelm analysis. To call this a distant opposition study is misleading, because the pawn field biases the operation of rules. Some effort at scientific classification has been made under the formula 'related squares', but as the determination of the proper square is as empirical as any triangulation manœuvre, the student is not greatly assisted. In the diagram position it is clear that White has lines of entry into the Black pawn field, at b5 and g5—h5. Equally obviously Black can effectively bar the access in either direction. But can White manœuvre so as to prevent Black from having his King available for both dangers? Thus, if the White King is at Q3 with the move, there is only one safe square for the Black King. If he is on QB2, he can meet an advance via QB4, and he can also meet the White King on good ground if the latter tries for g5. It follows that if the White King be on Q3, and Black King on QB2 with Black to move, Black must lose.

Study by Em. Lasker and
74   Reichelm

White to play and win

Exhaustive analysis has produced the following method:

1 K—Kt1!	K—Kt2	4 K—B2	K—Q1
2 K—B1	K—B2	5 K—B3	K—B2
3 K—Q1	K—Q2	(because K—B4 is threatened)

   6 K—Q3

and Black has to cede one of the avenues of approach.

According to the best opinion, Black, to move, from the diagram position, draws as follows:

| 1 .... | K—Kt2 | 3 K—Kt2 | K—R1 |
| 2 K—Kt1 | K—R2 | 4 K—B2 | K—Kt2 |

(five squares away on the same colour and not too far in file distance)

   5 K—Q2   K—B1

(not by formula, but by counting!) If now 6 K—B2, K—Kt2. Again, if 6 K—K file, K—Q file on corresponding colour. It just happens that Black's first move compensates for the relative lack of manœuvring space.

Cognate, in the theme of greater options, is a pretty study by that great English master of endgame study, the late T. R. Dawson, a man whose mathematical efforts in Chess were outshone, even redeemed, by the work of his creative imagination. Diagram 75 shows a position in which the White King is desirous of reaching Q4. If he arrives at K3 while the Black King is at Q4 and to move, evidently he will reach his objective. (Black's K—B4 will be met by K—K4, forcing K—B3 or K—Kt3.) Certain other truths follow. That if, when the Black King is at B3, the White King arrives at B3, White's triangulations will compromise Black. But if (and this is, from the opposition point of view, paradoxical) the White King gets first to B3, the reply K—B3 is perfect. If then K—K4, K—B4; alternatively, if K—K3, K—Q4 is adequate.

75   Study by T. R. Dawson

White to play and win

There is, however, one way of forcing an arrival at B3 when the Black King is at B3.

1 K—Q1

Black has a choice of two main lines of play (other moves lead to similar play). He has to choose K—B3 or K—B4. If

| 1 .... | K—B4 | 2 K—K2 |

If then

| 2 .... | K—Q4 | 3 K—K3 wins. |

If

| 2 .... | K—Kt3 | 3 K—K3 wins. |

If

| 2 .... | K—B3 | 3 K—B3 wins. |

If (the other variation)

| 1 .... | K—B3 | 2 K—Q2 | K—B4 |
| | | (K—Q4 is met by K—K3) |

3 K—K2   K—B3
(again K—Q4 is not playable)

4 K—B3
Now if

| 4 .... | K—Q4 | 5 K—K3 |

If

| 4 .... | K—B4 | 5 K—K4, etc. |

But there is more play in the position

| 4 .... | K—Kt3 |

(no difference in effect)

5 K—K3	K—B4	7 K—Q4	K—Kt3
6 K—K4	K—B3	8 K×P	K—B3
		with the opposition!

9 K—Q4	K—Kt3	12 K—B4	K—B3
10 P—B4	K—B3	13 P—B3!
11 P—QB5	K—B2

fulfilling its *raison d'être*. Black must retreat and lose. All the above play seems to constitute a mental movement more analogous to Draughts than to Chess. It is a manœuvring to avoid commitment.

This is not only true of King movements. Reflection will show that pawn movements are in the same category. If options should not be exhausted, then it follows that a pawn group that has altered its formation is at a disadvantage relatively to an undisturbed pawn group. Options in pawn moves lie with the unmoved ones: also, the access of conquering Kings is easier when the proles have been disturbed.

Let the reader set up White pawns at f2, g2, h2 and Black pawns at f5, g6, h7.

With P—f4, White reduces Black's options to two, h6 and h5.

If h5 is played, then g3 reserves two options for White, h4 reserves one. In both cases Black has no move left.

If h6 is played, instead, there comes h4, leaving only h5 to be played, then g3 creates *zugzwang*.

Imagine now that an opposition situation obtains on other parts of the board; it follows that the committed nature of the Black pawns will prove a factor for loss.

To illustrate this, I use a position for which I am indebted to Mr. Joseph, the Manchester master. Diagram 76 is of manifold interest.

76

First it shows a type of advantage that is very desirable, from the point of view of the player who wants to gain moves. (To gain ground while one's opponent is stationary is an advantage in most phases of the game.) White knows, here, that Black must lose a move in order to free his Knight. Further, not only has White a move in hand in addition to the normal benefit of turn to move: he also has positive purposes that he can fulfil. In particular he can alter the pawn position in his favour before exchanges and the opposition duel.

1 B—K4   P—Kt3

Note that 1 .... K—R2 (or K—Kt1) takes advantage of a technical feature, but one that in this case is ineffective for tactical reasons. Thus:

1 B—K4   K—Kt1   2 B × P   P—Kt3

cutting off the Bishop and being able to guard the BP with the Knight. But there is a rescue force to hand.

3 P—B4

The process is not simple.

3 ....   Kt—Q3   4 P—Kt4   K—Kt2

Now, *not* immediately 5 P—B5, because 5 .... P—Kt4; 6 P—B6 leaves the pawns in a less than optimum position. But 5 P—R4 makes 6 P—B5 into a winning threat. Therefore, in reply to 1 B—K4, Black must move a pawn. He has the choice of P—R3, P—R4 and P—Kt3. The last is reasonable.

This 1 .... P—Kt3 is met by 2 B—Q5, attacking another pawn. Black may play P—B3 or P—B4. The minimum move (i.e. preserving most options) is P—B3. Observe that were he to play P—B4 White would not be wise to hunt pawns in the conventional way with 3 B—Kt8, P—R3; 4 B—R7, because the freeing of the Knight makes victory difficult.

White's next manœuvre is with the King.

So after

1 B—K4   P—Kt3   2 B—Q5   P—B3

there follows

3 K—B2   K moves   5 K—Q3   K—B2
4 B × Kt   K × B   6 K—B4   K—B3

Clearly, now, White has in hand several pawn moves that he can lose for *zugzwang* purposes.

7 P—R4

(not the only move, but adequate. Note that in pawn exploitation it is frequently advantageous to move the pawn on the line where the other is least committed. E.g. if the pawns were at f7, g6, h5, White's most useful move would be with the Bishop's pawn).

7 ....   P—B4

(to stop 8. P—Kt4)

Delicacy is required; 8 P—B4 may throw away a neatly gained advantage. Thus if 8 P—B4, P—R3. If then 9 P—Kt3, P—R4 *zugzwang*. If, instead, 9 P—R5!?, P × P; 10 P—Kt3, Black turns the tables with 10 .... P—R5!; 11 P × P, P—R4!, the exploitation of doubled pawns mentioned above.

On the eighth move, therefore, be careful. P—B3 is playable because Black dare not risk P—B5, which gives the White King a square. But best is 8 P—Kt3.

Now the reader can work out Black's difficulties.

8 .... P—R4 is met by P—B4 or P—B3. 8 .... P—B5 is compromising. White could even win by ignoring it with P—Kt4. Then if 9 .... P—Kt4; 10 P × P, P × P; 11 P—B3.

The win, thereafter, would be delicate. White would go for the QRP. (The capture, 9 P × P, would also win—even more delicately —as the reader can work out for himself.)

Again,

8	P—R3	10 P—R5	P—Kt5
9 P—B3	P—Kt4	11 P—B4	

completes a *zugzwang*. The winning method will then be for White to win the QRP and promote before the Black King can organise the promoting Black pawn.

Before parting from this study, the reader should notice that in some variations, even after the win of the opposition, the win of the game is not automatic.

Games do not win themselves.

In this study the reader will have appreciated that all that technique offers is the information that there are possibilities. What the possibilities are must be worked out imaginatively, or laboriously with a counting of fingers, and, possibly, an abacus. (It has never been decided whether there is a penalty on a player who writes out a series of future moves on his score-sheet in order to confirm, or assist, mental counting.)

Every engineer will agree that in practical dynamics the formula does not save the labour, which is the study of detail.

A dynamic study by Grigorieff illustrates this for Chess. In Diagram 77 the important practical feature is that with P—Q4 White (the lesser force) is threatening to promote with check.

Therefore

| 1 .... | K—Kt4 | 3 P—Q5 | K—K4 |
| 2 K—B7 | K—B4 | 4 P—K4 | |

Now the threat is K—K7.

77 Study by Grigorieff	78 Study by Grigorieff

White to play and win	White to play and win

If 4 .... P—R4; 5 K—K7 will lead to promotions by both and check at KR8 by White! If 4 .... P—Kt4, the same promotions will take place, then Q6 ch, K × P, Q—K Kt6 ch decides the issue. Therefore

| 4 .... | K—Q3 | 6 P—K5 ch K × P |
| 5 K—B6 | P—R4 | 7 P—K6 |

and promotes in time to stop Black's promotion.

Two other studies by Grigorieff constitute fitting ornaments to a chapter on the play of Kings and pawns.

Diagram 78 is a delicate study in opposition play. The play is:

| 1 P—Kt4 | K—R6 | 3 K—Kt6 | K—Kt6 |
| 2 K—R5 | K—Kt7 | 4 K—Kt5 | |

and opposition play until 11 .... K—KB6; 12 K—KB5, K—Kt7; 13 K—Kt6, K—R6; 14 K—R5 wins. If 13 .... K—B6; 14 P—R3, K—B5; 15 K—R5 wins.

Diagram 79 is solved by the following process

1 P—B4

causing K—Kt5

79   Study by Grigorieff

White to play and win

2 P—R4	P—Q4	7 P—B7	K—K2
3 P—B5	K—B4	8 P—R7	P—Q7
4 P—R5	P—Q5	9 P—B8 = Q ch	K × Q
5 P—B6	K—Q3	10 P—R8 = Q ch wins.	
6 P—R6	P—Q6		

Two separate processes, BP drawing King, RP racing against QP, and both movements beautifully synchronised.

As a supplementary note to this chapter, a word may be useful on *zugzwang*.

Generally *zugzwang* is a characteristic of the manœuvres of short range pieces, Kings and pawns, and in certain circumstances the Knight. But, more generally it applies where there is any concentration of pieces in defence of a specific point or set of points.

Diagram 80 shows a neat restriction of the scope of a Rook, and a *zugzwang* resulting.

1 B—Kt6 ch   K—Q1   2 B—B7 *zugzwang*.

When major pieces are concerned, *zugzwang* and the cognate need to lose moves are less of a rarity than one might expect.

The following study by Réti (Diagram 81) illustrates how valuable the loss of a tempo can be, even on the part of a Rook. (The position is also valuable because it shows how quickly a distant King can get to close quarters.)

1 R—Q2

(R—Q3 also wins, but the important point is: *not* R—Q1, which only draws if 1 R—Q1, P—Q5; 2 K—Q7, K—Q4!)

80

81   Study by Réti

White to play and win   White to play and win

After

| 1 .... | P—Q5 | 2 R—Q1! |

The reason why this could not be the first move was that it had to be the second. Now Black yields ground to White.

| 2 .... | K—Q4 | 4 K—B6 | K—K6 |
| 3 K—Q7 | K—K5 | 5 K—B5 | |

and the attack on the pawn (before Black can attack the Rook) is decisive.

| 5 .... | P—Q6 | 6 K—B4, etc. |

In practical play there is an historic Rook and pawn ending by Alekhine against Sir George Thomas, in which the latter could have drawn if it had not been his move (Diagram 82).

Examine the White Rook's position. He dare not move from the file without allowing a winning pawn advance (P—Kt7, followed by P—R6 and R—R8). Nor can he move from the rank without allowing the Black King to approximate to the pawn, eventually win it, and move over to the aid of the Black pawns. Nor can the White King move, without allowing P—Kt7. If Black has to move, any King move can be met by a check that enables the position to be restored, e.g.:

1	K—B2	4 R—R6 ch	K—Kt2
2 R—B6 ch	K—Kt1	5 R—KKt6!	
3 R—Kt6 ch	K—R2		

Thomas—Alekhine
82   (Hastings, 1922)

(If after R—B6 ch, K—K2, then R—B1 cutting off the Black King.) Nor does Black win by 1 .... R—B7 ch; 2 K—K3. If now 2 .... R—B1 (e.g.); 3 K—K2! Not 3 R—Kt4, R—R1 and P—R6, R7, R8, cannot be stopped. But 3 K—K2 threatens this, e.g.:

3	R—B2	5 K—B1	P—R6
4 R—Kt4	R—R2	6 K—Kt1	

(obviously not R × P)

6 ....   P—Kt7
(threatening P—R7 ch)

7 K—R2
and this, with careful handling, amounts to a draw.

In the actual game there happened (with omission of unnecessary moves):

1 P—Kt6	K—R3	6 R—Q8 ch	K—B6
2 P—Kt7 ch	K × P	7 R—KKt8	K—Q7
3 R—Kt7 ch	K—B3	8 R—QR8	R—B7 ch
4 R—Kt6 ch	K—Q4	9 K—Kt4	P—Kt7
5 R—Kt8	K—Q5	10 R—R1	

(observe that Black's game is still not simple. If now 10 .... R—B8; 11 R checks wins the pawn.)

10 ....   K—K6

If now the Rook checks up the file, the King will approach it until checks are exhausted, and P—Kt8 will be unpreventable. Therefore,

| 11 K—R3! | R—K7 | 13 K—R2 | P—R6! |
| 12 R—KKt1 | K—B6 | and if this be captured, |

| 14 K × P | R—K1 |

creates a mating threat.

Zugzwang, in a case like this, is something that cannot be organised; it is an effect of pressure and lack of space. Let it be emphasised that it is not peculiar to the endgame; it can occur in the earlier game, on those rare occasions when the entire defence concentrating on one point, becomes paralysed. Then moves have to be made which either allow the opponent to run amok in other parts of the board, or involve retreat. There are some historic occurrences in the records of Chess. Nimzovitch reduced Sämisch to *zugzwang* in some 22 moves, and Alekhine, playing avenging Achilles, reduced the Hector of Chess to *zugzwang* in a game of comparable shortness (see p. 157).

More typical is the collapse under pressure in the late game, when one side has greater control of space than the other. Thus Diagram 83 shows a possibility that arose in a game in which the author was Black and in which recognition of *zugzwang* is necessary to victory, direct attack being less satisfactory.

83

Black to play

Thus:

1	R—QR6	2 Kt—B3	Kt—B2

with the threat of Kt—Kt4.

3 Kt—Kt1	Kt—Kt4

and White is movebound.   On the other hand

1	R—KR6

is less satisfactory.

2 Kt—KB3	Kt—B2	4 R—Q3
3 P—Q6	Kt—Kt4	

and White has more life than he need have been granted.   Exchanges here would lead to a draw.

A comparable position that occurred to the author (who was White), and is reprinted from the *New Statesman*, is Diagram 84. It is quite amusing because two Rooks are movebound in a most unusual way.

84

White to play

1 P—Kt6 ch	K—B3

(to prevent K—Kt5)

2 R—Q1	P—Q6

(in order to meet QR—K1 with R—Q5)

3 R × P	P—Kt3	5 R—K8! *zugzwang*.
4 R—Q5	R(1)—Q2	

CHAPTER IV
THE VARYING VALUES OF PIECES

On first principles one would expect that, whereas in the early game the values of the pieces are made unstable by tactical vicissitudes, in the endgame they should be relatively stable. Yet there are surprises and disappointments galore to delight or distress those who make these easy assumptions.

Thus no one will conduct his game in the belief that a Knight is more useful than a Rook in the endgame. Indeed, since a Rook can force mate and two Knights cannot, it is demonstrable that such a belief would be an absurdity.

Yet Diagram 85 shows a situation where a Knight achieves more than a Rook.

In this position, White to move can draw:

85

White to play and draw.
Substitute Rook for Knight and
White loses

1 Kt—Q4   P—Kt7   2 Kt—K2 ch

then captures one pawn and holds the other. Alternatively, 1 ....
P—B7 is met by Kt × KtP, holding the BP.

Now substitute, in the diagram position, a Rook. Even with the move this piece cannot stop these two pawns. Whichever it attacks from the rear can advance, or its companion can advance. Next move the rearmost one advances.

If the Rook works laterally, similar play (e.g. 1 R—K3, P—Kt7 (or B7); 2 R—Kt3 (or B3), P—B7 (or Kt7)).

And if

1 R—K1 ch	K—B7	3 R—QKt1
2 R—QB1	P—Kt7	

Now Black must be patient, not 3 .... P—B7; 4 R × P (with a pin), but

3 ....   K—K6

This last variation brings to mind one type of situation where the principle that two pawns on the sixth defeat a Rook does not hold good. That is when the position of Kings is tactically relevant.

Diagram 86 presents quite a sensational position from actual play.

Keres—Eliskases
86   (Noordwijk, 1938)

Black to play and draw

Black drew in the following way:

1	R—Kt3 ch	6 K—Kt1	R—Kt3 ch
2 K—B1	R—KR3	7 K—R2	R—R3 ch
3 K—Q1	K—Q6	8 K—Kt1	R—Kt3 ch
4 K—K1	K—K6	9 K—B1	R—KR3, etc.,
5 K—B1	K—B6		draws.

Observe that this extraordinary effect could only have been achieved with RP and KtP. If the pawns were not at the extreme wing there would be a point at which Black's mating threat could be thwarted by a promotion with check.

A subtlety of play is shown in Diagram 87. Here the mating threat is in a context which permits the capture of the pawns.

87　　　Study by Sapero

White to play and win

1 R—Q2 ch　　K—Kt8
(not R8 because of K—Kt3)

2 K—B3
Black now has a difficult choice. Best is

2 ....　　　　K—B8　　　3 R—QR2　K—Q8
(if 3 .... K—Kt8; 4 R—K2 creates *zugzwang*)

4 K—Q3　　　K—B8　　　6 R—R1 ch K—Kt7
5 K—K3　　　P—R7　　　7 R—R1!
and now the other pawn cannot advance because R × P will pin it. Consequently White has time for K—B3, etc.

If, on move two, Black plays P—Kt7, the sequence is also subtle:

3 R—Q1 ch　　K—R7　　　4 R—KKt1 with *zugzwang*.
To return to the Knight, Diagram 85 shows him in a preferential position. He does not always show to such advantage.

If you put a Knight on e1, a hostile Bishop on e4 paralyses him. (One is apt to forget that during that period the Bishop is also tied to a square, but only in the way that a slave driver has to stay by the slave.) Then the Knight seems a very ineffective piece. Yet there are very many positions where a Knight can do more than a Bishop. A Knight can help the promotion of a Rook's pawn, where a Bishop being of the wrong colour (not the colour of the promotion square) cannot evict an occupying King. A propos of Bishops of the wrong colour, it must not be said dogmatically that the Bishop fails to help home a Rook's pawn, working towards a square of the opposite colour. The rule so stated is too narrowly stated. I call the next diagram 'The Exception that Improves the Rule'. (A much better statement than the conventional mistranslation of *exceptio probat regulam*.)

88

White to play and win

White wins with 1 B—R7! momentarily blocking the pawn. But this gives the White King time to approach and gently to steer the Black King away. Observe that if the White King were further away than it is, for example if it were situated at h2, Black could still draw by 1 .... K—B3, threatening K—Kt4. This makes the Bishop move. If 2 B—Kt8, K—Kt3 draws. If 2 B—Kt1, 2 .... K—B2, threatening K—Kt1, forces 3 B—R7 and a repetition of the position and the play. It is, generally, true to say that when a Rook's pawn is left the player who has a Knight is usually more fortunate than one who has a Bishop of the wrong colour. In the late middle game it frequently happens that a Knight proves more valuable than a Bishop because it can operate against pawns on diverse-coloured squares with great destructiveness. A simple case is presented in Diagram 89. Here the Knight wins a pawn while the Bishop cannot even attack one. But observe the other aspect. Black to move can play B—B4. If now Kt × P, B—Q2 and the Knight is only extricated with difficulty.

89

90

White to move, wins a pawn.
Black to move, embarrasses
the Knight

White cannot win

Compare the position in Diagram 90. Here White cannot prevent the King from winning the pawn by K—Q3. If the Knight stood at K5, R5, Kt4 or Q4, it would be as effective as a pawn on Kt5 or Q5. In other words, the Knight must be behind the pawn in order to guarantee it against King capture. On the other hand, place in Diagram 90 a Bishop (instead of the Knight) on any square where it guards the pawn (R8, Kt7, Q7, K8), or behind the pawn, and the guard is permanent and effective. Also, what Knight action is comparable to that of a Bishop from a distance? Put a Bishop on h1, a pawn on a7, and the hostile King on c7. If the pawn is hostile to the Bishop, the Bishop stops it. If it is friendly the Bishop guarantees the promotion, keeping the King from b7.

Contrast Diagram 91. Here the Knight controls a field such that it captures the KP. Substitute for the Knight on g4 a Bishop on g5 and the pawn is defensible (by K—B2).

Not for nothing have practical players assessed an exchange of Bishop for Knight as no loss. Frequently the Bishop is tactically superior, less frequently the Knight. Wins dependent on the superiority which is the Bishop's greater range (13 squares against the Knight's 8) must be discounted when one considers wins due to the fact that the Knight can operate on squares that one particular Bishop cannot control. Diagram 92 shows the great power of a Bishop when the lines are open to its action, especially in combination with a Queen.

1 .... B—Kt4; 2 R—K1, Q—Q4; 3 K—B2, B—B3 is unanswerable.

91

White cannot save the pawns

92   (White)

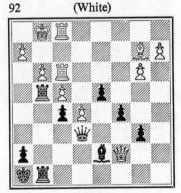

(Black)
Black to play and win

A Knight, be it noted, is also not useless on a diagonal. Visualise a Castled King (King side) with pawn having moved to g3 and no piece on g2. Then given a hostile Queen on e4 or d5 and a Knight on g5 or e5, mate is threatened at h3, or serious check at f3.

Another pair of examples may be useful. Diagram 93, from a game in which the author was Black, shows how Knights can be mobilised into activity and aggression, rendering a Bishop helpless, to say nothing of embarrassing a Rook. The play was 9 ....

93   Grob—Abrahams (1948)

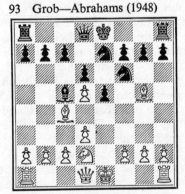

Black to play

Kt—Q2; 10 0—0, P—KB3; 11 B—K3, 0—0; 12 B × B, Kt × B;
13 P—B4, Kt—B4; 14 R—B3, P—QKt4; 15 B—Kt3, Q—K1;
16 Kt—B1, Kt—Q5; 17 R—K3, Q—B2, and Black wins a pawn.

On the other hand, Diagram 94 shows a position where a Knight
is quite helpless. Black has a pawn to the good, but loses through
zugzwang. If, e.g. 1 .... P—QKt4; 2 P—R5. Then after pawn
moves are exhausted, the Knight will fall. In Chess every dog has
its day. Always the consideration of value as between Knight and
Bishop is dependent on the particular position.

94

Black to move, loses

Diagram 95 shows a position where exchange of Bishop for
Knight can wind up the game. 1 .... B × Kt ch followed by R—
KR1 wins. If it is not played, then the Knight proves useful.
(1 .... R—R1; 2 Kt—Q1 sets up a defence.)

95　Lupi—Abrahams (1946)

Quite often short-range tactical considerations cause a player to exchange a Bishop for a Knight. Before he does that operation let him consider whether it will leave the opponent in control of some field of action. Every player has been at some time in a position where he would give his kingdom for a Bishop rather than a horse. Every exchange calls for an assessment in which the valuer is assisted if he has an idea what operations can be carried out in the absence of the piece he is giving up. The Knight may have such power that it is desirable to eliminate him at all costs. Especially a fianchetto pawn formation, or the open spaces behind advanced centre pawns, give scope to hostile Knights, to say nothing of heavier pieces, if the defender is lacking one or more Bishops. On the other hand, you may have a position which offers no such openings to the opponent. Always the details of the particular position form the decisive factor.

Apart from tactical points, if we wish to assess Knight against Bishop, certain considerations will show us that the difference is not a great one.

First, in King, minor piece, and pawn endings with one pawn left, the defending minor piece, whether Knight or Bishop, can usually sacrifice itself for the pawn, leaving the opponent without a mating force.

Assessing the impeding power of the minor piece, we find positions in which the Bishop is superior, and others in which the Knight is superior. Each can be found capable of stopping some pawn that the other could not cope with. A Knight can block the path of a Bishop, cutting it off from the pawn it seeks to capture. A Bishop, on the other hand, may succeed in chasing the Knight off some crucial square or set of squares. But, as a general proposition, it is true to say that both King and Knight against King Bishop (or Knight) and pawn, and King and Bishop against King Bishop (or Knight) and pawn, are likely to be drawn. On the other hand, King Rook and pawn, against either King and Knight or King and Bishop, in a vast majority of cases win. Again, King and Rook against King and Bishop is usually a draw. King and Rook against King and Knight is regarded as a draw, unless the Knight is badly situated. Diagram 96, a fine study by Auerbach, is in point. 1 R—KKt6, Kt—K1; 2 K—B5, Kt—Kt2 ch; 3 K—B6, Kt × P ch; 4 K—B7, Kt—B5; 5 R—Kt7 ch, K—R1; 6 R—Kt4, Kt—R6; 7 K—Kt6, K—Kt1; 8 K × P ch eventually wins the Knight. Diagram 97, by the same author, shows the limitation of the Knight, the shortness of its range. Here it is cleverly exploited by King, pawn, and Knight:

96   Study by Auerbach   97   Study by Auerbach

White to play and win   White to play and win

1 Kt—Q6	Kt—Kt2	6 K—B7	Kt—B4
2 Kt—K4	Kt—K1	7 Kt—K4	Kt—Kt2
3 K—B8	Kt—Kt2	8 Kt—Q6	Kt—B4
4 K—K7	K—Kt1	9 K—B8 wins.	
5 Kt—B6 ch	K—R1		

We know that, against a Rook, a Bishop is less likely to be 'in angustis' than a Knight, less likely to be forced on to a line where it can be pinned. But there is quite a large number of positions in which the Bishop is restricted.

Diagram 98 is a fairly easy case. 1 R—K1 forces 1 .... B—B4. Then 2 R—K8 ch, B—B1; 3 R—Kt8, P—Kt4; 4 R × P, B—Q3; 5 R—Q5, B—K2; 6 R—QR5 wins.

98

White to play and win

The relatively great power of the Rook reduces the issue, B *v* Kt, into perspective.

When one considers the power of the Rook, which in two moves can reach any square on the empty board from any other square, it is clear that the superiority of that piece to Bishop or Knight is in a different category from any superiority that Bishop may hold over Knight, and that the lesser differences cannot be the subject matter of any dogmatic pronouncement.[1]

Consider that a Rook and pawn can even defeat Bishop and Knight together if the Rook can attack, in one move, the Bishop and the Knight on differently coloured squares. E.g. a Rook moves to c6, forking, as it were, a Bishop on c5 and a Knight on a6. If Kings and pawns are out of the field, one piece will fall.[2]

As to the earlier game, Steinitz said that he wanted a Knight established on Q6. Who would not give a Bishop in exchange for such a force? But an attack would have to be serious indeed before one gave a Rook for it.

In the endgame the relevant limitations of a Knight are clearer, so that a player with an unpromising Knight will be reluctant to make the heavy exchanges that constitute transition to an ending. Thus you have six pawns against your opponent's six (yours on a2, b2, c2, f2, g2, h2, his on the corresponding squares). You have a Bishop on K2, he has a Knight on KB3. Your Rook is on K1, his on Q1, then you are not wrong to offer exchanges with R—Q1 (I do not say that that is the best move), but he would be unwise to make the exchange. Probably the outcome would be a draw, but Black's task would be heavier. Were his Knight and his King, however, better developed than yours, he might welcome the exchange.

---

[1] A realistic study by Havasi shows how, given a pawn superiority, a Bishop exploits the weakness of a Knight: 7K, 16, 3p4, 4kt1P1, 7k, P7, 7B.
1 P—Kt5, Kt×P; 2 B×P (controlling the Knight's field), 2 ....
K—Kt6; 3 P—R4, Kt—R6; 4 P—R5, Kt—B5; 5 B—B7, again in control, and the Knight can do nothing about the Rook's pawn.
A companion piece by the same composer shows the difficult task of two Knights reducing the Bishop: 16, Kt2b4, 8, K2Kt4, pPk5, 16.
1 Kt—Kt5 ch, K—Kt7; 2 Kt×P, B×Kt; 3 Kt—Kt4.
If the Bishop retreats 2 .... B—B1 the Knight develops from R3 to Q7, then the other Knight moves to B5, shielding the pawn.

[2] Of course there are a great many positions where a Bishop can do more work than a Rook. Everything depends on the configuration and scope. Here is a position where a Bishop wins the exchange very easily:
2r3k1, p4rp1, 2p2b2, 8, 4B3, 4B1P1, PP3P1P, 1R4K1.
By B—KB5, White wins the exchange. If Black plays R—K1, to prevent B—K6, then B—Kt6 is of equal effect.

When one side has a pawn to the good, the Bishop is frequently a better ally and a stronger opponent. But do not underestimate the power of a Knight to stop a pawn from promotion.

Diagram 99 shows how it can be done. The simple feature is revealed as follows:

1 Kt—Q2 ch   K—K7   2 Kt—K4
threatening the pawn. If the pawn promotes to Queen Kt—Kt3 forks the King and Queen.

If

1 ....   K—K8   2 Kt—B3 ch
and settles on KR2. Observe how difficult that makes the King's approach; e.g. K3 is taboo because of the fork at g4.

99   100

White to play and draw   White to play and draw

The movement is, however, one of delicacy. White must not play 1 Kt—K3 ch. There would follow 1 .... K—K7; 2 Kt—B5, contemplating the fork at g3.

But this is thwarted by 2 .... K—B6; 3 Kt—Q4 ch, K—Kt5; 4 Kt—B2, K—B5, and the Knight is helpless.

We have already seen that a Knight can operate against two joined pawns.

Diagram 100 shows a possibility that may surprise many. White draws by 1 Kt—B3 followed by Kt—K2. E.g.:

1 Kt—B3   P—R6   2 Kt—K2
                              and occupies g3.

If

| 1 .... | P—Kt6 | 3 Kt—Kt1 |
| 2 Kt—K2 | P—Kt7 | |

holds everything.

Observe that if the Knight were on R3 instead of R4, it could not save the game, because it could not strike at g3 and g1 on the second move.

1 Kt—B2   P—Kt6   2 Kt—K3(K1 or Q4) P—R6

From R2 on the other hand it can stop the pawns.   Also from Kt4—viz.:

| 1 Kt—Q3 | P—R6 | 3 Kt—R1 |
| 2 Kt—B2 | P—R7 | |

If

1 ....   P—Kt6   2 Kt—B4

and settles on R3.[1]

The next Diagram (101) is an ending by Grigorieff which is a very instructive study in Knight-paths.

101   Study by Grigorieff

White to play and draw

The first move is

1. Kt—B7

(not Kt—Kt6, which leads nowhere)

[1] The importance of the Knight's power to control an advancing pawn makes itself felt in the middle game—and in the stages of transition to the endgame.   Thus in the position 16,PK6,2Kt2rp1,2R5,r6k,16, White can allow exchange of Rooks.   Then King and RP will hold the opposing Rook and the Knight will attend to the pawn.   Thus:
1 R—QR4, R—B3 ch; 2 K—Kt5, R×R; 3 Kt×R, P—Kt5; 4 P—R7, R—B1; 5 Kt—B3, P—Kt6; 6 Kt—K2, P—Kt7; 7 K—Kt6, draws.

If

| 1 .... | P—R6 | 3 Kt—Q4 ch |
| 2 Kt—Kt5 | P—R7 | |

Observe, now, how many squares the Knight controls in the King's field.

If

| 3 .... | K—K5 | 4 Kt—B2 |

and the King cannot cross the Queen's file. It is as if an invisible ray were guarding the access. If 3 .... K—K6; 4 Kt—Kt3 has a similar effect. The King cannot cross via d3 or e2 and d1. So he must move via f2, e1, d1 to c2, by which time the White King has arrived, and this is so in the case of 3 .... K—B7.

If he does not wish to save a move (or does not see how to save a move in that unobvious way) something quite pretty can happen.

3 Kt—Q4 ch	K—K6	7 K—Q4	K—B7
4 Kt—Kt3	K—B7	8 Kt—R1 ch	K—Kt7
5 K—K6	K—K8	9 K—Q3	K × Kt
6 K—Q5	K—Q8	10 K—B2 stalemate.	

This kind of ending is a feature of King chases when the attacking King ends its course on the Rook's file.

To return to the diagram position. Suppose that Black decides to use his King earlier, the play is instructive.

| 1 Kt—B7 | K—K5 | 3 K—K5 | K—B5 |
| 2 Kt—Kt5 | K—Q6 | 4 Kt—R3 ch | |

and this Knight cannot be eliminated from the defence.

If

| 4 .... | K—Kt6 | 6 Kt—Q4 |
| 5 Kt—Kt5 | K—Kt5 | still stopping the pawn! |

| 6 .... | K—B5 | 8 Kt—R3 *Da capo*. |
| 7 Kt—B2 | K—B6 | |

An interesting defect in the Knight's powers is shown in Diagram 102. Here Black, to move, loses. Simple is:

| 1 .... | P—R7 | 2 Kt—Kt3 mate. |

Less simple is

1	K—R7	3 Kt—B1	P—R7
2 Kt—K2	K—R8	4 Kt—Kt3 mate.	

But White to move cannot force this.

If

1 Kt—K2	P—R7

draws immediately.

If 1 Kt—Kt3 ch, K—R7, and the Knight may wander away where it likes, but (if Black has not availed himself of P—R7) it will always return to Kt3 with check, which is useless. *In other words, a Knight cannot lose a move.*

102

Black to move, loses.
White to move, draws

103   Study by Bron

White to play and win

This interesting fact is beautifully exploited in Diagram 103, a study by the Czech composer Bron.

The first manœuvre is a slight triangulation.

1 K—B7	Kt—R3 ch

(if 1 .... P—R3 we reach more quickly a position which occurs in the main play later)

2 K—B8	Kt—Kt1	3 Kt—Kt4	P—R3

(if Kt—R3, not 4 Kt × Kt, but 4 Kt—K5 with mate next move)

4 K—B7	K—R2	5 Kt—K5	K—R1

Here we have the problem. If the King were now at R2, Kt—Kt6 would force Black to move and lose. Unhappily, the Knight cannot force this denouement because he cannot lose a move.

But a King can lose a move! By triangulation, as we have seen. We must therefore place the Knight where it covers all exits, bring the King out for a triangulation, then return it and start again, having lost a move.

6 Kt—B4	K—R2	8 Kt—K8	K—R2
7 Kt—Q6	K—R1	9 K—K6	

(the exits of the King and Knight being closed)

9	K—R1	11 K—Q7	K—R1
10 K—Q6	K—R2	12 K—K6	

('Operation Triangulation' completed)

12	K—R2	15 Kt—K6	K—R1
13 K—B7	K—R1	16 Kt—B8 *zugzwang.*	
14 Kt—B7	K—R2		

When the dominant force is King, Rook and Bishop against King and Rook, there are more chances of victory than there are with King, Rook and Knight against King and Rook.

One 'set-up', however, is technically important. (Diagram 104.) That combination of Knight and Rook against a King in the corner is quite paralysing, and Rook and Bishop can very rarely organise so terrible a mating threat. (Note that a similar terror would exist if the White Rook were on the seventh rank, instead of the seventh file.)

104

Black to play. What result?

Black cannot extricate himself with an offer of exchanges at g7 because then R—R1 ch forces mate. He is driven to the back row, and with R—f8 he can force the White Rook to g6. Then he has a resource. The Rook endeavours to sacrifice itself with checks, leaving stalemate. Were the White King able to reach g6, this process would fail, because check on g5 would be met by K × R. But, with g6 occupied, Black can cheerfully (but carefully) check. (1 .... R—R1; 2 K—B3, R—KB1; 3 R—KKt6, R—B1 ch; 4 K—Q4, R—B5 ch!—*not* R—Q1 ch.)

Incidentally, a Knight in combination with a Bishop can, as is known, force mate.

From any position, by using Bishop, Knight and King as an edge to the board (e.g. King on d4, Bishop on e4, Knight on f3, opposing King on e6), one can coerce the King to the real edge of the board and gently muster him to the corner controlled by the Bishop. One aims at a position like the following: 4k3, 8, 4K3, 5Kt2, 7B, 24.

Then if White is to move:

1 B—Kt5	K—B1	6 Kt—K7	K—R1
2 B—K7 ch	K—Kt1	7 Kt—Kt6 ch	K—R2
3 K—B6	K—R2	8 Kt—B8 ch	K—R1
4 K—B7	K—R1	9 B—B6 mate.	
5 B—Kt5	K—R2		

Mate with two Bishops is much easier and needs no treatment.

No one need be ashamed at having difficulty in forcing mate with Bishop and Knight against King within a reasonable number of moves. A slight inaccuracy can add half a dozen moves to the solution all too easily.

Combinations resulting in mate are easier, given the imagination that sees them, than are long technical processes.

The next diagram (number 105) is a study showing a neat exploitation of the combined power of Bishop and Knight. White ignores Black's operations, while he organises a mate. 1 B—K2, K—Kt2 ch; 2 K—Kt2, B—Q5; 3 Kt—Kt3, B × Kt; 4 Kt—R5 ch, K—R1; 5 Kt—B6, B—B6; 6 B—R6, P—Kt4; 7 K—B3, and via Kt4, etc., to QB8. This study constitutes, also, a rather striking example of a win *with Bishops of opposite colour*.

Diagram 106 shows a brilliant 'save' by Knight against Bishop. 1 K—Q5, K—Q2; 2 P—R4 threatens to free the Knight. 2 .... P—R4; 3 K—B4, K—B3; 4 Kt—B7, K × Kt; 5 K—Kt5, B—Kt3; 6 K—R6 wins the pawn or achieves stalemate.

Another interesting combination of Knight and Rook is shown in Diagram 107. They achieve a perpetual check.

| 1 Kt—B6 ch | K—B1 | 2 Kt—R7 ch | K—K1 or Kt1 |

105   Study by Ratner

White to play and win

106   Study by Mattison

White to play and draw

107

White to play and draw

108 Abrahams—Christoffel (1946)

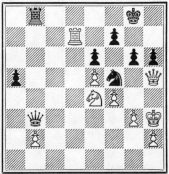

White to play

3 Kt—B6 ch, etc.

The King dare not move to h8.

Diagram 108 shows how this power can be used in a middle game to liquidate a difficult position into a draw. If he wishes White can play 1 Q × P ch, P × Q; 2 Kt—B6 ch, K—B1; 3 Kt—R7 ch, K—K1; 4 Kt—B6 ch, etc.

Given a Rook each, if a choice of extra minor pieces were offered, the offeree would be well advised to choose the Bishop. We have seen a position where Rook and Knight constitute a fatal attack. But this is a feature of corner-of-the-board play. In the middle Knight and Rook operate less forcefully than Rook and Bishop.

Let it not be assumed that Rook and Bishop always win against

Rook. The test is whether the defending King can be driven to the side of the board and kept there long enough for the attacker to achieve the framework of the winning attack.

Classical is the Philidor position (Diagram 109), of which Lasker says that the only difficulty is how to bring it into being. And it must be brought into being with the right player having the move.

Black to move can relieve all pressure by checks, and so draw. White to move must be very exact. Not, e.g. B—B6 or B—K6, because of 1 .... R—Q2 ch, a type of sacrifice often available to a Rook.

109   Study by Philidor

White to play, wins.
Black to play, draws

Best play is as follows:

| 1 R—B8 ch | R—K1 | 2 R—B7 | R—K7 |

(so as to be able to check on a Black square if the Bishop moves)

3 R—KKt7

(causing the Black Rook to alter its position)

| 3 .... | R—K8 | 5 B—Kt3 |
| 4 R—Kt7 | R—QB8 | (the point of move three) |

5	R—B6	7 B—Q5	R—QB6
6 B—K6	R—Q6 ch	(if 7 .... K—B1; 8
		R—QR7 wins)

8 R—Q7 ch   K—B1
(if 8 .... K—K1; 9 R—KKt7 wins)

9 R—KB7	K—Kt1	11 R—Kt4
10 R—Kt7 ch	K—B1	(threatening B—K6 ch)

11	K—Q1	13 B—K6 (or R6) ch K—Q1
12 B—B4	K—B1	14 R—Kt8 ch forces mate.

This pretty study, incidentally, is not the only important research into Chess conducted by the famous French eighteenth-century musician. He also contributed to the theory of Queen against Rook and pawn, and gave his name to an opening Defence and to a neat process of smothered mate.[1]

To return to our sheep, an interesting set of data derives from Szen (working on Philidor's position).

Put the Black King on e8, White King on e6, White Rook on b6, White Bishop on e5, and Black Rook on d2. This is, in effect, the Philidor position. Now move the Black King to d8 (the same colour as the Bishop's diagonal) and the Black Rook to c2. This is drawn, because when the White King moves to d6 it interferes with the action of the Bishop. Let the reader experiment. However, move the whole position further left, White King on d6, Rook on a6, Bishop on d5, Black King on c8, Rook on b2. Then White wins, notwithstanding the colour of the King's square. Thus:

1 R—R8 ch	R—Kt1	4 R—B8 ch	K—R2
2 R—R7	R—Kt8	5 R—R8 ch	K—Kt3
3 R—KB7	K—Kt1	6 R—Kt8 wins the Rook.

Here the determinant is the accidental circumstance that the Black King is too near the edge of the board. This is the kind of feature that makes rules impossible to draft.

Very hard, also, is the play of Rook and pawn against Bishop and pawn. A study by Emanuel Lasker shows all the difficulties. (Diagram 110.) An exhaustive analysis is beyond the scope of this volume, but the main play is as follows:

[1] This last, called Philidor's legacy (but possibly due to Deschapelles the eighteenth-nineteenth-century expert on board and card games), calls for a Queen on the diagonal leading to the defending King (say on g8). Place Black Rook on f8, Black pawns on g7, h7. White's Knight has just captured at f7. There follows: 1 Kt—R6 d ch, K—R1; 2 Q—Kt8 ch, R × Q; 3 Kt—B7 mate. This is an important feature to be remembered when King side attacks are impending. 'Smothered mates', be it remarked, are not the monopoly of Knights. Such a mate inflicted by a Bishop is seen in Diagram 161 on p. 159.

110   Study by Lasker

White to play and win

1 R—KR8	B—B4	3 K—Kt2	K—Kt4
2 R—R4 ch	B—Kt5	(K—B4 compromises the	
		Bishop)	

4 K—Kt3	B—B4	7 R—K8	K—B3
5 R—R8	B—Kt3	8 K—B4	
6 R—KB8	B—K5		

(the purpose of previous moves is becoming clear. White wants his King at K5)

8	B—Kt7	10 K—K5	B—K5
9 R—QR8	K—B2	11 R—R7 ch	K—K1

(Black is trying to achieve a position where the sacrifice of Rook for Bishop and pawn will leave a draw. Against this, White's aim is to drive the Black King to the QKt file or KB file, so that when the Rook captures at its Q5 and is exchanged, White will have a winning ending.)

12 K—K6	K—Q1	14 R—R8 ch	K—Kt2
13 K—Q6	K—B1	15 R—KKt8	

(aiming at QB5 while the King is cut off).

15	B—B6	18 R—QB5	any
16 R—Kt3	B—K5	19 R × P and wins.	
17 R—QB3	B—Kt7		

A special weakness, and at times a saving grace, of Bishops is that two opposing ones may find themselves unable to attack each other. They operate each in a different diocese, and ignore each other. One position has been seen (Diagram 105) in which a

Bishop must move about irrelevantly while the opposing Bishop, Knight and King construct a mating net.

But frequently the neutrality of two Bishops to each other's affairs is an advantage to the lesser force. Very many games in which there is an advantage of one, even two, pawns are drawn because the surviving pieces are Bishops of opposite colour. Diagram 111 is typical. Obviously Black, with pawn advantage, cannot achieve anything against a Bishop settled on e4 and King on g2.

111

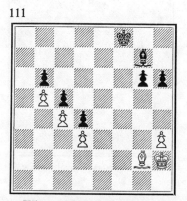

Whoever has the move can
only draw

Moreover, let the reader add a Black pawn on e5. Black now has two pawns to the good, and what can he achieve?

Add a further Black pawn, say on a7, then after laborious preparations, manœuvring of the Black King down to f4 and the Black Bishop to b8, a breaking up process might start with a7—a6. But the win would be exceedingly difficult.

On the other hand, if the diagram were altered by the moving of the central banks of pawns one square up the board, Black pawns at b7, c6, d5, White Pawns at b6, c5, d4, then Black, to move, would win and if it were White to move Black could still win because, before White could organise any captures, Black would be capturing and eventually would be left with an extra pawn on each of two separate sectors of the board. The truth of the matter is that Bishops of opposite colour do not guarantee a draw if there are weaknesses in the position, or in the pawn structure, that lend themselves to exploitation by pressure on both flanks.

The next two diagrams show wins achieved by the author where there were Bishops of opposite colour.

Diagram 112 shows a position reached in 1938. Black need not have been allowed to win, but inferior play by the opponent made it possible. Observe that Black is actually a pawn down, having sacrificed a pawn in order to bring his King into an aggressive position.

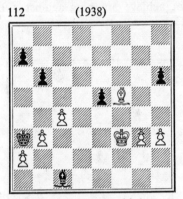

112   (1938)

White to play, should draw

The play was:

1 B—K6
(observe that this defends the pawn on a2, because if K × P; 2 P—B5!, P × P; 3 P—Kt4 ch, and the tables are turned)

| 1 .... | B—Q7 | 2 K—K2 |
| | | (not the best) |

2 ....   B—Kt5
(a good example of blockade)

| 3 B—Q7 | K × P | 5 P—Kt4 |
| 4 B—R4 | K—Kt7 | (indifferent) |

5	K—B6	8 K—B5	B—Kt2
6 K—K3	B—K2	9 K—K4	
7 K—K4	B—B3		

(a feature is now discernible, if K—Kt6, P—K5!)

| 9 .... | K—Kt5 | 10 K—B5 | |
| | | (not good) | |

10	P—R3	14 K—B5	P—QR4
11 B—B6	K × P	15 K × P	P—R5
12 B—Q5	K—Kt5	16 K—Q4	B—B4 ch
13 K—Kt6	B—B1	17 K—Q3	K—Kt6 wins.

A few observations are to be made:

1. If one can put the defending Bishop out of play or force its loss and be left with a pawn or pawns, one wins.

2. It is usually necessary to have threats, however distant, on more than one part of the board, in order to be able to coerce the defending Bishop.

3. The diagram position could easily have been drawn by White, had he seen the possibilities.

1 B—K6 is correct. Then play the King to the centre. If Black blockades at b4, which he can only do by letting the KP fall, White can afford P—B5! guarding the all-important b3, and now Black is in danger! To put the Bishop out of play at a4 was a major concession and totally unnecessary.

But there are positions whose exploitation is not mediated by bad play on the part of the opponent. Such is that in Diagram 113 reached by the author against no less a defender than the late W. Winter.

113   (1946)

Black to play and win

At an early stage Winter had allowed pawns to fall, relying on the Bishops-of-opposite-colour ending for a draw. But Black is in a position to win the defending Bishop and be left with a pawn. There

happened: 53 .... P—Kt6; 54 P × P, P—R6; 55 B—Kt1, P—K4 ch;
56 K × P, K—Kt5; 57 B—R2, K—B6; 58 P—Kt4, K—Kt7 and wins.

Before the reader moves to other topics, a further remark on
Bishops of opposite colour is worth making.

If you have defensive ideas, obviously the best formation is
with pawns untouchable by the opposing Bishop, i.e. on squares
of another colour as in Diagram 114. But the aggressive position
is with pawns on the same squares as the hostile Bishop, inhibiting
his movements. Diagram 114 is in point. Black plays 1 ....
B—Q4. If 2 P—R3, K—B5 and on to Kt6. If 2 P—Kt3, P—B5!
is decisive.

Theoretically, when opposing Bishops are active on the same
colour, then the side with a pawn to the good should have better

114

Black to play, wins

115   Study by Centurini

White to play and win

chances than in the case of Bishops of opposite colour. Certainly,
the draw is not so easily demonstrable. But those wins that
occur usually involve difficult play. The obvious difficulty is
that one player has to prevent his opponent from sacrificing the
Bishop for the pawn, and a determined sacrificer, like an assassin
with a taste for suicide, is almost unthwartable.

Clearly success is more likely when the pawn is far advanced
than when it has a long way to go. But even after far advance,
victory is a rarity. How it can come about is shown in a position
published a century ago by Centurini (Diagram 115). The process is:

| 1 B—K8 | B—Q8 | 3 B—B4 |
| 2 B—Kt5 | B—R4 | |

and cuts the Bishop off with B—B7.

This seems easy enough, but how delicate the threads are on which victory hangs is shown by a slight alteration. Diagram 116, a study from the same period by Horowitz and Kling, shows a position producing only a draw.

Study by Horowitz
116   and Kling

White to play, can only draw

1 B—K8   B—Q8   2 B—Kt5   B—R4
produces nothing.

Therefore (here the composers restore the original)

2 B—Kt6   B—R5
How else to get the White Bishop to d7?

3 B—R5   K—K4
(not 3 .... K—K3; 4 B—K8 followed by B—Q7 ch)

4 B—Kt4   K—Q3
and the cut-off is no longer possible.

The slightness of the difference between the two positions is quite fascinating. In Diagram 115 the attacking Bishop has one more square for play on the side occupied by the Black King than it has in Diagram 114. That one square is decisive.

Before we move from the light pieces to the heavier pieces, the reader should consider the final claim to superiority of Bishops to Knights. Bishop and Knight, or two Bishops, can force mate. Two Knights cannot. That is not to say that two Knights cannot mate. They can. Put Kings on g6 (White) and g8 (Black). Knights

on e5 and e7 (giving check). If the Black King is obliging enough
to go to h8, Kt—f7 gives mate.

But that cannot be forced. Set up the position: White King on
g6, Black King on h8, White Knight on e7. This position is stalemate. White cannot bring it about and play round with the other
Knight. He could only have forced this position into being if the
last move K—h8 had been inevitable, i.e. if there had been a Knight
on d7, e6 or h7; namely, not one that can go straight to f7.

But place a Black pawn on a7. Now the second Knight has
time to manœuvre itself to f7. In other words, King and two
Knights cannot force mate against a lone King: but King and two
Knights can force mate in some circumstances against King and
pawn. Obviously, to force a mating net against a player who has
a pawn is pretty difficult. One of the Knights has to employ itself
blockading the pawn, stopping it from moving and from either
promoting or forcing its own capture.

A century of research has investigated the possibilities, and the
great Russian composer Troitski has done much to the working
out of the conditions in which the process is available.

For the purposes of a relatively elementary work a full survey
is out of the question. But one diagram (117) shows a compara-
tively easy instance, and, from it, the method can be seen in action.

117   Study by Troitski

White wins, whoever has the move

If it be White's move the main line of play is:

1 Kt—Q3 ch	K—R7	4 K—Kt3		P—B6
2 Kt—K2	P—B5	5 Kt—K1 (or Kt4)		P—B7
3 Kt—B3 ch	K—R8	6 Kt—B2 mate.		

If it be Black's move:

1	K—B8	7 Kt(B4)—Q3	P—B5
2 K—B3	K—Q8	8 K—Kt3	P—B6
3 Kt—B2	K—B8	9 Kt—QB4	P—B7
4 Kt—K3	K—Kt8	10 Kt—Q2 ch	K—R8
5 Kt—B4	K—B8	11 Kt—Kt4	P=Q
6 Kt—QKt2	K—Kt8	12 Kt—B2 mate.	

In this it will be seen that the blockading Knight is helping, even from its fixed position, to keep the Black King from freedom and is near enough to come quickly into the mating complex.

Theoretically, there are a large number of positions in which King and one Knight can muster the opposing King to the edge of the board, then to the corner, and, at that stage, a blockading Knight can abandon the blockade of the pawn and hurry across to help in the mate. The undertaking can be of such great difficulty that it belongs to the field of vision rather than to the methods that are technique.[1]

When the larger pieces are in play the operations are tactical rather than technical. But there are some features of Rooks, Queens, etc., that should be known.

Thus Philidor has given us a better legacy than the smothered mate in his researches into King and Queen against King, Rook and pawn.

The position in Diagram 118 is only a draw because White can do nothing to prevent the Rook from oscillating between c6 and e6.

This method of defence is obviously available with all pawns except the Rook's pawn. (In that case, however, there is the compensating advantage that the Queen can operate only from one side; but then, it is better for the defence if the pawn is on a6 rather than a7.)

From Diagram 118 move the pieces one or more squares down the board and the position need no longer be a draw (Diagram 119). The process is that the Queen gets behind the King and eventually drives it between the two squares on which the Rook operates. Thus:

1 Q—B7 ch   K—B3

(if to the back row, the Queen will arrive at c6 or e6)

[1] It adds to the margin of draw which characterises Chess, that a player may be able so to exchange and sacrifice as to leave his opponent with two Knights to the good and no win. Three Knights, incidentally, can defeat one Knight. This comes about when the pawn promotes to Knight in order to check and fork. This has occurred in tournament play.

TECHNIQUE IN CHESS

White to play, can only draw · · · · · · White to play and win

2 Q—QR7	R—Q4 ch	7 Q—B8 ch	K—Q4
3 K—K4	R—K4 ch	8 Q—Q7	R—B5 ch
4 K—B4	R—QB4	9 K—B5	R—B4
5 Q—K7	R—K4	10 K—B6	
6 Q—Q8	R—B4		

and the Rook must leave its moorings. However, even if White
allow Black to manœuvre down the board, to reach the position in
Diagram 120 he should still win. For this position, which for so
long was thought to be a draw, has now been shown a win for White.

120

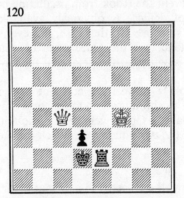

White to play and win

1 Q—Kt3   R—K8
(other file moves endanger the Rook because of checks)

2 Q—Kt2 ch	K—Q8	4 Q—B3	R—Q7
3 K—B3	R—K7	5 Q—B4 *zugzwang.*	

(If K—K8; 6 Q—B1 ch, R—Q8; 7 Q—K3 ch, etc.)

Care must be taken to avoid the situation with the White King on its back row, say at d1, with the Rook at c2 or e2, pawn at d3 and Black King behind the pawn, and the White Queen at large. This is rather a tricky draw. A possible development with the advanced pawn is the following danger:

White King at KB2, Queen at Q4, Black King at QKt6, Rook at QB8, and pawn at Q6. Black plays P—Q7, and it cannot be captured because of the pin. There are numerous situations in which a pawn is defended by a Rook indirectly, because the capture results in a pin. It should also be added that a well-advanced pawn with a Rook behind it holds a Queen. (The extreme case is a pawn at the seventh, holding the Queen tied to the back line.)

For the benefit of those readers to whom the Philidor study (with some analysis due to the Frenchman, Chéron) appears hard, it must be made clear that Queen and King against Rook and King must win, except in very special cases.

The win is not easy. Diagram 121 shows one difficulty. If

1 K—K6	R—B3 ch!

So the King must play K—Kt6. Now 1 .... R—Kt2 ch, drawing the King to R6.

121

White to play

Afterwards the Queen has to drive the King from the back row and so manœuvre as to make the Rook part from its mooring and allow itself to be won by the King-Rook fork, at the end of a series of checks. An amusing position consists in a study by Ponziani (Diagram 122) showing one of the special cases.

122   Study by Ponziani

Black to play and draw

1 .... R—R2 ch; 2 K—Kt2, R—Kt2 ch; 3 K—B3, R—B2 ch; and it is clear that White cannot cross the K file. 4 K—Kt4, R—Kt2 ch; 5 K—B5, R—B2 ch; 6 K—Kt6, R—Kt2 ch. And now if 7 K—B6, R—Kt3 ch; and if 7 K—R6, R—R2 ch, in each case uncapturable.

And now let us take the normal case (that can be won), Diagram 123. This is quite hard. The technique is to keep the King from those squares on the back row that are most favourable.

123

White to play and win

1 Q—R8 is as good an approach as any. If 1 .... R—B1, the Queen can obtain a series of checks which will ultimately enable K—K6 and an easy mate (e.g. 2 Q—Kt7 ch, K—K1; 3 Q—Kt8 ch, K—K2; 4 Q—B7 ch, K—K1; 5 K—K6, and mate follows). Accordingly, the Rook is better advised to go down the file, say 1 .... R—B8.

Then a possible sequence is:

2 Q—R3 ch	K—B2	8 K—K6	R—KKt4
3 Q—QKt3 ch	K—Kt2	9 Q—KB4	R—Kt3 ch
4 Q—Kt3 ch	K—B2	10 K—K7	R—KR3
5 Q—R4	R—QR8	11 Q—B7 ch	K—R1
6 Q—QB4 ch	K—Kt2	12 K—K8	R—KKt3
7 K—B5	R—R4 ch	13 K—B8	

And there is no further stalemate resource.

This particular way of playing it is copied from an actual game, and seems quite clumsy.

There are innumerable variations in this study, including forking threats on the KKt and KR files. Suffice it to say:

1. That Queen against Rook constitutes a win, not a draw.

2. The technique is to separate the King and Rook.

3. The edging ranks and files can, for a long time, be advantageous to the defender because of the resources by way of stalemate.

The decisive factor is the long-range checking power of the Queen.

With the Queen we enter a realm where the scope of the tactician is so great that technique seems trivial and unhelpful. Yet a few observations on the Queen's power and the limits of her power can furnish a useful corrective to the natural tendency to overvalue.

A Queen is not materially equivalent to two Rooks. A simple test is that if a Queen attacks a pawn, a Queen can defend it completely. If two Rooks attack a pawn, the Queen cannot defend it.

Yet a Queen can, in the proper setting, draw against Queen and Rook, even against two Queens (Diagram 124). The King cannot escape from the checks at c3 and e1.

But given only little mobility, Queen and Rook can extricate the King from check. Contrast two positions.

First, place the White King on QR1, Queen on KR2, Rook on QKt1. A Black Queen checking on the squares d4, d1, a4, gives perpetual check.

124   125

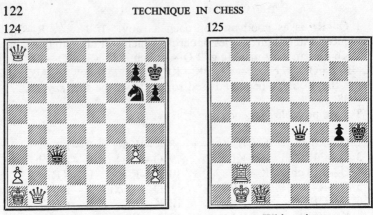

Drawn game   White wins

Second, Diagram 125. Here White gets out of check. The process involves the changing of places, Queen with Rook.

1 R—B2
(K—R1 and K—R2 are of no avail)

1	Q—Kt5 ch	8 Q—B2	Q—Kt4 ch
2 Q—Kt2	Q—K8 ch	9 K—B1	Q—B8 ch
3 K—R2	Q—R4 ch	10 Q—Q1	Q—B5 ch
4 Q—R3	Q—Q4 ch	11 Q—Q2	Q—B8 ch
5 Q—Kt3	Q—R4 ch	12 K—B2	Q—B4 ch
6 K—Kt2	Q—K4 ch	13 K—Q1	Q—B8 ch
7 R—B3	Q—K7 ch	14 Q—K1	

and even if this were not itself check, it would terminate the checks.

Of the resources of the Queen when there is any material on the board that can be compromised, Diagram 126, reached by the author, is a good illustration. Materially, White is better off, but his move 87 R—B4 (the fact that it was the 87th is explanatory) surprisingly loses. After

| 87 .... | Q—R6 ch | 88 K—Q5 | |

loses by

| 88 .... | Q—Q6 ch | 89 K—B5 | |

(R—Q4 allows mate at b5)

89	P—Kt3 ch	91 R—Q4	Q—B6 ch
90 R×P	Q—K6 ch	92 R—B4	Q—K4 ch
			wins a Rook.

It should be added that Mieses was avenged by the late Landau, at the same tournament, against whom the author failed, somehow, to draw with King and two Knights against King and Queen. It is matter for argument whether that force is adequate.

By way of contrast it happens frequently that the Queen proves less of a force than might be expected. She gets pinned, or captured, when the King is 'stabbed in the back', or she gets cut off from important squares, or gets herself, as the composers say,

Mieses—Abrahams
126   (1939)   127

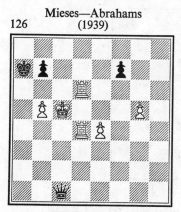

White to play   Black to play and win

'dominated'. From the early game (as played by the author in 1923) here is an example.

1 P—K4	P—Q4	4 P—Q4	Kt—KB3
2 P×P	Q×P	5 B—Q2	Kt—B3
3 Kt—QB3	Q—R4		

(this is an experiment inspired by Mieses, but is inferior to the normal 5 .... P—B3)

| 6 B—QKt5 | B—Q2 | 7 Kt—Q5 |

wins the Queen.

Typical and fairly elementary, is the next diagram (127) from the later stages of a game. White has made the mistake of R—Q7. Now:

| 1 .... | R×R | 2 Q×R | R—Q1 |

and the Queen cannot get back to the defence of d1.

Frequently it happens that a Queen cannot take a pawn, or re-capture something on d7, e7, or such squares because a Rook move to the adjacent square d8, e8, etc., leads to capture or mate on d1 or e1, as the case may be.

A set-up frequently seen in endgames is shown in Diagram 128. (If the Bishop and Knight were reversed, this would probably be a drawn position in any event.)

128

White to play and draw

1 B—Q5 ch draws because if Q × B; 2 Kt—B4 forks. If 1 .... K × B; 2 Kt—K3 forks.

This is usually exploited in complex settings. But it must not be thought that ideas like this are fantasies of the composers. The practical game is very rich.

An amusing opening variation showing domination is the follow-ing (from a game by the author):

1 P—QKt4	P—Q4	5 P × P	B × P
2 B—Kt2	Kt—KB3	6 P—K3	Q—Kt3
3 Kt—KB3	P—K3	7 Kt—QB3	
4 P—QR3	P—QB4		

and if

7	Q × B	8 Kt—R4 wins the Queen.

This is a piquant example of a possibility that is always to be thought about when Queens are attacking Knights' pawns in the vicinity of Knights.

But domination is seen in its beauty when a craftsman like Rinck reveals it on the relatively empty board. Some striking dominant play is seen in Diagram 129, and the position is not unrealistic. It might have occurred after heavy skirmishes.

1 R—R8

immediately takes a large number of squares away from the Queen.

| 1 .... | Q—Kt4 | 3 R—R6 ch | K—K4 |
| 2 Kt—B5 ch | K—B3 | 4 R—K6 ch | K—Q4 |

(if 4 .... K—B5; 5 R—K4 ch!)

| 5 P—B4 ch | Q×P | 7 Kt×Q and wins |
| 6 Kt—K3 ch | K×R | |

129   Study by Rinck

130   Botvinnik—Minev
(Amsterdam 1954)

White to play and win

Before we part from the Queen, let it be said that one of the hardest fights in Chess is between King, Queen and pawn against King and Queen.

Diagram 130 shows a position reached by Botvinnik. He has admitted that much of his play was tentative. It is not clear to what extent he was assisted by his opponent's belief that the best squares for the defending King were on the opposite Rook's file. (This has been argued.)

The play was:

1	Q—R1 ch	5 Q—B5 ch	K—R5
2 K—Kt6	Q—B6	6 K—R5	Q—R1 ch
3 P—Kt4	Q—Q7	7 K—Kt4	Q—KR8
4 P—Kt5	Q—Q5		

(observe that he can't check on the 4th rank!)

8	Q—B4 ch	K—R4	14	Q—K3	Q—B2 ch
9	Q—K5 ch	K—R5	15	Q—K5	Q—B8 ch
10	P—Kt6	Q—Q8 ch	16	K—B5	Q—B1 ch
11	K—Kt5	Q—Q1 ch	17	K—Kt5	Q—Q1 ch
12	K—B5	Q—QB1 ch	18	Q—B6	
13	K—B4	Q—B8 ch		(he could have done this at	
				move twelve)	

18	....	Q—Q4 ch	20	K—R5	Q—K1
19	Q—B5	Q—Q1 ch			

This pin is characteristic of the difficulties of this type of position.

21	Q—B4 ch	K—R4	24	K—Kt5	Q—K2 ch
22	Q—Q2 ch	K—R5	25	K—B5	Q—B1 ch
23	Q—Q4 ch	K—R4	26	K—K4	
				(the only square 'out of check')	

26	....	Q—R3	28	P—Kt7	Q—R8 ch
27	Q—K5 ch	K—R5	29	K—Q4	
				(note the extraordinary detour)	

29	....	Q—Q8 ch	33	Q—Q5	Q—K7 ch
30	K—B5	Q—B8 ch	34	K—Q6	Q—R7 ch
31	K—Q6	Q—Q7 ch	35	K—B5!	
32	K—K6	Q—R7 ch			

Out of check in every variation, Black resigned. Minev was evidently too exhausted to try the following:

35	....	Q—QB7 ch	37	P = Q	
36	Q—B4 ch	K—R6		(not Q × Q stalemate)	

If now

37	....	Q—B7 ch

White could allow him fun with

38	K—Q6	Q—Q5 ch	39 Q(Kt8)—Q5, etc.

That endgame is typical of the difficulties. Without dogmatism it is evidently impossible to say that Queen and pawn must defeat Queen. But the cases where it does not happen are those where the configuration of Kings lends itself to perpetual check. Also RPs are likely to be the most difficult to exploit.

Chéron combines these thoughts in Diagram 131.

131   Study by Chéron

Black to play and draw

132

White to play and draw

1 ....   Q—B6 ch   2 K—R4

(if K—R2, Q—B2 ch, and the Queen cannot intervene without losing the Pawn)

2 ....   Q—B3 ch   4 K—Kt5   Q—Kt2 ch
3 K—R5   Q—B2 ch

and the King cannot escape.

With these studies we are forced to the realisation that Chess is a set of difficult tactical operations. Technique tells us that we can expect certain results with certain material, and shows us some devices. But from the vast range of possibilities the dominant feature of Chess endgames that emerges is the degree to which they are not predictable on technical lines. Thus any player who had Black in the position in Diagram 132 would be sadly disappointed for apparently accidental reasons.

1 B—B3, K—Kt7; 2 K—Kt4, K—B7; 3 K—B4, K—Q7; 4 K—Q4, K—K8; 5 K—K3, K—B8; 6 B—K2 ch, K—K8; 7 B—B3, etc.

Following are some tactical conflicts. The first (Diagram 133) reveals an idea which, being absorbed, will enrich technical equipment. It is variously described as a composition by Saavedra, and as the ending of a game between two strong London players, Fenton and Potter, who failed to see the ultimate point.

The reader will see that if the King goes to the Bishop's file he

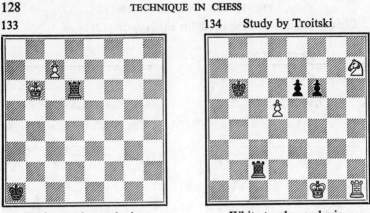

133   134   Study by Troitski

White to play and win   White to play and win

will be thwarted by R—Q8, capturing the promoting pawn. Nor can the King go to Kt7 because of R—Q2, nor to the Rook file.

A minor feature is the control of the eighth rank by the pawn. Rooks are frequently defeated in this way. The play is

| 1 K—Kt5 | R—Q4 ch | 3 K—Kt3 | R—Q6 ch |
| 2 K—Kt4 | R—Q5 ch | 4 K—B2 | |

and it looks as if Black is thwarted. But the resources of Chess are hard to exhaust.

4 ....   R—Q5

If

5 P=Q   R—B5 ch

will force a stalemate. However, White, too, has his resources.

5 P=R

threatening mate. This forces

5 ....   R—R5

Now comes

6 K—Kt3

with a double threat of K × R and Rook mates, and they cannot both be prevented.

Inspired by this, but having great beauty of its own, is one of Troitski's greatest compositions (Diagram 134).

White's first move is P × P, and Black seems to have more than one defence.

However, direct efforts against the pawn fail.

1 P × P	R—B3	3 Kt × P	
2 P—K7	R—K3	(guarding the pawn!)	

3	R × Kt ch	4 K—Kt2	R—Kt3 ch
		(if R—K3; 5 R—R6!)	

5 K—B3	R—Kt1	9 K—B6	R—KR1
6 R—K1	R—K1	10 K—Kt7	R—K1
7 K—B4	K—B2	11 K—B7 wins.	
8 K—B5	K—Q2		

But it appears that Black can do something simpler: exchange the Rooks and bring the King quickly to the pawn. The Knight will have to guard it from KB8, and will quickly be extruded.

But White has a quite revolutionary treatment of that line of defence.

1 P × P	R—B8 ch	2 K—B2!	

One of the most beautiful moves in Chess.

2	R × R	3 P—K7	

and now commences a multiple Saavedra duel.

3	R—R7 ch	8 K—B5	R—R4 ch
4 K—B3	R—R6 ch	9 K—B4	R—R5 ch
5 K—B4	R—R5 ch	10 K—B3	R—R6 ch
6 K—B5	R—R4 ch	11 K—K2	R—R7 ch
7 K × P	R—R3 ch		

Now White marches up the other line.

12 K—Q3	R—R6 ch	15 K—Q6	R—R3 ch
13 K—Q4	R—R5 ch	16 Kt—B6!	
14 K—Q5	R—R4 ch		

(One of the beauties of this move is that if now 16 .... R—R1; 17 Kt—Q7 ch and 18 Kt—B8!)

16	R × Kt ch

and the Saavedra setting is complete. The King returns to Q3 and at K2 terminates the checks.

Not the least amusing and instructive of endgames are those in which interferences disrupt the defence.

Here (Diagram 135) is a crude but useful example of mutual interference. The Rook controls the RP. And when White plays 1 P—Q7, B—R4 controls that pawn. But in doing so the Bishop has interfered with the Rook. So that if 1 P—Q7, B—R4 is met by RP=Q. However, in this position Black has play, not 1 .... B—R4, but 1 .... RR7!, answering QP=Q with B—R4 dis ch.

135

White to play. What result?

136

White to play

White has to play, 2 K—B1 (not K—Kt1, which allows the Bishop to check and go to Kt3). Now 2 .... R—R8 ch; 3 K—K2. R—K8 ch does not work because the pawn controls K8.

But quite simply Black plays 2 .... K—B6 threatening mate. White must play 3 K—Kt1. Then B—K6 ch (or even B—Kt4) solves Black's problem.

Many brilliant problems have been composed to show how one side causes the other to be involved in mutual interference.

Diagram 136 is a crude example. In this position P—QB7 is met by R—B5 and then P—KB7 by B—Kt5, so that both promotion squares are covered by defending pieces.

But White plays

1 B—Q5
threatening P—QB7. If 1 .... R × B.

2 P—QB7   R—B4   3 P—KB7

and Black's Bishop is obstructed at Kt5 by the Rook at B4.

137

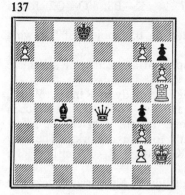

138   Study by Birnov

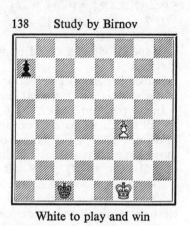

White to play and win

If at move 1 .... R—Q6, 2 P—QB7 will cause the Rook at B6 to obstruct the Bishop.

Cognate a piece of play much loved by problemists is an interference that not only obstructs but misleads.

Of this, Diagram 137 is a crude but useful example. Both promotion squares are controlled.

To this 'problem' there are other solutions than the following: and the thing is not presented for its difficulty.

1 R—Q5 check is very effective as well as amusing. If

1 ....   B × R   3 P—Kt8 = Q ch
2 P—R8 = Q ch B × Q
If

1 ....   Q × R   2 P—Kt8 = Q ch

Problemists call this a Nowotny interference. A similar idea can be executed on the rank or file with Rooks or Rook and Queen. Then it is called a Plachutta.

Diagram 138 is a study which incorporates much of the learning of these chapters, and affords a good introduction to the next. Diagram 138 by Birnov involves some modern pawn *v* pawn technique, also Queen *v* Queen, and an old mating demonstration that derives from the ancient Lolli.

The solution is: 1 K—K2 (the immediate pawn race is not won), P—R4; 2 K—Q3, K—Kt7; 3 P—B5, P—R5; 4 P—B6, P—R6; 5 P—B7, P—R7; 6 P = Q, P = Q. And now 7 Q—Kt4 ch leads to mate.

If 7 .... K—R7; 8 K—B2. If 7 .... K—B8; 8 Q—Q2 ch and 9 Q—B2 mate.

A special chapter could be written on the subject of 'Drawing Devices'.

Suffice it here to give two examples of a spectacular stalemate and a spectacular perpetual check.

In the position 32, 5k2, 8, 1q6, R5KR (a study by Rinck), White, for all the slight material advantage of two Rooks against a Queen (a definite plus), is in danger of being mated. Nor can he safely move the attacked Rook off the rank for fear of forks. The play is: 1 R—K1, Q—Q7; 2 K—B1!, K—Kt6; 3 R—K3 ch!, Q × R; 4 R—R3 ch, K × R stalemate.

Very surprising is the following study by Kasparian, one of the cleverest of the Russian composers:

8, Q7, r4q2, 7k, r7, 3R4, 8, 3K4.

The draw is achieved as follows: 1 Q—R7 ch, K—Kt4; 2 R—Q5 ch, K—Kt5; 3 Q—R5 ch, K—B5; 4 Q—R2 ch, K—K5; 5 R—K5 ch!!, Q × R; and now, having given up a third of his force, White has a 'merry-go-round' perpetual check—a movement to enrich the technical equipment of all players. (6 Q—K2 ch, K—Q5; 7 Q—QKt2 ch, K—Q4; 8 Q—Kt5 ch, etc.).

CHAPTER V

THE RELATIVE MERITS OF SOME PAWNS

In studying Chess technique the reader must not hope to acquire a set of rules governing types of position, and perpetually valid. The game is too rich in tactical complexities, even when material is at a minimum.

This truth is well illustrated in a classic study by Horowitz and Kling analysed over a century ago (Diagram 139).

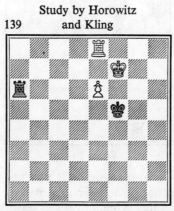

Study by Horowitz
139   and Kling

White to play.   What result?

White cannot win by 1 R—KR8 because after R × P; 2 R—R5 ch is met by K—Kt5.

And if he tries 1 P—K7, R—B3 ch; 2 K—Kt7, R—Kt3 ch (not 2 .... K—K3; 3 R—KB8!); 3 K—R7, K—B3 threatens R—Kt2 ch and can meet R—B8 ch with K × P.

The solution (the recognition that the game is drawn) involves the perception of checking and capturing possibilities, not the application of any formula.

If this position be moved one square to the left, White wins with R—KR8, because the White pawn is now taboo.

The field of Chess which is Rook and pawn against Rook is so extensive and varied that it has failed to be analysed algebraically by more than one Caissic Descartes. All that can be done is the appreciation of some essentials, and these can be very hard to isolate and recognise.

That creative analyst Grigorieff has pointed out that so great a player as Alekhine mishandled a Rook and pawn ending, and so powerful an opponent as Dr. Euwe failed to take advantage of the inaccuracy.

The position (Diagram 140) occurred in the World Championship Match of 1935.

Alekhine—Euwe
140   (Match of 1935)

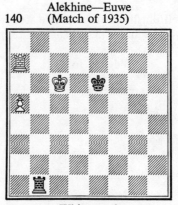

White to play

A technical feature of the position is that Black's King is pretty well placed (this is not obvious at first glance). Also, the pawn is a Rook's pawn so that King moves can leave White constricted. Indeed, Black, to move, would draw, thus:

| 1 .... | R—B8 ch | 3 K—Kt8 ch | K—Q1 |
| 2 K—Kt7 | K—Q2 | | |

threatening R—B1 ch, followed by R—B2 ch with a Rook exchange on a7 and K—B2 to follow, with a draw.

    If

| 4 R—QKt7 | R—B4 | 6 K—R7 | |
| 5 P—R6 | R—B3 | (not P—R7, Rook mates!) | |

6 ....   K—B1 draws.

If (instead of 4 R—QKt7)

| 4 R—KR7 | R—QKt8 ch | 6 R—R5 | K—B2 draws. |
| 5 K—R7 | R—QR8 | | |

But White, with the move, can alter the position.

1 P—R6

If now

| 1 .... | R—B8 ch | 2 K—Kt7 | |

There are many variations; but to adopt the line of play that Black uses when he has the move, let us try

| 2 .... | K—Q2 | 4 R—KR7 | |
| 3 K—Kt8 ch | K—Q1 | | |

and Black's R—QR8 is evidently useless. (The pawn is too near home.)

Therefore,

4	R—Kt8 ch	7 K—Kt7	R—B2 ch
5 R—Kt7	R—QB8	8 K—Kt6	K—B1
6 R—Kt2	R—B1 ch	9 Either R—KR2 or P—R7

                                                       wins.

To attempt to make a formula from this, postulating Kings in opposition and pawns at R6, would be unhelpful.

What can be learned is the idea of the defensive power of the Black King, even far away from the pawn, on the other side of an intervening King. Evidently Alekhine was not considering this when he played 1 R—KR7. Black could have replied:

| 1 .... | R—QR8 | | |

An interesting point now is that if 2 R—R5, R—B8 ch, the Rook cannot interpose, e.g.:

| 3 R—B5 | R × R ch | 4 K × R | K—Q2 |

catches the pawn or forces the King to block its progress. An interesting example of the King's speed.

(If Kings start a Knight's move apart, the higher King cannot be headed off by the lower one.)

So after

| 1 R—R7 | R—QR8 | 3 P—R6 | R—Kt8 ch |
| 2 K—Kt6 | K—Q3 | 4 K—R7 | K—B3 |

and this is a draw. Not the easiest of draws, therefore worth studying.

5 R—QKt7	R—KR8	10 P—R7	R—QKt8
6 R—Kt2	K—B2	11 R—KR2	K—B2
7 R—B2 ch	K—Q2	12 R—R7 ch	K—B1
8 K—Kt7	R—Kt8 ch	13 R—R8 ch	K—B2
9 K—R8	R—QR8	14 R—QKt8	R—QB8

and White can do nothing.

To revert to the actual event (Diagram 140). In answer to

1 R—R7
Black played

| 1 .... | R—B8 ch | 3 K—B8 |
| 2 K—Kt7 | R—Kt8 ch | |

Perhaps the point that Black had missed. If now R—QR8;
4 P—R6! is playable.

3	R—B8 ch	7 P—R6	K—B4
4 K—Kt8	R—Kt8 ch	8 K—Kt7	R—R8
5 R—Kt7	R—QR8	9 R—B6 ch	Resigns
6 R—Kt6 ch	K—Q4		

From this and previous diagrams the reader will be aware that Rook's pawns are the least reliable units as margins of victory, especially when the defending King is within a notional striking distance, i.e. when it is on the lee side or close on the windward side of the attacking King.

Move the Alekhine-Euwe position one square to the right, and it is clear that White has fewer subtleties of defence to cope with, and Black, given the move, cannot draw because one essential feature, the constriction of the King, is not among the possibilities.

Certain very general propositions are useful in connection with all pawns.

Thus it is desirable to hold the defending King as far away as possible, by cutting it off, either horizontally or perpendicularly.

If a King is cut off in the vertical plane, the seriousness of the situation varies inversely with the distance of the pawn from promotion; and something depends on the nature of the pawn's file.

Thus Diagram 141 reveals disappointment, as follows:

1 K—Kt2	R—Kt1 ch	3 K—Kt3	R—Kt1 ch
2 K—B3	R—QR1	4 K—B4	R—B1 ch

(not R—QR1; 5 R—R1, with a winning position)

141

White to play, can only draw

5 K—Kt5	R—Kt1 ch	7 K—Kt7	R—B6!
6 K—B6	R—B1 ch	8 R—Kt8	R—KB6!
			(not R—QR6, met by
			9 R—QR8!)

9 P—R4	R—B2 ch	10 K—Kt6	

(K—Kt8 would compromise the pawn to 10 .... R—B5, etc.)

10	R—B3 ch	15 R—QR8	K—Kt3
11 K—Kt5	R—B4 ch	16 K—Kt2	R—KB6
12 K—B4	R—B5 ch	17 P—R5	K—Kt2!
13 K—Kt3	R—B6 ch	18 R—R7 ch	
14 K—B2	R—QR6!		

(if the pawn advances to R7, a well-known draw is reached)

18	K—B1	20 R—Kt6	R—B4
19 R—QKt7	R—B3	21 P—R6	R—QR4 draws.

The Black King cannot be kept out.

The above, largely an analysis by Chéron (whose endgame collations are beyond praise), shows the difficulties latent in the apparently easy.

Other pawns than the RP are more useful, because in the final approximation to promotion the aggressive King is not compressed against the side of the board.

Nevertheless, Diagram 142 shows another pawn holder being tantalised.

142   Study by Chéron

Black to play and draw

The Black King is separated from the pawn's file by four files, yet can draw.

1	K—Kt4!	5 K—Q4	R—QKt1
2 K—B2	R—B1 ch	6 R—QKt1	K—B3
3 K—Q3	R—QKt1	7 P—Kt4	
4 K—B3	R—B1 ch	(K—Q5 is met by 7	
		R—Kt6)	

| 7 .... | K—K3 | 9 R—QR1 | R—B1 ch |
| 8 K—B5 | K—Q2 | 10 K—Q5 | R—B7 |

draws easily.

Another line of play illustrates the failure of a horizontal scission: 1 .... K—Kt4; 2 R—B3, K—Kt5; 3 R—B6, K—Kt4; 4 R—QR6, K—B4; 5 K—B2, K—K4; 6 K—B3, K—Q4; 7 P—Kt4, R—B1 ch; 8 K—Kt3, R—B3; 9 R—R7, R—B8 (if 9 R—R8, R—B2). In all cases White can achieve nothing.

As it happens, White with the move, would win from the diagram.

     1 R—B3   R—KR1

(if 1 .... K—Kt4; 2 K—R2 followed by R—QR3 and to QR6; then King and pawn can advance more rapidly)

2 K—B2	R—B1 ch	9 P—Kt3	K—Kt4
3 K—Q3	R—QKt1	10 K—B5	K—Kt5
4 K—B3	R—B1 ch	11 R—Q3	K—B5
5 K—Q4	R—Q1 ch	12 P—Kt4	R—B1 ch
6 K—B5	R—B1 ch	13 K—Q5	R—Q1 ch
7 K—Q5	R—Q1 ch	14 K—B4	R—B1 ch
8 K—B6	R—QKt1		

(Exchange of Rooks loses because, though the defending King can reach its QKt, the resulting ending is lost)

15 K—Kt3	R—QKt1	17 R—QR6	K—Q4
16 R—Q6	K—K4	18 K—R4	

and Black, being unable to get his Rook to c6, in time to cover the King's entrance, must lose.

White will play K—R5, P—Kt5, R—R7, K—R6.

If Black tries to avoid this sequence, there might happen: 18 . . . . K—B5; 19 R—B6 ch, K—Q4; 20 P—Kt5, R—R1 ch; 21 K—Kt4, R—R8; 22 R—B2, K—Q3; 23 P—Kt6, R—Kt8 ch; 24 K—R5, R—R8 ch; 25 K—Kt5, K—Q2; 26 P—Kt7, R—Kt8 ch; 27 K—R6, R—R8 ch; 28 K—Kt6, R—Kt8 ch; 29 K—R7, R—R8 ch; 30 K—Kt8, R—Kt8; 31 R—QR2, K—B3; 32 K—B8!, wins.

It is clear from the above example that the power of the defending King to approximate is vital; and in most cases great delicacy is required in the handling.

143

Black to play and draw

Diagram 143 shows a draw that may surprise the reader.

1 . . . .   K—Kt3

(not 1 .... K—Kt1, because then after R—K2 the Black Rook is tied to the file because of the possible pawn check)

| 2 R—K2 | R—QR8! | 4 P—B7 | R—R2 ch draws. |
| 3 R—Kt2 ch | K—R2 | | |

Nearer the centre, and often, paradoxically, at the fifth rather than the sixth rank the draw is harder of achievement, because there is more nanœuvring space for the aggressive King.

Of Rook and pawn endings, generally, certain propositions are useful technical knowledge.

1. The defending Rook is better placed behind the pawn than in front of it.

2. It departs from the pawn's file for specific purposes, (*a*) to check the aggressive King into a temporary blockade of the pawn; (*b*) to attack the Pawn laterally.

3. The attacking Rook so places itself as to fulfil several functions, of which the most important are:

(*a*) To act as umbrella to the attacking King (as in the Lucena position).

(*b*) To cut off the defending King.

4. The attacking King prefers to be in front of the pawn. Failing that, its next best placing is between the pawn and the defending King.

5. The defending King prefers to be in front of the advancing pawn. Failing that, it should be beside the pawn or on its heels.

6. If the defending King has to be placed at the side of the pawn, not immediately adjacent, then it prefers the short side, not the long side. (Diagram 139 is one instance of the advantage of the short side.)

7. If a Rook is tied to a rank rather than a file, the Rook prefers the long side to the short (Diagram 144). In this diagram White, to move, plays

1 K—B6
(not 1 R—B6, R—Kt3!; 2 K—B5, R—Kt8 draws)

| 1 .... | K—Q2 | 2 K—B7 |

If 2 .... R—K1; 3 R—K6 wins. Now transfer the Rooks to the long side. With the White Rook at QR6 and Black Rook at QKt1 or QB1, no *zugzwang* play is available.

But observe that this diagram illustrates a further special proposition.

8. The back row can be the worst, as well as the best, for defensive purposes on the part of the defending King. Best, because of the possibilities of stalemate, worst, because of the possibilities of checkmate.

The reader must realise that in all Rook and pawn endings there are tactical elements which, being apprehended, render general statements academic. If they are not apprehended, general statements are useless.

144

White to play and win

145

White to play. What result?

In point is Diagram 145. White, to move, can only draw against the best defence. But the best defence is not easy defence.
Suppose

| 1 R—Kt1 ch | K—B1 | 2 K—B6 |

Black must now resist the temptation of pinning the pawn with

| 2 .... | R—R3 |

If

| 2 .... | R—R3 | 3 R—QKt1 |
| | | with threat of mate. |

If, then,

| 3 .... | K—Kt1 | 5 K—B7 |
| 4 R—Kt8 ch | K—R2 | |

with cut-off King and ability to force the Lucena method of promotion, e.g.: 5 .... R—R7; 6 P—K7, R—B7 ch; 7 K—K8, and 8 R—Q8 (in answer to R—Q7) will enable the King to emerge.

So, in this variation, Black is forced to

3 ....   R—R1
Now with

4 R—Kt7
White has something very advantageous. Black must mark time with

4 ....   R—B1
Then comes

5 R—B7 ch   K—Kt1
(if 5 .... K—K1; 6 R—KR7 is fatal)

6 R—Kt7 ch   K—R1
(Obviously K—B1 is met by P—K7 ch followed by R—Kt8 ch, etc.)
After

6 ....   K—R1   7 R—Kt1
cuts the King off. So we must go back and reconsider Black's
second move.
After

1 R—Kt1 ch   K—B1   2 K—B6
the only move is R—R2, because of tactical resource.

3 R—QKt1   R—B2 ch   4 K—K5
                           (P × R gives stalemate)

4 ....   R—B7
and the Black King cannot be prevented from occupying K1 or K2.
   This study is important because it shows the defending Rook
in two lines of action, along the rank and on the file behind the
attacking force. The latter placing is normal in these endings.
   The next study (Diagram 146), by Chéron, is one of the most
valuable of Rook and pawn models, revealing, as it does, the
delicacies that can be involved.
   Let it be White's move. If he moves the Rook from the Rook's
file (say to QB6), then

1 ....   R—QR1
Now if

2 K—Q6   K—K5

forces the loss of the pawn.

If, instead,

2 R—B5

(R—B1 would actually lose.)

146   Study by Chéron

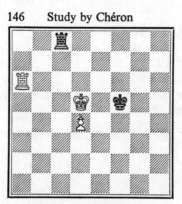

Black to move, loses
White to move, draws

2 ....   R—R3

and progress is at a standstill.

If White tries

1 R—R7   R—Q1 ch

lets the Black King in.

If

1 K—Q6   K—K5   3 K—B5   R—Q4 ch
2 R—R4   R—Q1 ch

However, if it be Black's move the *zugzwang* operates in favour of the attacker.

Any move down the Bishop's file makes 2 K—Q6 into a good move. Any move off the Bishop's file makes 2 K—B5 effective. Black King moves are also harmful.

One variation of this study will constitute useful learning in the annals of KR and pawn *v* King and Rook.

1 ....   K—B5   3 K—B5   R—R4 ch
2 R—QB6   R—QR1   4 K—Kt4!

Not K—Q6, which permits K—K5.

4	R—R1	5 R—K6

(the point—the Black King is cut off)

5	R—Q1

(to stop P—Q5)

6 K—B5	R—B1 ch	10 R—B5	R—R2
7 R—B6	R—QR1	11 R—B7	R—R4
8 P—Q5	R—R4 ch	12 K—B6	K—B3
9 K—Q6	K—B4		

(Observe the importance of the Rook's ability to check the Black King off the King's file)

13 P—Q6	K—K3	18 P—Q7	R—Q7
14 R—K7 ch	K—B3	19 K—B7	R—B7 ch
15 R—K1	R—R3 ch	20 K—Q8	R—KR7
16 K—B7	R—R2 ch	21 R—QB1	
17 K—Kt6	R—R7		

(not K—K8, R—R1 mate) and the White pawn will be promoted.

The last ten moves of this solution are fairly easy, but useful illustrations of the method of exploiting a cut-off King. Incidentally, reflect, at move 17, that if the pawn were the KP the Black Rook would be harder to embarrass.

Many elaborate statements have been made of the requirements for victory by pawns in Rook and pawn endings. The list of situations is so large that no practical purpose is served by this. Suffice it here to say each file has disadvantages as well as advantages.

A Knight's pawn stands next to a Rook's file on which either an attacking or defending King can be embarrassed, and on one side there is lack of manœuvring space.

Very pointed is the following position, played by Rabinovitch:

8,5K2,8,2R3P1,6k1,8,6r1,8.

Black, to move, draws:

1	K—R4	3 R—B6	R—Kt8
2 P—Kt6 ch	K—R3	4 R—B6	

(with the threat of R—B2 and R—R2 ch)

4	R—Kt4!	6 R × R stalemate.
5 R—B1	R—B4 ch	

Two other studies show the inferiority of Knight's pawn to other pawns further from the edge (including the Bishop's pawn, though that sometimes involves special variations due to mating threats).

Diagram 147 shows a King cut off by two files, but the ending is a draw.

147   Study by Chéron

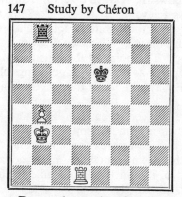

Draw, whoever has the move

Black, to move, plays:

1	K—K4	5 K—R4	R—R1 ch
2 R—Q7	K—K3	6 R—R5	R—QKt1
3 R—QB7	K—Q3	7 R—R7 ch	K—B3
4 R—B5	K—Q2	8 K—R5	R—Kt4 ch

drives the King back.

If it be White's move,

1 R—Q4	K—K4	3 R—B5 ch	K—Q3
2 R—QB4	K—Q4	4 K—B4	R—Kt2

and

5 P—Kt5

allows R—B2 with exchanges and a draw.

Now move all the pieces one to the right. White wins, whoever has the move. The White play is sufficient to reveal the point.

1 K—Kt4	R—Kt1 ch	2 K—R5

(note that this kind of space is not available when the pawn is the KtP)

2	R—QB1	5 R—QB1	K—K2
3 K—Kt5	R—Kt1 ch	6 K—Kt7	R—B4
4 K—R6	R—QB1	(K—Q2 would lose the Rook)

| 7 K—Kt6 | R—B1 | 8 P—B5 and wins. |

This contrast shows the relative defect in Knight's pawns. Other factors are always relevant. If the Black King were lower down in Diagram 147 and the White Rook higher up (White Rook on d7, Black King on e4), White would win by making a Rook cover for the King. The point of the illustration, however, is that similarly handicapped as to Rook and King placing, the player with BP, QP, KP may win, while the player with KtP would only draw.

Best pawns are the centre pawns. But here a defending King and Rook have their maximum scope.

The merits of the file are relatively less than the merits of the rank on which the pawn stands. A fairly advanced pawn, with the King in front of it, and Rook available to shelter the King, is a pawn that bids fair to win. It is necessary for the defence that the defending King be adjacent, at worst, not cut-off by more than one file. Whether a cut-off by one file is sufficient for victory depends on the effectiveness of the defending Rook and the distance of the pawn from promotion.

In order to get some experience of the problems of this frequent endgame the reader would be well advised to think about Diagram 148 and experiment with the material shown there.

148

White to move, wins
Black to move, draws

As it stands, White, to move, wins by R—Kt1 ch, followed by K—B6. But Black, to move, can draw by checks.

Move Kings, White Rook and pawn one square to the right and Black cannot draw by checks because the space is limited; the King can drive the Rook off the rank and still be not too far from the pawn.

Now revert to the diagram and alter it by transferring the White Rook from c1 to e1.

Can Black draw? Let us investigate.

1 ....   R—R3 ch
Now not 2 K—K(or Q)7, because of K—B4, but

2 R—K6	R—R4	3 R—K5	R—R2

If now

4 K—K6	K—B4	5 P—K6 ch	K—B3 draws.

Therefore try

4 R—K7	R—R4	6 R—B7 ch	K—Kt3
5 K—K6	K—B4	7 P—Q6	R—R3 ch

leads to a draw.

Also playable, it seems, is

3 ....   R—R3 ch
(instead of R—R2)

4 K—Q7	K—B4	5 P—Q6 ch	K—Kt3

(obviously K—K5 would be very bad; in general, a horizontal cut-off is more serious than a perpendicular one)

6 R—K6	R—R1	8 P—Q7 ch	K—B2 draws.
7 K—K7	K—B3		

(if the White Rook were lower down the file, P = Q ch would win, but the play has involved keeping the White Rook on the sixth. So P = Q ch does not win a Rook by subsequent check)

No rules about the relative merits of pawns emerge from these studies except the general one that side pawns are, on the whole, inferior to central ones.

This is evident when we consider that two joined passed pawns on the Rook and Knight files frequently fail to produce victory. (Cases on other files exist, but are rare.)

As long ago as 1851, Horowitz and Kling published a study

showing the possibilities, or impossibilities. (Diagram 149.) The obvious try is

1 R—Kt8   R—R5 ch   2 K—K3
(if 2 K—K5, R—R4 ch; K—K6, R × P)

2 ....   R—R2   3 R—Kt8 ch   K—R2
and White has nothing.

Obviously, King, Rook and two pawns only fail when the defending King is excellently placed and the pawns badly placed.

Study by Horowitz
149   and Kling   150

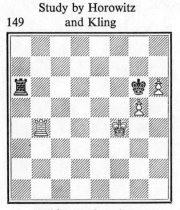

White to play, draws   White to play and win

Diagram 150 shows the pawns better placed. 1 K—B3 drives the Rook off the file (otherwise the King makes for f6).

1 ....   R—QKt5   2 K—Kt3
(to keep the Rook from the R file as well)

2 ....   R—QR5   3 R—QKt7
threatens P—R6 with a mating process. Black cannot stop this by R—R3, because that lets the White King approach.
Best is:

3 ....   R—B5   4 P—R6   R—B1
The White King has not really wanted h6, and if it makes approaches via g5 with a view to h7 ch, the Rook chases it away. If the pawn checks first and then the King approaches, there may happen:

| 5 P—R7 ch | K—R1 | 7 K—Kt5 | R—B4 ch |
| 6 K—Kt4 | R—B5 ch | 8 K—R6 | R—R4 ch |

The chances of stalemate through Rook sacrifice are always to be borne in mind. Therefore, P—R7 ch must be held back until it is fatal.

The winning process is a delicate one. (Forcing Rook exchanges.)

The King goes to the fifth rank on the Queen's side of the board and moves on to the sixth when there is no pawn-winning check available to Black and then to the seventh. Vertical cut-off is impossible because the King has Rook protection. E.g. after 5 R—Q7, R—R1; 6 K—B4, R—QKt1,

7 K—K5	R—R1	11 K—Kt6	R—QB1
8 K—Q5	R—R4 ch	12 K—Kt7	R—K1
9 K—B4	R—R5 ch	13 R—QB7 wins.	
10 K—Kt5	R—R1		

Alter Diagram 150 by putting the Black Rook at g3 and the White King at a1. In an exhaustive analysis Kasparian has claimed that the winning move is K—Kt1! But that is another story.

A well-placed King and Rook at times hold off divided pawns. The most favourable pair, for the defender, is RP and BP.

151

The defence is exceedingly difficult. Diagram 151 shows a position defended by the author in 1924 and drawn. I am indebted to the American researcher Frink for the following point of play:

| 1 .... | R—R7 ch | 3 R × P ch | K—Kt6 |
| 2 K—B1 | K—B5 | 4 R—R8 | P—B5 |

5 R—Kt8 ch	K—B6	6 K—Kt1

reaches a standard draw. But the King must not move the other way. E.g. if 6 K—K1.

6	R—R8 ch	8 R—KB8	K—Kt7 wins
7 K—Q2	R—KB8!		

e.g. 9 R—Kt8 ch, K—B7, and after 10 .... P—B6 White is helpless.

One way of stating the results of this is that in King and Rook *v.* King and pawn the defending King should stand on the short side and let its Rook check laterally on the long side. (This is subject to the danger of mating threats to be perceived.) Diagram 152 shows the difficulty where the two pawns remain uncapturable.

152

White to play. What result?

Many players, including the author, have experienced difficulty with this ending. It tends to occur at a phase of great fatigue.

It is unlikely that K—R1 draws (it would if the Rook's pawn were at a5), but the following line definitely loses.

1 K—R3	R—KR7	3 K—R2	K—Q6
2 R × P	R—R8	4 R—R8	P—B6

with the threat of P—B7.

5 R—R7

is useless because after P—B7 the King can be checked away from Kt7.

If 5 R—Q8 ch, K—B7, threatening K—B8 and P—B7.

If 6 R—QB8, K—Q7; 7 R checks K—B8 and 8 .... P—B7.

Distinguish this position from that in Diagram 151, where the attacking King is prevented from settling on its B7 or B8.

The holding of options on B8 is the more important.

Thus one point of technical importance which emerges in this ending is that when KR and BP are playing against Rook and a King on the Rook's file, the attacking King, in order to win, should try to establish itself on B8. Similarly the position in Diagram 153 is a win for White, whoever has the move.

153

White wins, whoever has the
move

But place the White King at B7 and Black, to move, draws with R—Kt2 ch and K—Kt3.

Or place the White Rook on R7 checking the Black King and K—Kt3 draws. Thus 2 P—B7, R—Kt1 ch; 3 K—K7, K—Kt2.

In working out the exact placing of the pieces in such endgame play great accuracy in timing and a degree of subtlety are required in addition to technique.

It is hoped that the student of this chapter learns from it some 'sense' of pawn values. Attempts to classify all cases of Rook and pawn are hopeless. Formulae only prevent concentration on the subtleties of actual endgame play.

PART THREE: THE STRUGGLE FOR ADVANTAGE

CHAPTER VI

SOME EARLY INITIATIVES AND EXPLOITATIONS

The question is frequently asked: Why and how do good players lose? As to the why, many suggestions can be made, including the proposition that many games are lost because the loser was trying to win: or (to put it another way) was trying to do too much. Also a great many are lost because the loser did not do enough. And some are lost through sheer misguidedness, to say nothing of short range error.

More useful to the student of technique is the question: How? By studying how specific losses came about, one can learn to avoid dangers and to exploit weaknesses.

Here are a few examples of type of win and loss.

Very interesting is Diagram 154. This shows a position reached by a strong player, the lamented Dutch Master Landau, against an opponent whom he would have readily admitted to be of a higher class than himself (Salo Flohr).

What has happened here?

Well, Flohr has wasted a lot of time. He played the Nimzovitch Defence (1 P—Q4, Kt—KB3; 2 P—QB4, P—K3; 3 Kt—QB3, B—Kt5). That is orthodox now: but this defence places a Bishop on the Queen's wing; which Bishop becomes a displaced person when White castles on the King's side. So it behoves Black not to waste time with it. Flohr wasted time with that Bishop before exchanging it, and dallied with his Queen to regain a gambit pawn. Then he exchanged a Bishop for a Knight at f3, giving White an open line, instead of challenging the centre at e4. White was granted time to bring a Rook via QKt1, QKt5, KKt5 to KKt2, and to establish Bishops on excellent diagonals. In other words, thinking to win an endgame with a Q-side pawn majority, Flohr now finds that he has given his opponent time to build up all the necessary pressure for a winning K-side attack.

Landau—Flohr
154   (Bournemouth, 1939)

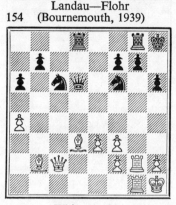

White to play

There followed:

29 B—R7	QKt—Kt5	32 R—Kt7	Kt—Kt5
30 Q—KB5	P—KKt3	33 KR × Kt dis ch.	
31 B × R	P × Q	(better was 33 R—R7 double ch,	
		K × B; 34 R—R8 mate)	

33	P—B3	35 R × R resigns.
34 R—Kt7	R—Q2	

White won that game through benefit of tempo. He had used his time (i.e. his number of moves) more constructively than his opponent. His opponent had used time on irrelevant play, repetitious play, unincisive play.[1]

The lesson in technique taught by that example is the importance of relevant play.

The next diagrams are other examples of consequences of 'irrelevance', the moving of important pieces from the scene of action.

[1] A psychological explanation may be that Flohr, in August 1939, being a Czech, was more disturbed by the political situation than the Dutch Landau. It happens that Flohr eventually escaped into Russia. Landau was murdered by the Germans. (Incidentally, Landau had a good record against Flohr.)

Diagram 155 shows the consequences of a White excursion to the Q-side in search of pawn gain, while the opponent builds an

155

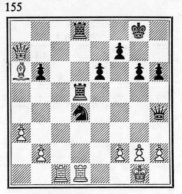

White to play

attack in the centre. 1 R—K1 (in order to prevent Kt—K7 ch) is met by Kt—B6 ch. There follows:

| 2 P×Kt | R—Kt4 ch | 4 K—K2 | R—K4 mate. |
| 3 K—B1 | Q—R6 ch | | |

The next diagram, No. 156, shows the end of a fine game by Broadbent, in which he demonstrates that Black has no time to mobilise a defence (R—Kt1 ch was contemplated). There came:

Broadbent—Bogoljubov
156   (Cheltenham, 1951)

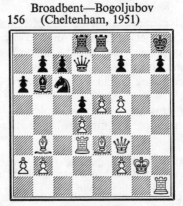

White to play

27	R × P ch	K × R	30	P—K6	Kt × P
28	Q—R5 ch	K—Kt1	31	R—Kt3 ch wins	
29	B—R6	Kt—K2			

This position is particularly interesting because it develops, though not of necessity, from the interesting situation shown in Diagram 157. Black has not lost in this compromised position, though many good players disapprove of the compromising of the centre. But Black did lose the game in question because he thought he had tactical chances and overestimated them. His manœuvres were unproductive against a correct defence conducted by a player with the technical advantage of a better centre.

157 Broadbent—Bogoljubov

Black to play

From Diagram 157 the play was:

12	....	P—Q4	15	Kt—Kt3	Kt—Kt4
13	P—K5	B—Kt5	16	R—Q3	B × Kt
14	R—K3	Kt—K5	17	P × B	B—R4

(in order to move against White's Q4)

| 18 | P—B4 | Kt—K5 | 20 | RP × Kt |
| 19 | Q—B3 | Kt × Kt | | |

and now White has disposed of all Black's tactical threats, gaining a stronger centre than ever and an important open file.

But the centre, in itself, is not a guarantee of victory. Indeed, a formidable appearing centre may give the opponent an objective for attack.

In the position shown in Diagram 158 Nimzovitch has played B—B4 inviting P—Q4, and proceeds to attack that square. His Knight is well placed at K3 because Black has no KBP.

Black can hold this position if he plays very economically as to tempo. Against 8 B—Kt3, followed by 9 P—QB4 and later by Kt—QB3, Black must mobilise his Bishop to QKt5, his QKt to KB3 and his KKt to K2. Then with Bishop at K3 and Queen at KB2 he can hold the game. Nimzovitch's opponent did not play profoundly enough, and eventually Nimzovitch sacrificed at Q5 and won elegantly.

158   Nimzovitch—Behting

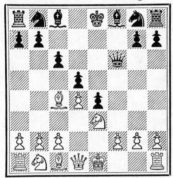

159   Landau—Klein

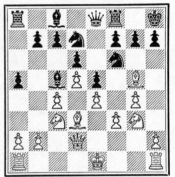

Black to play

Many games of Chess are decided by struggles for particular points. A whole game can collapse if a venture fails.

Diagram 159 shows Landau, the hero of the game against Flohr, being completely outplayed by that excellent strategian Klein, who, for so many years, kept the minor masters of the Chess world in total subjection.

Against a Nimzovitch defence White has built up a centre with P—B3 and P—K4, and Black has counter-developed with P—Q3 and P—K4. This leads to a centre block and Black mobilises better. So long as there is space in the interstices of the advanced pawns the second player has *Lebensraum*.

The game continued 12 .... Kt—KKt1. This manœuvre (technically important) is not a retreat but a freeing of pawns.

13 Kt—B5	P—KB3	15 Kt—Kt3	B × B
14 B—K3	P—KKt3	16 Q × B	Kt—B4
			(well established here)

| 17 P—KR4 | Kt—K2 | 19 KP × P | P × P |
| 18 0—0—0 | P—B4 | | |

and Black, not White, is attacking. There followed:

20 P—B4	Kt—Kt3!	24 R × Q	P × Kt
21 B × P	P × P	25 B—B5	Kt—K4
22 Q—Q4 ch	Q—K4	26 KR—Q1	P—KR4
23 B × B	Q × Q	with a winning position.	

This is the result of White's pushing forward and being pushed
back, a very frequent pattern of loss in high-class Chess. Observe
that in this position both players have a claim on the centre. But
Black is doing more effective work there.

Very different is Diagram 160. Here, as often in the French defence,
White occupies plenty of space and is able to manœuvre more freely.
Black has not played the best possible sequences, but is not lost.

Alekhine—Nimzovitch
160   (San Remo, 1930)

Black to move

Here, however, instead of fighting on the Queen side with 14 ....
P—R4 (if 15 P—Kt5, Kt—Kt5; if 15 B—Kt5, P × P), Black played
14 .... P—B4, and the following impressive play unfolded itself:

15 P—R5   Kt—B1
(if P × P; 16 P—Kt5 is good)

16 Kt × B	Q × Kt	18 B—Kt5	Kt(B1)—K2
17 P—R6	Q—KB2	(otherwise a White Rook will	
		occupy c7)	

19 0—0	P—R3	21 R—B2	Q—K1
20 KR—B1	KR—B1		

(Kt—Q1 is met by Rook exchanges and R—B1, and the Queen reaches c7)

22 QR—B1	QR—Kt1

(to meet B—R4 with P—Kt4)

23 Q—K3	R—B2	26 Q—B 1	R(Kt1)—B1
24 R—B3	Q—Q2	27 B—R4	P—QKt4
25 R(B1)—B2	K—B1		

(the reader is left to analyse the speculative Kt × QP which only just fails)

28 B × P	K—K1	30 P—R4	*zugzwang*
29 B—R4	K—Q1		

(Eventually K (or Q)—K1 will allow P—Kt5 to win.)

This position is the result of the defender's allowing to the opponent too much space and himself too little space.

In this particular game the centre takes the form of a pawn thrust into the opponent's territory, restricting the movements of the defender. Contrast this centre with that in the game Landau-Klein, where the pawn formation does not prevent a mobilisation by the player with the apparently smaller manœuvring space.

So far we have seen two or three clear (not unrelated) types of loss.

1. Loss through waste of time.

2. Loss through surrender of space.

3. Loss through irrelevant play or inadequate play: play that seemed relevant but turned out to be waste of time and/or abandonment of space.

There are other varieties of loss, including all those in which one player misses a tactical point.

Thus Diagram 161 shows Van Scheltinga losing to Alexander through missing a neat mating device—which should be in the awareness of combative players. (Technically, it is a case of 'smothered mate'.) In the diagram position White can play

33 Q—Q2	R—Q1	35 B—Q2
34 Q—KB2	R—Q6	

with victory in sight. Instead, he played

33 R—B3	R—Q1	35 B—Kt1 Q × R wins.
34 B—K3	R—Q8 ch	

Van Scheltinga—Alexander
161   (Cheltenham, 1951)

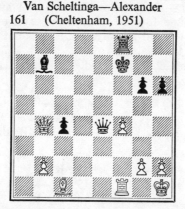

Diagram 162 shows an opponent of the author's playing happily along, unaware of what can happen to him.   The play was:

31 KR—Q1	R—KKt4	36 R—QR8	Q—KB6
32 R(1)—Q5	R—Kt2	37 Q × Q	P × Q
33 P—R5	R—K3	38 R—Q1	R × P ch
34 Q—R3	R—KKt3	39 K—R1	R—K5
35 R—Q8 ch	K—R2	and R—R5 forces mate.	

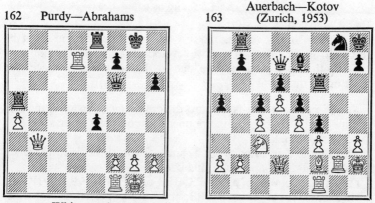

162   Purdy—Abrahams

163   Auerbach—Kotov
(Zurich, 1953)

White to play   White to play

More spectacular is Diagram 163.   After hours by both players of threatening nothing with great subtlety, Black has accidentally emerged with advantage and is threatening R—R3.   Playable in

defence are: 30 P—KR4, followed by Q—K1 and R—Kt4, with
eventual R—R1 and K—Kt1. Black can exert pressure with R—
R3, R—R4, Q—Q1 and Kt—R3, but it does not win. Also playable is 30 R—Kt4.

However, Auerbach, undoubtedly fatigued, played 30 Kt—K2,
allowing

30	Q × P ch	32 K—Kt4	Kt—B3 ch
31 K × Q	R—R3 ch	33 K—B5	

(not 33 K—Kt5, R—Kt1 ch; 34 K × R, R × R, threatening B—B1
mate)

33	Kt—Q2	38 K—B5	Kt—Kt1 ch
34 R—Kt5	R—B1 ch	39 K—Kt4	B × R
35 K—Kt4	Kt—B3 ch	40 K × B	R—B2
36 K—B5	Kt × QP ch	41 B—R4	
37 K—Kt4	Kt—B3 ch	(to stop eventual mate by the Knight on K2)	

41	R—Kt3 ch	44 K—R4	Kt—B3
42 K—R5	R(2)—Kt2	45 Kt—Kt3	R × Kt
43 B—Kt5	R × B ch	46 Q × QP	

(Why did Black need to capture the QP at move 36? Had he not
seen the entire movement?)

46	R(6)—Kt3	48 Resigns.
47 Q—Q8 ch	R—Kt1	

If this possibility of loss requires technical description let it be
described as due to a cramping of development. (It is worth observ-
ing that this cramping may be due to the crowding of pieces for
one's own attack.)

More important, perhaps, than the cramping of space is the loss
of time which enables your opponent to compress your space, or
to attack material.

Amusing is a position from a game of the author's from which
two other citations appear in this book:

r1bq1rk1,p3bppp,2p1p3,3ktP3,4Kt3,6P1,PP3PBP,R1BQ1RK1.

In answer to 13 .... B—R3, the author played 14 Q—Kt4,
with the threat of B—R6. Black (as anticipated) snatches a tempo
now with:

14	P—R4

There followed:

15 Q × P   B × R   16 B × B

But now the tempo is returned with interest.

16 ....   P—KB4   17 P × P e.p.   Kt × P

with reliance possibly on exchanges. But White with Q—R3 is able to ignore the attack on the Knight. After

18 Q—R3   Kt × Kt   19 Q × P ch

regains the Knight with a strong attack.

In this class are all those gains which are made when a player is able apparently to ignore a threat to a piece.

Thus one is attacking a King-side pawn and the opponent counters against the QBP. Perhaps that counter amounts to nothing. There may be Q—R4 ch to follow, picking up the capturing piece. And similarly it happens that many an apparently good counter is met by a fork or some other violence.

The essence of Chess is seeing the move after; and many gains of tempo accrue to those who see that they need not make defensive or preparatory moves. Aggression with subsequent consolidation can be better than slowly prepared aggression.

In the classifying of reasons for loss and victory (and the means of stealing marches), mention should also be made of those moves, seen by one, unseen or inevitable to the other, which, when they are made, threaten two processes, both of which cannot be prevented. The threats may be immediate or may constitute the refutation of a move that the opponent wishes or needs to make. The effect is equally important. In point is Diagram 164.

(Simultaneous Exhibition)
164   Abrahams (White)

White to play

White plays:

15 P—B5	P × P	16 P × P

If now

16	B × P	17 Q—B3

attacking Bishop and Queen and tying the latter to the defence of the Knight.

If, then,

17	B—Q3	18 R × B wins.

If, instead,

17	Q—K2	18 R—Q7

wins imaginatively, quite apart from the logical win by B × Kt ch followed by the gain of a Bishop.

Therefore

16	B—K2

is forced, and, if he so wishes, White can win the exchange by

17 Q—K3, Kt—Q4.	19 Q—Kt3
18 B—R6 ch K—Kt1	(again an attack on two things)

19	B—R3	20 B × R

and Black cannot play

20	B × R

because of B × B followed by K × B with a piece to the good.

This last variation introduces the useful idea of the 'desperado', also of *zwischenzug*, of both of which Diagram 165 affords examples. White plays 15 Kt—Q5, forcing Q × Q, but White need not stop to recapture. Before he recaptures White can use his Knight to play 16 Kt × B ch (met by K—B1). Then he recaptures the Queen with his Bishop. So far the actual game. At that point Black can, and does, play K × Kt. But he need not. The Knight has no escape. Playable is 17 .... B × P. If White replies to this with 18 P—B3, Black retreats B—R2, the only square on which the 'desperado' Knight cannot capture it. (19 Kt—B5 suggested.)

In the diagram the Black Queen is, in the continental expression, a 'hanging piece'; it is loose—an unconsidered trifle for Autolycus. Instances of this type of larceny are innumerable in Chess. If, in the diagram, there had been a Black pawn at d5, the position of Black's Queen would have caused its loss. Had the Rooks been at d8 and c8, the Bishop at g6, a piece would have been lost. As to the excursions of desperadoes, their dangers account for something that may puzzle the student of openings.

In the Sicilian, after 1 P—K4, P—QB4; 2 Kt—KB3, Kt—QB3; 3 P—Q4, P × P; 4 Kt × P, Kt—B3; 5 Kt—QB3, P—Q3; 6 B—K2, P—KKt3; 7 B—K3, B—Kt2; White frequently plays

Penrose and Clarke
165   (B.B.C. 1961)

Fischer

    8 Kt—Kt3
Why? Because if he castles,

    8 ....   Kt—KKt5
can lead to a wild process. If 9 B × Kt, B × B; 10 Q × B, Kt × Kt. If

    9 Kt × Kt   Kt × B   10 Kt × Q   Kt × Q
Now Black is threatening Kt × Kt. At this point 11 Kt × Kt, K × Kt leaves Black with two Bishops against Bishop and Knight.

This variation needs a good deal of analysis, but players avoid the complexities with 8 Kt—Kt3, removing temptation from the opponent.

The 'desperado', be it said, is the hero of many attacks when one player finds himself with a piece that has gained something and is momentarily unrecaptured. In a sense the 'desperado' is the opposite of the piece with too much to do. He has relative freedom from anxiety. Whatever gain he makes is profit.

Cognate to the idea of double threats is the fact that, frequently in Chess, pieces are performing two or more functions. Thus visualise a pawn on d4 supporting a pawn on c5 and a Knight on e5. If a hostile Queen or Bishop or Rook is operating over the square e5, then some other piece may capture the pawn at c5, because if it be captured by the pawn the Knight will fall. It may be that that Knight will use a tempo capturing a pawn at f7, because it is 'desperado', or it may not be able to do so. This is typical of many apparently sacrificial attacks. They amount to exploitations of a double function on the part of some piece or pawn.

Diagram 166 illustrates a double function which is not immediately apparent, but which it is very important to recognise.

166

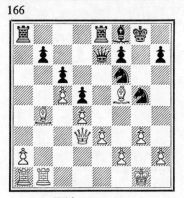

White to move

The position, from a correspondence game by the author, starts with an interesting point of order. Should White play P—KR4, or K—Kt2 or B—K1 first? White decided against P—KR4 (inter alia) because of Kt—B6 ch, and a counter sacrifice, Kt × RP. B—K1 is met by check and exchange of Knight for Bishop.

The play was:

22 K—Kt2   Kt(B3)—K5

If now

23 P—KR4   Q—B3

and if

24 P—KKt4   Kt—R6!

However, White decides to protect (or over-protect) KB2. He can do this with B—K1 or R—Kt2. Now R—Kt2 would be exploited because that Rook would be doing a double function. It is guarding the Bishop at Kt4. So R—Kt2 would allow P—Kt3!

This is the kind of danger for which one must be ever vigilant. The expression 'double function' does not really help the Chess player to see these things. It is a name given to a feature which has to be seen before it is named. No one looks round the board asking himself what pieces may or may not be fulfilling double functions. But if the player is aware that a certain piece is over-working, he should consider its future relief, even if there is no present danger. At this stage let it be said that no one can draft a set of rules for attack. Writers have expressed themselves on the topic of 'outposts', 'strong points', 'weak points', etc. But in practice the recognition of strength and weakness of squares or pieces is tactical. Diagram 167 shows Yates wreaking on Tarrasch his wrath at the latter's opposition to his entry to the Tournament. Black played 1 .... Kt × P. If 2 P × Kt, Q—Kt4 gives a winning attack! There is no formula to describe this combination. The fact that White's mobilisation is less dynamic than Black's describes the position when one has seen the possibilities. Thus, vary the position slightly: put the White King on R1: Black still stands well, but the specific sacrificial line fails.

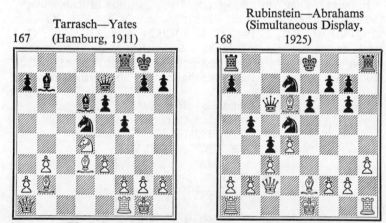

Tarrasch—Yates
167   (Hamburg, 1911)

Black to play

Rubinstein—Abrahams
(Simultaneous Display,
168   1925)

White to move

Even more demonstrative of the absence of formula is, if I may say so, Diagram 168. Rubinstein,[1] playing at the speed of simultaneous play, failed to see why (in answer to Black's Q(B1)—B3) B—R2 was a better move than B—Kt3. Geometrically B—Kt3 gives the Bishop's pawn a double function that is hard to see,

[1] Unhappily deceased while this book was in the press.

because no piece is yet attacking the Bishop, and one of the guarded squares is a vacant one. Black played Kt—K6! This move was not made for technical reasons. (Important moves on to empty squares are, incidentally, harder to see and classify than captures.) It was perceived as a vigorous and effective attack with perceptible lines of play to follow it. The mental activity in Chess is a constant awareness of what one's pieces can do. The habits of a player's mind select for him the relevant possibilities, and, if he is not a very good player, the field of relevance will be more limited than that of the good player. The need for seeing what can be done is not supplied by technical equipment. It is, of course, possible for the teacher of Chess to say, 'observe that unusual idea', and a pupil learns something from this. But in general, the teaching and the technique show methods of achieving certain known objectives. They leave to the sensitive mind of the player the task of recognition. They classify, but do not create, ideas.

This is mentioned because some great players, including Lasker, have canvassed the possibility of stating rules for combination in Chess.

In point is Diagram 169, which shows a position of Rubinstein's, famous in Chess literature. The play was 21 B—Kt1, Kt—B5; 22 Q—B2, B—Kt1; 23 P—Kt3, Kt × RP; 24 R × P, Q—Q3; 25 Q—Kt6! It has been said of this that Rubinstein made 'the most restraining move' or 'the most restrictive move'. If that means that Rubinstein sought out the move that carried him furthest into the

Rubinstein—Hromadka
(Mährisch-Ostrau,
169   1923)

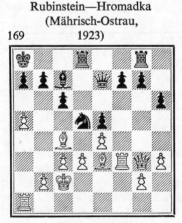

White to play

opponent's position, in terms of distance, then it is an absurdity.
There are many long Queen moves in many games that are completely useless, and many very effective moves are very short in
range.

The truth is that, when tactical movements are being considered,
adequate technical rules are not available. Important to the attacker is the feeling that he has some advantage of tempo, some
greater degree of mobility than his opponent. But he has to work
out lines of play, bearing in mind that he may be forcing into
activity the latent resources of his opponent's position. For that
reason, except for generalities about time and space and relevance,
there are no rules to guide one to successful attack or defence.
These are matters of awareness, vision, imagination, not of technique.

Awareness cannot be taught. Nevertheless, in experience we
encounter events that make us more sensitive to possibilities. Thus
everybody knows about Knight's forks and Bishop sacrifices at
B7. But not everybody is fully aware of all the possibilities at
crucial moments. (Who, indeed, is, on every such occasion, aware
that the moment is crucial?) In point is the following short line
of play from the opening

| 1 P—Q4 | Kt—KB3 | 3 P—KKt3 | B—Kt2 |
| 2 P—QB4 | P—KKt3 | 4 B—Kt2 | P—Q4 |

Now 5 P × P, Kt × P seems to give White the opportunity of
quick centralisation, notwithstanding that the pawn at d4 is going
to need protection, not to say overprotection. At this stage, has
White considered 6 P—K4, Kt—QKt5?

If he thinks that this is well answered by 7 Kt—K2 he is mis-
taken, because the pawn at d4 is still underdefended, viz.:

| 7 .... | B × P | 9 Q × Q | Kt—B7 ch |
| 8 Kt × B | Q × Kt | | |

Knowledge of the Knight's fork by itself would not make a
novice see this. Suppose he has seen it and relied on 7 Q—R4 ch.
(Or, more likely, he has not seen this because he has not considered
Kt—Kt5, but now looks to the Queen's move as a resource.)

| 7 .... | QKt—B3 | 8 P—Q5 | Kt—Q6 ch |

(the unanticipated effect of moving the KP when the Bishop has
fianchettoed itself).

If 8 K—B1, Kt × B; 9 P × Kt, 0—0 leaves Black with a winning
attack.

If 8 K—Q2, Kt × KBP (inter alia) leaves a serious situation. Evidently 7 Q—R4 ch comes to nóthing.

To be considered are: 7 P—Q5, met by P—QB3; 8 P—QR3, Q—R4 and White may now or later, with P × Kt, sacrifice the exchange for freedom and counter-play. Also 7 P—QR3 is to be considered. White must work out the effect of

7	B × QP	9 K—K2	Q × Q ch
8 P × Kt	B × BP ch	10 K × Q	

which, happily, is not terrible for White.

The likely response to 7 P—QR3 is KKt—QB3. Then 8 P—Q5 (necessary) allows 8 .... Kt—K4, or Kt—Q5, and Black has command of the diagonal.

In considering this variation the reader may be reminded of the maxim that one should not move the same piece or pawn more than once before development is complete. That is a valuable maxim. But it is not a dogma. In this piece of play the essence is the destruction of White's centre. Rules of general development can be subordinated to this. Moreover, White has wasted tempo in this way: that he has furnished two outlets for his KB instead of one. Further, from the point of view of the actual play, some of White's development is irrelevant.

Development, be it remembered, is a relative term. You can win on occasion with a quick attack by very few pieces, with several heavy pieces undeveloped. The opponent's force is relatively less developed. When the opponent is playing a steady development, then, admittedly, one must be chary of the repetitious, of the un-economical, of doing in two moves what should be done in one. But sometimes it is unwise to try and do in one what may be done in two.

Thus in the Queen's Gambit, Black plays P—K3 and later P—QB3. Then he tries to get in P—QB4 or P—K4, after preparation. To try and save time, by not moving the QBP unless, or until, it can move two squares, is to adopt a dangerous policy.

In the same opening White allows a Bishop to move twice, but with strategic compensation. Thus:

1 P—Q4	P—Q4	4 B—Kt5	QKt—Q2
2 P—QB4	P—K3	5 P—K3	
3 Kt—QB3	Kt—KB3	(threatening to win a pawn)	

5 ....   B—K2   7 QR—B1   P—B3
6 Kt—B3   0—0   8 Q—B2   P—QR3

(a strategic preparation for pawn play on the Queen side). 8 ....
P × P here or earlier enables White to do in one move what he can
do in two. But good players have played it.

9 B—Q3   P × P   10 B × P

The Bishop has moved twice, but there is a gain (momentary at
least) of better centre control. Black now develops with 10 ....
Kt—Q4 expecting, after exchanges, to get in P—K4. He also has
to consider 10 .... P—QB4 or 10 .... P—QKt4 followed by
P—QB4. Moves like Kt—QKt3 followed by QKt—Q4 are also
playable. At this stage pieces are beginning to make second moves
without detriment to the position.

But the importance of tempo, and the ease with which points
of tempo can be missed, are illustrated in the following piece of
play: 1 P—Q4, P—Q4; 2 P—QB4, P—K3; 3 Kt—KB3, P—QB3;
4 P—K3, P—KB4; 5 P × P, KP × P; 6 B—Q3, B—Q3; 7 0—0,
Kt—KR3; 8 P—QKt3.

At this point the tempting 0—0 was played and caused the loss
of a move, because after 9 B—R3 Black cannot develop his QKt
without exchanging Bishops (i.e. moving the Bishop twice). If,
however, 8 .... QKt—Q2; 9 B—R3, Kt—B3, without loss of
tempo, and 0—0 to follow. (Black has no need to fear that 8 ....
QKt—Q2 may be met by 9 P—K4!? This comes to nothing.)

To revert, however, to the theme, which is the awareness of the
powers of groups of pieces (rather than individual pieces), the well-
equipped player acquires from experience, not from the learning
of rules, an appreciation of what attacking pieces can wreak by
way of damage, also what points are weak points that require to
be watched and warded.

Relatively elementary is the weakness at KR2, which is exploited
in the 'Greek Gift' sacrifice. The Diagram 170 is justified because
it occurred in a tournament. The sacrifice is sufficiently well
known to be regarded as 'technical'.

After exchanges at e4 Black played 11 .... P × P. There followed 12 B × P ch, K × B; 13 Kt—Kt5 ch. Observe, now, that had
Black's Rook been at KB1, the game could be held with K—Kt1
and Kt—B3. Indeed, K—Kt1 seems natural here. (It loses to
14 Q—R5, Kt—B3; 15 Q × P ch and 16 R—K4!). However, Black
played: 13 .... K—Kt3. A simple move like Q—Kt4 would win
now. But Colle played: 14 P—KR4, R—R1; 15 R × P ch, Kt—B3 (if

Collé—O'Hanlon
170   (Nice, 1930)

15 .... P × R no interposition is possible when the Queen checks at d3); 16 P—R5 ch, R × P. And now Colle, though he won the game, missed a smothered mate by

17 Q—Q3 ch   K—R3   18 Kt—B7
The whole line of play is so familiar as to be conventional. But a player should not be restricted in his outlook by the one specific form of the sacrifice that he has been shown. An important added feature is present in the following position:
r1b2rk1, pp2q1pp, 1ktp1pp2, 8, 3P1P1P, 2PB1KtP1, P4P2, R2QK2R.
White may play as follows:

1 B × P ch   K × B   3 RP × P ch   K—Kt1
2 Kt—Kt5 ch   P × Kt
Now 4 Q—R5 looks good, but is thwarted or delayed by R—B4. White, however, has an interesting *zwischenzug*.

4 R—R8 ch   K × R
(K—B2 is met by 5 Q—R5 ch, P—Kt3; 6 R—R7 ch)

5 Q—R5 ch   K—Kt1   6 P—Kt6
and Black cannot vacate enough squares to stop the mate unless he sacrifices his Queen at h4. Less conventional is the attack against KB7 that so strong a player as Koltanowski overlooked (Diagram 171).[1]   Black played

[1] Something similar was inflicted on the great Tarrasch by the minor master von Holzhausen.

8 ....   R—K1

(less unenterprising here than it was in Collé-O'Hanlon. The idea
is B—B1)

9 B × P ch   K × B   10 Kt—K6
                               with an overwhelming attack.

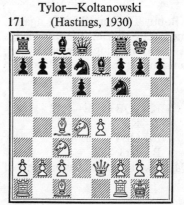

Tylor—Koltanowski
171   (Hastings, 1930)

Abrahams—Herrick
172   (Manchester, 1948)

Another attack on KB7, that is frequently overlooked by players
thinking at a distance, is the one expressed in Diagram 172.

In answer to 16 Kt—K4, Black played B—B5. When 17 Kt—K5
was played, he saw the danger of

17 ....   B × R   18 Kt × P

so played 17 .... B × Kt, losing to 18 Q × P ch, which forces
mate.

The moral is that the conventional weak points are not always
recognised for their exact weaknesses when other features of the
board are occupying attention.

In this psychological difficulty—of achieving an adequate and
relevant attention—we have the reason why the cleverness of the
board cannot be taught. Yet something can be learned by the
player who, when shown an idea, appreciates it. His sensitivity
will be enhanced to the fine points of play.

What degree of sensitivity one has can be gauged by looking at
such a position as the following: 5r2, p4R2, 3p4, 1p4pk, 1P5r, 6qP,
P2B4, 5Q1K. White (Simagin), to move, appears to be hopelessly
lost. If he plays R—R7 ch, his checks very quickly cease. But

there is an idea available. 1 Q—K2 ch, P—Kt5, and now 2 R—B5 ch!, R × R; 3 Q—K8 ch, forcing mate. That is a brilliant perception. I would say that a problemist, experienced in the geometry of mating angles, might have it as part of his composing equipment. The practical player will only see it if he has a mind that is sensitive to the subtleties of the board. This he will have acquired from the apprehension, and the learning, of ideas totally different in shape!

Finally, let the play of prodigy Bobby Fischer (White), against prodigious Samuel Reshevsky, demonstrate that all the knowledge of weak squares, pins, angles, etc., to say nothing of great vision, does not prevent the occasional omission of even great players to see a possibility.

1 P—K4	P—QB4	5 Kt—QB3	B—Kt2
2 Kt—KB3	Kt—QB3	6 B—K3	Kt—B3
3 P—Q4	P × P	7 B—QB4	0—0
4 Kt × P	P—KKt3	8 B—Kt3	

(to prevent Kt × P, Kt × Kt, P—Q4, a well-known exploitation of 'fork').

8 ....　　　　　Kt—QR4　　　9 P—K5　　　Kt—K1
(if 9 .... Kt × B; 10 KP × Kt, Kt × R; 11 P × B, Kt × P ch, and when the desperado is removed, White shows profit. But what happened was worse!)

10 B × P ch
(one of many different kinds of sacrifices that happen on this weak square, a square which seems at this moment to be strengthened!)

10 ....　　　　　K × B　　　　　11 Kt—K6!
winning the Queen; incidentally a study in domination.

CHAPTER VII

CONTROL OF THE CENTRE IN THE EARLY GAME

One way of looking at Chess development is to regard it as a fight for freedom. You want to have at least as much action for your pieces as your opponent has for his. Recognition of this should lift a player above much useless detail, just as if he had vision, from an aeroplane, of a crowded town. When the groundwork of opening theory is surveyed, much of the crowded terrain can be safely ignored if one discerns the common purpose in the planning. What does this opening give you? A frequent question is, what kind of centre? Before appreciating any opening line, it is necessary to visualise the central development that results. So let us consider, first of all, the centre as developed in a modern opening.

Diagram 173 shows a position from a King's Indian Defence, a very popular opening system. White has to make his eleventh move.

173

White to play

Examine a few features. White has plenty of space and seems to be controlling more squares. But Black has placed his pieces where most of them can be made effective. Thus the Knight on

Black's QB4 is well placed. Black has played earlier P—K4 inducing White's P—Q5, then, with P—QR4 and P—QKt3, has made a square snug at QB4.

Note that White cannot quickly disturb the Knight with P—QR3 and P—QKt4. The pawn takes three moves, not two moves, to arrive at QKt4. (If 11 P—QR3, P—QR5 paralyses the Knight's pawn, so the proper method would be first P—QKt3, then P—QR3, finally P—QKt4.)

White must be quite careful about this. It does not appear, at first glance, that the Black Bishop at Kt2 is very active. But look at this possibility:

11 P—QKt3	Kt(B4) × KP	14 Q—Kt1	P—K5
12 Kt × Kt	Kt × Kt	15 Kt—Q2	
13 Q × Kt	P—KB4		

Note that 15 Kt—Q4 seems bad because of 15 .... P—B5. Always be aware of the possibility of the defence being undermined. However, there is more to it than undermining. There is a good deal of play in this alternative variation.

| 15 Kt—Q4 | P—B5 | 16 Kt—B6 | Q—Kt4 |

with an exceedingly strong King side attack.

There can follow:

17 P—KR4

(This can be called a 'decoy' if one wishes to give names to moves.)

| 17 .... | Q × RP | 19 P × P |
| 18 B—Q4 | P—B6 | |

(Observe P—Kt3, Q—R6, a well-known mating net.)

| 19 .... | P × P |

wins back the sacrificed piece.

At move 15, then, it seems, on analysis, that

15 Kt—Q2

is tactically best.

There follows:

| 15 .... | B × R | 16 Q × B . |

and Black has given two Knights and Bishop for Rook, Knight and pawn, not bad value if one has the attack. But here it may well be that White with control of the long diagonal has plenty of play. If Black risked

16 ....   P—KKt4

White would play

17 B—R5   P—B5   18 B—Q4

(not B × R, because P × B leaves two pieces threatened) and Black, not White, is in serious trouble.

The technical interest of that play is considerable. In the diagram position a pawn that looks firm enough is not a rock.

Some players would advocate a move like 11 Kt—Q2. That is called 'over-protecting', and they might continue with P—B3. Then they would not feel grave doubts about the moving of any one of the defending pieces.

There are other features to be discerned in Diagram 173, if the reader will revert to it.

Note White's pawn on KR3. In general one does not use time to move Rooks' pawns one square. To prevent B—Kt5 or Kt—Kt5 it may be necessary. But if it is not strictly necessary, the move uses time to little purpose, and the opponent has a free move which he can use, if he wishes to put the piece in question on a square where it will remain developed.

P—R3, when unnecessary, or unpurposive, is called 'the country move' or 'the provincial move' (presumably by London players who never heard of Blackburn, or Yates, or Atkins, or other distinguished non-Londoners). In the diagram position it has been a useful move. First, it has enabled the Bishop to settle on K3 without being threatened with exchange by Kt—Kt5. Secondly, in a strategy which involves neutralising the Black pieces, this move helps to keep Black's QB out of the game. Further, there may come a time when White requires P—KKt4. In many games when the centre is closed, Black gets relief, and some attack, by manoeuvres, like Kt—KR4 (or K1 if that square be free) and P—KB4. Technically, that is a proper procedure if it be tactically possible. It may result in a further push to KB5 or in the opening of the Bishop's file for attack along it. Moreover, P—KKt4 will prevent a manoeuvre like Kt—R4, followed by Kt—B5. If the Knight be exchanged at B5, the long Diagonal is open to Black's Bishop. Indeed, if, in the diagram position, White plays 11 P—KKt4, he is making a good move, rendering safer, inter alia, a future P—QKt3. Also, the move can be followed up with a King move and the occupation of the Knight file with a Rook. Other possible manœuvres, in conjunction with P—KKt4, are a tour of the Knight via KB1 to KKt3. Eventually, when Rooks are stationed on the KKt file Kt—B5 may prove a useful sacrifice.

Also to be borne in mind is that in the struggle for Black's KB4, White can exchange the Bishop on K3, for the Knight on Black's QB4, so as to play B—Q3. In considering this one assumes that this Bishop is slightly better and freer than the Knight it captures. But that Knight is not lifeless. Much has to be done to drive it from its square, and then it will be active. E.g. after White has played P—QKt3, P—QR3 and P—QKt4, and after pawn exchanges, Black can play Kt—R3 attacking the pawn at White's QKt4.

Another point is that if now B × Kt, a piece that has moved once is exchanging itself for a piece that has moved twice. In some games, where tempo is of the essence, this matters. Here, where the position has taken a relatively rigid shape, the gain of a single tempo is not among the important strategic considerations.

Another line of thought from this position is that if White can somehow free his Queen from the task of guarding the KP he can then play Q—Q2 and enable his Bishop to reach KR6. At least he will prevent P—KR3 by Black, with moves like K—R2 to follow. Clearly B × Kt does not enter into this scheme, and Kt—Q2 also does not cohere. White's problem is to form a plan —not a way of winning, but a way of bringing all his pieces to integrated activity—and to work and carry out this plan while coping with Black's activity, whatever it is. That thinking, how-ever, takes us beyond technique.

One technical feature of the diagram we have been considering is the closed centre. This is not peculiar to QP openings.

The position in Diagram 174 has developed from the Ruy Lopez after 14 or 15 moves. Black, who has done some clever timing of moves, is threatening to (i.e. 'is in a position to') retreat his Knight to Kt1 (not a bad square, although on the back row) and play P—KB4. If he achieves this, he will have a better control of the board than White has (an outcome which I believe to be normal in the close forms of the Ruy Lopez). White may well play here P—KKt4 and Kt—Kt3. I give this diagram in order to show, among other things, that the strategy of KP openings is not funda-mentally different from the strategy of QP openings. One of the most important technical features of the two positions seen is the closed centre, with which is involved the idea of a flank-attack on

it by the KBP.   A technical difference between the Lopez and
the Queen's Pawn openings is, paradoxically, that the QP openings aim at centre control, with a view to King's side attack.   In
the Lopez White frequently achieves a strong centre with an attack
on Black's QBP which, in many variations, is in danger of remaining backward.   Therefore, in the Lopez, Black must beware of
exchanging KP for QP on d4; it is usually wrong to do so if his
QBP is backward, and attackable along the open file.

174

White to play

An opening like the King's pawn (played by both players—
P—K4, P—K4) brings into being a centre which is easier to attack
than the centre generated by P—Q4, P—Q4.   This is quite a serious
matter in respect of choice of openings, because the player who
controls the centre can usually build up a strong attack against
the castled King.   It is, indeed, a paradox of Chess, that you are
not likely to succeed on the wings unless you have a strong central
control.   This is really not hard to understand, because the opponent will be able to interfere, using his centrally placed pieces, or
to block lines of action, or to organise an attack of his own.   It
follows that a good centre should not be conceded except for some
compensating advantage, such as material.

The King's Pawn openings can lead to quick attack on the
centre, the QP to slower attack.   To the various attacks there are
several attitudes that have been and can be adopted.

One can yield partially on the centre, in exchange for compensation, and be involved in heavy combat.   Typical is the accepted
Evans Gambit.   (An opening, this, of the "open" kind.)

1 P—K4	P—K4	5 P—B3	B—R4
2 Kt—KB3	Kt—QB3	6 0—0	P—Q3
3 B—B4	B—B4	7 P—Q4	
4 P—QKt4	B × P		

Black has to be careful now. Threats include 8 Q—R4, to be followed by P—Q5. That makes moves like Kt—B3 and B—KKt5, etc., unplayable. 7 .... B—Kt3 comes into consideration. 8 Q—R4 is to be met with B—Q2. This (B—Kt3) introduces us to a manœuvre which is so important that it should be reckoned part of technique. If White plays 8 Q—Kt3, Black has Kt—R4. Now 9 B × P ch simply loses a piece. (The Queen cannot guard the Bishop for longer than one move.) However, 7 .... B—Kt3 may be met by 8 P × P.

With the reply 8 .... P × P Black can lose a pawn after Queen exchanges, but has not lost the game. However, after 8 .... P × P; 9 Q—Kt3 is strong because after Kt—R4; 10 B × P ch, K—B1; 11 Q—Q5 saves the Bishop. Since the Black Queen going to K2 or KB3 can now be attacked on the Black squares, Black's defence is awkward, though the game can be held. Many players choose, therefore, 7 .... P × P; 8 P × P, B—Kt3 (Diagram 175).

175

The centre is compromised to Black's detriment, but he has a pawn for compensation. White now has an attack, not nearly so easy to play as it looks. Moves like R—K1, Kt—QB3 and B—Kt2 (even B—R3) maintain pressure, and Black has to play hard to achieve a full development.

Let this be added: that if he does develop successfully under attack, he will have winning chances.

Similar reasoning applies to the long popular King's Gambit.

(Be it mentioned that this is still a good opening, if White does not expect miracles from it.)

| 1 P—K4 | P—K4 | 3 Kt—KB3 | P—KKt4 |
| 2 P—KB4 | P × P | | |

Black is attempting to hold the pawn. Of the lines that can develop, such as the Allgaier (4 P—KR4, P—Kt5; 5 Kt—Kt5, P—KR3; 6 Kt × KBP), and the Muzio (4 P—KR4, P—Kt5; 5 B—B4, P × Kt), suffice it to say that a good player should defeat these sacrificial attacks, but a great many good players have frequently failed to do so. The wiser ones do not try to seize too much for Black. This leads us to consider a second attitude: 'Do not compromise the centre for pawn gain.' To revert to the Evans.

| 1 P—K4 | P—K4 | 3 B—B4 | B—B4 |
| 2 Kt—KB3 | Kt—QB3 | 4 P—QKt4 | B—Kt3! |

Does this lose a pawn?

| 5 P—Kt5 | Kt—Q5 | 6 Kt × P | Q—Kt4 wins! |

e.g.

| 7 B × P ch | K—B1 | 9 R—B1 | Q × KPch |
| 8 B × Kt | Q × KtP | forces mate. | |

A simpler form of this pitfall is

| 1 P—K4 | P—K4 | 3 B—B4 | Kt—Q5 |
| 2 Kt—KB3 | Kt—QB3 | | |

So done, nobody 'falls for it'. But when Black is forced to play Kt—Q5, as in the Declined Evans, the danger is psychologically easier to miss.

After

| 1 P—K4 | P—K4 | 3 B—B4 | B—B4 |
| 2 Kt—KB3 | Kt—QB3 | 4 P—QKt4 | B—Kt3 |

moves like 5 P—QR4 met by P—QR4 achieve nothing. Black easily gets full development.

Similarly, as we have seen, if one starts 1 P—K4, P—K4; 2 P—KB4, the King's Gambit, the centre is being shaken quickly. The gambit can be accepted and battle done to hold the pawn for a time (not for ever), or it can be accepted and the pawn immediately thrown back with P—Q4, or it can be declined with the aggressive 2 .... P—Q4 (Falkbeer) or the quieter 2 .... B—B4.

Perhaps the most determined of early attacks on the centre is in the Scottish system.

1 P—K4	P—K4	2 P—Q4

The order is important. If 1 P—K4, P—K4; 2 Kt—KB3, then a player anxious to avoid immediate compromise can play Philidor's Defence, 2 .... P—Q3, to be followed by Kt—Q2, or 2 .... Kt—QB3. But the immediate attack gives no time for this and can hardly be declined.

If 2 P—Q4, P—Q3; 3 P × P, P × P gives White the option of Queen exchanges, preventing Black from castling; not a fatal handicap; but, for a time, a disadvantage.

If

2 P—Q4	Kt—QB3	4 P—KB4
3 P × P	Kt × P	

and White has gained some tempo. Consequently 2 .... P × P is considered necessary. If

3 Q × P	Kt—QB3	4 Q—K3

Black has gained a slight advantage of tempo and has no anxieties. With 4 .... B—K2 or 4 .... P—Q3 he rapidly achieves a good development.

More serious are the lines in which the pawn is not immediately recaptured. There are many attacking variations in this system. Possible, but not useful, is

3 B—QB4	B—B4	5 Q—R5 ch
4 B × P ch	K × B	

which leads to nothing for White. Black emerges more developed. Quite popular at one time was the Danish Gambit. (It is far from extinct.)

1 P—K4	P—K4	4 B—QB4	P × P
2 P—Q4	P × P	5 B × P	B—Kt5 ch
3 P—QB3	P × P	6 K—B1	

White has a tremendous development for two pawns. Without saying that this wins for White, the experts tend to refuse the third pawn and throw material back with 4 .... P—Q4. Or they refuse the second pawn with P—Q4. It may be mentioned that on King-side openings of the open type, Black's P—Q4 is frequently a liberating move; and the ability to make it without loss is often the test of his development.

The usual play in the Scotch is

| 1 P—K4 | P—K4 | 3 Kt—KB3 | Kt—QB3 |
| 2 P—Q4 | P × P | | |

(the order of moves 2 and 3 is very often reversed because White does not fear the Philidor)

4 B—QB4

This makes a gambit of it.
If now

| 4 .... | B—B4 | 6 P—K5 | P—Q4 |
| 5 0—0 | Kt—B3 | | |

and we are in the delightful adventure world of the Max Lange, which is also not without technical interest.

| 7 P × Kt | P × B | 9 Kt—Kt5 |
| 8 R—K1 ch | B—K3 | |

(with the threat of Kt × B followed by Q—R5 ch)

9 ....   Q—Q4

(the only move: if 9 .... Q—Q3; 10 P × P, R—Kt1; 11 R × B ch, P × R; 12 Q—R5 ch, followed by Kt—K4 wins a piece)

10 QKt—B3

(not the only case in the openings in which a pin facilitates development)

10 ....   Q—B4   11 QKt—K4

From this position Rubinstein played

11 ....   KB—B1

allowing

12 Kt × BP   K × Kt   13 Kt—Kt5 ch   K—Kt3

and held off the subsequent attack. Normal is 11 .... B—Kt3, and eventually Black castles Q side with a good game.

The following line shows the resources of a quicker defence:

11 ....   0—0—0   12 P—KKt4   Q—K4

(batteries are frightening but not always fatal)

13 Kt—KB3	Q—Q4	19 Kt × R	Kt—Kt5
14 P × P	B × P!	20 P—QB3	Kt—Q6
15 Kt—B6	Q × Kt	21 P × P	B × P
16 Q × Q	B × Q	22 B—Kt5	B × KtP
17 P × R(= Q)	R × Q	23 R—Kt1	P—B6 wins.
18 R—K8 ch	R × R		

(A game played in 1909 by the late Dr. Holmes.)

The moral of these cautionary tales is twofold. Because of these 'wild' possibilities, Black is apt to play moves like P—Q3 instead of B—B4. Also, White is apt to play the attack at a slower pace. But the slowness of one move may be deceptive. Very strong for a long series of moves is the Möller:

1 P—K4	P—K4	4 P—B3	Kt—B3
2 Kt—KB3	Kt—QB3	5 P—Q4	P × P
3 B—B4	B—B4	6 P × P	

6 .... B—Kt5 ch can be played; but Black is not wise to try and win a pawn after 7 Kt—B3 by Kt × P, because 8 0—0 leaves White with plenty of open lines against the Black King as well as the power of constricting Black's development with P—Q5. A good principle is: 'Do not get compromised.'

On the other hand, timidity is not a good policy. Over forty years ago an opponent with White played, against the author, an attack on the King file, and lost interestingly.

1 P—K4	P—K4	7 0—0	Kt × P
2 Kt—KB3	Kt—QB3	8 Kt × Kt	Q × Kt
3 B—B4	B—B4	9 R—K1	Kt—K5
4 P—B3	Kt—KB3	10 B—Q3	P—Q4
5 P—Q4	P × P	11 P—B3	P × P ch
6 P—K5	Q—K2	12 K—B1	Q × RP
			and won.

Black can avoid the problems of the Möller effectively as follows:

1 P—K4	P—K4	4 P—B3	Q—K2!
2 Kt—KB3	Kt—QB3	5 0—0	P—Q3 (or QR3)
3 B—B4	B—B4	6 P—Q4	B—Kt3 (or R2)

Then exchanges are not adverse to Black, and a move like P—Q5 drives the Knight to remobilisation via Q1 and B2, but this is not diasdvantageous. In general Black can always find some way of not becoming too compromised.

The nature of Chess is happily such that neither player can seize advantage by mere reason of moving first or second. Those attacks that start fiercely are, against adequate defence, destined to frustration. They burn out. The important considerations for the defender are to make relevant moves and not lose tempo.

Instructive is the following:

1 P—K4	P—K4	4 Kt × P	B—B4
2 Kt—KB3	Kt—QB3	5 B—K3	Q—B3
3 P—Q4	P × P		

White can now 'start something' with

6 Kt—Kt5

and there can follow:

6	B × B	9 QKt—B3	Q × R
7 P × B	Q—R5 ch	10 Kt × P ch	K—Q1
8 P—Kt3	Q × KP	11 Q—Q6	Kt—B3!

But Black can avoid all this with

7 ....   K—Q1

and Black has not used more time than White.

Slower and better is

| 6 P—B3 | Kt—K2 | 7 B—B4 |

Observe now that

7 ....   0—0

loses a piece through

| 8 Kt × Kt | B × B | 9 Kt × Kt ch (*zwischenzug*). |

The principle is not to leave checks and captures uncontrolled. Another aspect is the unwisdom of leaving pieces 'hanging'.

In answer to 7 B—B4 Black can counter with Kt—K4. If then 8 B—Kt3, P—Q4 gives Black very interesting attacking chances. In any event he must play in order eventually to move his pawn to Q4, rather than Q3.

A vigorous line against 7 B—B4 is, indeed,

| 7 .... | P—Q4 | 9 P × Kt | B—Kt5 ch |
| 8 P × P | Kt × Kt | 10 Kt—B3 | 0—0 |

and the QP will be regained without difficulty.

The technical aspect of this is that Black plays vigorous move for vigorous move, and, that way, holds at least equality.

Another general method is to avoid centre conflicts by partial surrender, either with the French Defence (P—K4, P—K3), the Sicilian (P—K4, P—QB4) or Caro Kahn (1 .... P—QB3). The strategy of the French is that White is allowed to hold K5 until Black can break the line of pawns. Black concentrates on White's Q4 (Diagram 176).

176

White to play

Mention of this opening serves to introduce a technical point of considerable importance. The French Defence, like the defence to the orthodox lines of the Queen's Gambit, seems to put Black's Queen's Bishop out of the game. Theoretically the ideal in Chess would be to move both one's centre pawns two squares in order to give development to both Bishops. In many of the King's pawn openings Black achieves easy development for both his Bishops. If he has difficulty it is more likely to be with his KB than his QB (e.g. in the Lopez, according to the best opinion, the KB should stay on K2, not venture to QB4, where White gains tempo at its expense). In the Q.G.D. and French Defence Black's QB suffers. But opening theory these days does not regard this suffering as tragic. Indeed, one of the achievements of modern theory and practice is the recognition that undeveloped pieces do eventually become developed. Also it is now recognised that a Bishop masked by pawns is actually doing work. In the French Defence, if and when White's centre is dissolved, the Queen's Bishop will achieve play.

The technical methods of the French Defence consist mainly in an attack on White's centre at his Q4. Sooner or later the KP goes to K5. That square, occupied or empty, remains for some time in White's power, but Black has plenty of useful work on the Queen's wing. This may be initiated after

1 P—K4	P—K3	4 B—KKt5	B—K2
2 P—Q4	P—Q4	5 P—K5	KKt—Q2
3 Kt—QB3	Kt—KB3	6 P—KR4	P—QR3

with a view to P—QB4. (The author has played, with success, 7 P—QKt4, but does not call it safe.) Another approach is

1 P—K4	P—K3	3 Kt—QB3	B—Kt5
2 P—Q4	P—Q4		

(Winawer's variation, once popular with Botvinnik). White can attack the King's wing after

4 P—K5	P—QB4

(safer is Kt—K2); and Black presses on the Queen's wing.

Similar effects follow

3 P—K5

(Nimzovitch's recommendation). In these lines, White can let his QP fall so long as he maintains control of K5. Indeed, QBP × QP by Black may leave White an excellent Bishop on Q3.

These things are the subject matter of much analysis in books of Opening Variations (which the reader is advised to consult, but not to attempt to learn!). Suffice it here to say that this form of development is reasonable for both players. Nobody loses merely because of choice of an accepted opening, whether for Black or White.

However, some players prefer to develop their Queen's Bishops early. Thus, the Caro-Kahn (1 P—K4, P—QB3; 2 P—Q4, P—Q4) endeavours to secure play on the White squares for Black's Queen's Bishop. Suffice it here to say that White's initiative against this play does not last for ever.

A form of the defence that is popular at the moment, having been played (in 1960) by Botvinnik against Tal, is as follows:

1 P—K4	P—QB3	6 KKt—K2	Kt—Q2
2 P—Q4	P—Q4	7 P—KR4	P—KR3
3 Kt—QB3	P × P	8 Kt—B4	B—R2
4 Kt × P	B—B4	9 B—B4	P—K3
5 Kt—Kt3	B—Kt3		

Chess openings, like women's hats, are affairs of fashion.

In the return match (1961) 3 P—K5, P—QB4; 4 P × P, P—K3 turned the thing into a sort of French.

Another form of the defence is determined by White, who exchanges pawns at move 3. This exchange, as also when it is played against the Slav Defence to the Q.G.D. (P—Q4, P—Q4; 2 P—QB4, P—QB3), leaves Black free, but weak on the Queen's wing. But it is hard for White to exploit this weakness; which ceases to exist if and when Black becomes castled and develops his QR at QB1. (In the French Defence 3 P × P frees Black.)

More dynamic is the Sicilian (1 P—K4, P—QB4), an opening of which it is said that both players have the initiative in it. Normal is

| 1 P—K4 | P—QB4 | 3 P—Q4 | P × P |
| 2 Kt—KB3 | Kt—QB3 (or P—Q3) | 4 Kt × P | Kt—KB3 |

regarded as important because it induces

5 Kt—QB3

(5 P—KB3 is also playable, but is not popular.) Now White cannot get in P—QB4 (the Maroczy attack). Yet observe that, in the King's Indian, the following sequence:

1 P—Q4	Kt—KB3	4 P—K4	P—Q3
2 P—QB4	P—KKt3	5 Kt—B3	0—0
3 Kt—QB3	B—Kt2	6 B—K2	P—B4

results in a Sicilian Defence ('Dragon' form) in which the Maroczy pawn is in being. This position is not avoided! (It is also reached from the Réti-Zuckertort 1 Kt—KB3, Kt—KB3; 2 P—QB4, etc.) In general the Sicilian tends to be played nowadays with King's fianchetto for Black, and in a way that reproduces the kind of position studied earlier, the type of position that develops from King's Indian Defences. So KP leads to QP thought.

The popularity of the Indian Defences is derived from the desire to avoid central skirmishes and to develop lines of play for both Bishops. The fianchetto of the KB, or for that matter the QB, is now held good policy, because the fact that its action is delayed is now recognised not to be a defect.

From the ordinary Queen's Gambit White develops considerable pressure on the centre. This can happen after the 'Pillsbury line'.

| 1 P—Q4 | P—Q4 | 3 Kt—QB3 | Kt—KB3 |
| 2 P—QB4 | P—K3 | 4 B—Kt5 | |

White develops Bishop and Queen on the diagonal pointing at KR7, and, eventually, after Rook moves, may advance his pawn from K3 to K4. Exchanges give White plenty of play.

An interesting point of Chess learning is that people have played

1 P—Q4	P—Q4	2 Kt—KB3

(in order to prevent the Albin Counter P—K4 to 2 P—QB4)

2	Kt—KB3	4 B—Kt5
3 P—QB4	P—K3	

This, however, can be met by P—KR3, more or less forcing an exchange (not necessarily to White's detriment, for he develops a good centre). The alternative after

4	P—KR3

is

5 B—R4	P—KKt4	7 P—K3 (or Kt—B3)	P—KR4
6 B—Kt3	Kt—K5		

Now White is constrained to a move of his KRP, after which Kt × B creates a doubled pawn and a target at g3.

That is why, usually, White moves his QKt before B—Kt5. And the normal form is, therefore,

2 P—QB4	P—K3	3 Kt—QB3

Black (as already mentioned) has the option of the Albin Counter Gambit.

2	P—K4	3 P × P	P—Q5

which cannot be met by P—K3 because of B—Kt5 ch followed by P × P.

But 4 P—QR3 gives White a good game: and White also has a King's fianchetto movement; Black has to spend time recapturing the pawn.

To avoid these things 2 Kt—KB3 is played by players who are content with a slower form of the opening. This move can also be played after 2 P—QB4 and 3 Kt—QB3. Indeed, it was once fashionable (before Pillsbury popularised 4 B—Kt5). Also popular at one time was the following:

1 P—Q4	P—Q4	3 Kt—QB3	Kt—KB3
2 P—QB4	P—K3	4 P—K3	

and White develops a slow strong thrust against the centre.

Diagram 177 is one of many possible illustrations. White is not winning, but has the initiative. And although initiative must be distinguished from an attack, most players prefer to have it themselves rather than leave it to their opponents.

177

Black to play

Note one danger in this position. If Black plays 8 .... P × KP; 9 Kt × P, Kt × Kt; 10 B × Kt, he cannot play the tempting 10 .... P—K4 because of 11 P × P, Kt × P; 12 Kt × Kt, B × Kt; 13 B × P ch, K × P; 14 Q—R5 ch wins a pawn. That possibility against KR7 is something to be borne in mind.

In the QP the movements against the centre are less rapid than in the KP, but slight initiatives are valuable. That is why many strategians have adopted systems like the King's Indian, and the Nimzovitch and the Queen's Indian.

In answer to 1 P—Q4 they play Kt—KB3. If 2 P—QB4 follows (to build up control of Q5), then 2 P—KKt3, or 2 .... P—K3, or 2 .... P—QKt3 (not, be it noted, 2 .... P—Q4, which loses tempo to 3 P × P, Kt × P; 4 P—K4).

This 'silly' variation is not irrelevant because a similar move can be played on move 3, when it is not at all 'harmless'.

| 1 P—Q4 | Kt—KB3 | 3 Kt—QB3 | P—Q4 |
| 2 P—QB4 | P—KKt3 | | |

—the Grünfeld System. Perhaps the best course is to ignore it with Kt—KB3, B—B4, P—K3, etc.

But if

4 P×P	Kt×P	6 P×Kt	P—QB4
5 P—K4	Kt×Kt		

Black has initiated a strategical process, which is very important theoretically, because it reveals the weakness as well as the strength of the centre. If

7 Kt—B3	P×P	8 P×P	B—Kt2

The resultant position (Diagram 178) shows an ambivalent centre. It has features of weakness as well as of strength. This theory of abandoning the centre squares to hostile pawns that are eventually prone to attack is what underlies puzzling openings like Alekhine's Defence (P—K4, Kt—KB3, a defence scrupulously eschewed by its inventor) as well as the Indian systems.

178

Alekhine's Defence is worth mentioning, if only for one technical reason, viz. move saving.

1 P—K4	Kt—KB3	4 P—Q4	P—Q3
2 P—K5	Kt—Q4	5 P—KB4	P×P
3 P—QB4	Kt—Kt3	6 BP×P	Kt—QB3

Now 7 B—K3 is preferred to Kt—KB3. Why? Because 7 Kt—KB3 can be met by B—Kt5 and B—K3 must still be played, whereas in answer to 7 B—K3 Black has no better than 7 .... B—B4 and 8 Kt—KB3 goes unpinned, because Black cannot spare the tempo. Let it be added that in this opening Black has given White rather too much time-space, but has not lost.

A different kind of concession in the centre is the Benoni system. In this Black plays P—QB4 inviting White's QP to Q5.

A possible line is

1 P—Q4	Kt—KB3	4 Kt—QB3	P × P
2 P—QB4	P—QB4	5 P × P	P—Q3
3 P—Q5	P—K3		

Black has the strategic advantage now of three pawns to two on the Queen's side. In an endgame this might become the advantage of remote passed pawn.

On the other hand, White has a strong middle-game position. A frequently played continuation is as follows: 6 P—K4, P—KKt3; 7 Kt—B3, B—Kt2; 8 B—K2, 0—0; 9 0—0, R—K1; 10 Kt—Q2, Kt—R3; 11 P—B3, Kt—B2; 12 P—QR4, P—Kt3; 13 Kt—B4, and White has more potential than Black for the time being.

Cognate to both French Defence and Alekhine's Defence is the Nimzovitch Defence proper. (It is certainly superior to the second mentioned, for all that the inventor of the latter was the stronger player.)

1 P—Q4	Kt—KB3	3 Kt—QB3	B—Kt5
2 P—QB4	P—K3		

To this there are two attitudes.

4 P—QR3

seems to waste a move; but it gets rid of the Bishop and commits Black.

One technical development from this is the exploitation of the 'Sämisch Pawn'. Black sooner or later plays P—QB4 and P—QKt3. Then with Bishop from R3 and Knight from R4 and Rook from QB1 (if Black's QBP gets exchanged) he concentrates on the isolated QBP with varying success.

The other main lines against the Nimzovitch are P—K3 and/or Kt—KB3, or King's Fianchetto by White. These seem right on the theory that the Black KB is not doing much if White castles King's side. It serves a useful purpose, however, pending the completion of that process. One technical aspect of the Nimzovitch system is that White finds it hard to play his KP to the fourth.

In this connection a neat piece of play is worth noting. Let Black delay his pin:

1 P—Q4	Kt—KB3	3 Kt—QB3	P—QKt3
2 P—QB4	P—K3	4 P—K4	

is playable because

    4 ....   B—Kt5
is met by

    5 P—K5
and

    5 ....   Kt—K5
by

    6 Q—Kt4
Black wins material on the Queen's side:

| 6 .... | Kt × Kt | 8 K—Q1 |
| 7 P × Kt | B × P ch | |

but is now faced with the impending terror of Q × KtP. There
may follow:

8	K—B1	11 R—Kt3	B—R4
9 B—R3 ch	K—Kt1	12 Q × KtP ch	K × Q
10 R—QKt1	B—Kt2	13 R—Kt3 ch	

and Black is quickly mated.

    The logic of this play will remind the reader of lines in the
Winawer form of the French Defence (1 P—K4, P—K3; 2 P—Q4,
P—Q4; 3 Kt—QB3, B—Kt5), which was resuscitated by Alekhine
in his match against Capablanca, and thereafter became fashionable.[1]

    Another treatment of the Queen's Gambit is the temporary
abandonment of the centre by the acceptance of the gambit.

| 1 P—Q4 | P—Q4 | 2 P—QB4 | P × P |

With 3 P—K4 White does not achieve much. Valid against it
is such a move as 3 .... P—K4. If 4 P—Q5 Black has plenty of
squares. If 4 P × P Queen exchanges are in Black's favour. Usually
White plays more slowly with P—K3 or Kt—KB3 (to stop P—K4)
and Black prepares to defend the square e4 with moves like B—B4
or a Queen's fianchetto.

    It is worth mentioning that old fianchetto systems (the Italian
name suggests their age) have regained a great deal of favour in
modern times; and play from KKt2 and QKt2 is normal. The

---

[1] Alekhine showed that if White exchanged pawns, Black obtained good
development for the KKt at K2. Since then 3 P—K5 has superseded
3 P × P.

method is effective, both in support of centre pawns and against them. Moreover, experience shows that even a Bishop closed in behind a diagonal of pawns eventually develops a real activity. Indeed, it happens in many openings where the Bishop has emerged via the K2-Q3 line or the Q2-K3 line that it returns later to B1 and re-emerges at Kt2. This has been done even with the Lopez Bishop.

On the topic of fianchetto it is worth mentioning that, against a King's fianchetto, pawns at Q4 and QB3 make a good defence. On the other hand, a player should be able to counter-attack the centre with P—QB4. Let, then, the defensive pawn at QB3 not be an article of dogma.

If vigorous ideas suggest P—QB4 the player who abandons them because of a hostile fianchettoed Bishop is conceding power to that piece, enabling it to support a move to K4 or other manœuvre.

To resume; the experience of a few generations of Chess players suggests that the centre is not a thing in itself. It must be functionally regarded, not formally. The test is whether one has lines of play, and squares on which to post pieces so that they can co-operate. If one has that, then it matters not whose pawns stand on the central squares.

Technically, if pawns are wanted on the centre squares it is better for them to be joined than isolated. But no less a player than Tarrasch used a system which allowed a pawn to be isolated.

1 P—Q4	P—Q4	3 Kt—QB3	P—B4
2 P—QB4	P—K3		

If now 4 BP × P, KP × P; 5 Kt—KB3, Black is ill advised to play P—B5; and, eventually, with P × BP, White will isolate the Black QP and blockade it with a Knight at Q4; or, at all events, prevent it from advancing. Strategically, the thing has its merits and defects. Given vigorous play by Black, White should not be able to win the isolated pawn; but Black will have more anxiety than White in contemplating processes of liquidation that lead to Rook and pawn endings if an isolated pawn is a feature of the game.

The Masters' attitude to the centre, then, is not a dogmatic one. The centre may be defended, or conceded. If one wants to hold it in QP openings a good method of holding it strongly for Black is the Stonewall. A possible approach to this is:

1 P—Q4	P—Q4	3 Kt—QB3	P—QB3
2 P—QB4	P—K3	4 P—K3	

(Kt—B3 is met by P × P, and the difficulties of 'Abrahams' Defence')

4 ....   P—KB4

Black continues with B—Q3, Kt—KR3 (so as to be able to re-capture the QP with the KP), 0—0, QKt—Q2, and QKt—B3. Not an easy opening, but equally hard to play against.

As a matter of general policy the reader is not advised to pre-pare openings that prevent complications. Complication is of the essence. If one does not waste time, one is always ready to fight for freedom tactically, whenever it is endangered.

Diagram 179 shows a position arising from the Sicilian, in which White's pawn barrage proves less formidable than it appears.

Lupi—Abrahams
179   (London, 1946)

Black to play

In this position Black played

10	B × Kt	12 P—B5	P—Q4
11 RP × B	P—K4	13 P × QP	Kt—Q5

If now

14 B × Kt	P × B	16 Q × Kt	B × Kt ch wins.
15 Q × P	Kt × QP		

The resources available to Black are comparable to the force of an uncoiling spring. This is not an unusual phenomenon in Chess. Unless a game is badly played by one player, i.e. with irrelevant (wasted) moves, the development of both sides will contain latent strength. No miracles of exploitation will be possible. Then the player whose development is subtler than that of his opponent, who plans it in the light of ideas that his opponent fails to see, will eventually secure some advantage.

Steinitz and Lasker wrote about Chess that it was governed by principles of Cause and Effect, and by laws comparable to those of Newtonian Physics (that every action has its equal and opposite reaction, etc.). All this may well be true, but is as remote from the practicalities of Chess as it is from the routine of ballroom dancing. Some moves are more purposive than others, more effective than others, because of their strategic effect. Other moves are less effective because they do not help the tactical purposes of attack or defence, or are not strategically useful. But in each case this is not judged *a priori*. The effect of a move depends on the circumstances in which it is made, on the position that it is designed to create or alter, and on the possibilities in the time-space of the particular game.

Nevertheless, good players are guided in all games by a certain common sense (i.e. an intelligence obvious in all games) that can be partially distilled into words. Thus

1. A good player likes to have control of space; not mere empty space, but the lines in the position where activity is possible.

2. A good player likes to have control of time. That means that he wants his position to be as well integrated as it can possibly be in the moves that he has had at its disposal.

3. A corollary to both of these proportions is that a good player likes the space-time balance to be in his favour, or at least level. He wants to be as capable of action as his opponent in the developing battles of the game. What is essential and what is not essential: these are empirical questions dependent on the position. Very advanced pawns, for example, may be exerting effective threats and pressure, or they may be idly waiting for eventual capture. They may even be defending the opponent. Similarly, tempo gained in movements to nowhere is tempo lost.

This being said, it is useful to ask oneself at all times: Am I behind in my development? Have I wasted any particular move? These questions are a useful guide in the openings. And another question is usually pertinent. Am I exerting as much pressure on the centre as he is?

The first two questions emphasise the time factor; the other question expresses the space factor. The latter question may be harder to answer because the control of the centre is not a simple question of having pawns there. However, all these questions are useful, and they express something of the good player's sense of balance.

The questioning can be illustrated from the characteristic of normal opening play.

White plays vigorous developing moves, and Black develops with him equally purposively. Is the latter likely to be overwhelmed?

In many players there is a feeling, which the author is convinced to be unjustified, that Black is always in danger. This is the error of confusing a temporary initiative with an advantage.

One manifestation of this feeling of inferiority is the obsessive fear of pins (e.g. of Knight against Queen); and players make moves like P—KR3 to prevent these.

Certainly there are times when one may use such a move because it is essential to one's plan to keep a square vacant. But the move should not be employed as mere prophylactic. In Chess there is little time for such luxuries.

Certainly, if a Bishop is on KKt5 it may be difficult to eject. Moves like P—KR3, followed by P—KKt4 in front of the castled King, invite a dangerous Knight sacrifice (Diagram 180).

180

Black to play

Here

7	P—KR3	9 Kt × P	P × Kt
8 B—R4	P—KKt4	10 B × P	

and Black is in trouble, because heavy pressure is developing with Kt—Q5 and Q—B3. White will have full value for his material deficits.

In order to appreciate this better, consider how Metger defended the Four Knights: 1 P—K4, P—K4; 2 Kt—KB3, Kt—QB3; 3 Kt—QB3, Kt—KB3; 4 B—Kt5, B—Kt5; 5 0—0, 0—0; 6 P—Q3, B × QKt; 7 P × B, P—Q3; 8 B—Kt5, Q—K2; and Black developed his QKt via Q1 to K3.

The important test of the justification of anxiety is the calculation whether you have lost tempo or not.

If no tempo has been lost, concentrate on the tactical lines for dangers to weak spots; but don't assume that there are weaknesses merely because a hostile piece looks aggressive.

In the last diagram position Black has good moves like B—KKt5 (adventurous) or B—K3 (safer), and the move Kt—K2 allowing White to play B × Kt is strategically quite good.

One must, thereafter, prevent White from establishing a Knight on his KB5, where it would be very strong. But there is a Bishop for that purpose.

These considerations show that there is no need for anxiety about aggressive moves, and no need to use tempo in preventing them.

To take an elementary example:

| 1 P—K4 | P—K4 | 3 B—B4 | B—B4 |
| 2 Kt—KB3 | Kt—QB3 | | |

Now Black, with B—B4, has done as much as White. But before considering whether White can attack against this, let us examine an alternative:

3 ....   Kt—KB3 (instead of B—B4)

This, too, is a developing move, exerting pressure on the centre. But it allows White a dangerous-looking thrust:

4 Kt—Kt5

putting great pressure on one of the sensitive spots of the board, f7, where only the King guards the pawn. The Knight that could defend it from g8 by Kt—R3 has committed itself in another direction. One is tempted to say: 'Kt—KB3 (although a developing move) was a bad move.' But it wasn't. White, in order to attack so early, used two moves with one piece, while other pieces stood undeveloped. If the move is not terribly effective, then, perhaps it is wasted. So Black plays vigorously:

4 ....   P—Q4

Is this good? The test is, can White gain any advantage by capturing it? Let us see:

5 P × P

(evidently B × P, Kt × B, P × Kt, Q × P would develop Black tremendously). Can Black recapture? Owing to the peculiar weakness

of KB7, Black is unwise to play Kt × P. This involves the King in a
situation that is vulgarly called the 'Fried Liver'.
  If

  5 ....   Kt × P   6 Kt × BP!
a sacrifice which, if not sound to mathematical demonstration, is,
nevertheless, worthwhile, because it brings about an exposure of
the King among White's developing pieces. That, surely, is value
for the sacrifice of Knight for pawn that White has ventured.
There might follow:

  6 ....   K × Kt   7 Q—B3 ch
forcing the awkward

  7 ....   K—K3   8 Kt—QB3
developing, and forcing Black to a move that retards development.

  8 ....   QKt—K2
(8 .... QKt—Kt5; 9 P—QR3, Kt × P ch; 10 K—Q1, Kt × R,
commits the White Knight to a capture that may prove irrelevant,
because with B × Kt ch, K—Q3; P—Q4, White is getting homicidal)
  In answer to the best line (QKt—K2) White goes on developing.

  9 P—Q4   P—QB3
(P × P is obviously bad, in the light of Q—K4 ch)

  10 0—0
If Black lives, with greying hair, he may win an endgame. He is
not, however, certain to live that long. The technical lesson is that, in
order to expose a King, sacrifices of varying value can be profitable.

  To sacrifices there are two possible attitudes, varying with the
position, as well as with temperament. Some sacrifices should be
accepted and the attack beaten off, others avoided. Some players,
forced with sacrifices of uncertain outcome, welcome them, others
avoid them.
  The one in the text is to be avoided. What, then, on move 5,
should Black do? The answer is:

  5 ....   Kt—QR4
The outcome of this is unpredictable because it leads to Chess
in which good play on either side will defeat bad play on the other
—i.e. it's a sound opening!

One possibility is as follows:

5	Kt—QR4	7 Kt—KB3	P—K5
6 P—Q3	P—KR3	(taking advantage of the double function of the White QP)	

8 Q—K2	Kt × B	9 P × Kt

And now Black seems to have value for the loss of half a pawn, but the game is hard (9 .... B—QB4; 10 KKt—Q2, 0—0; 11 Kt—QKt3, has been played).

A wild and woolly game develops from

6 B—Kt5 ch	P—B3	8 Q—B3
7 P × P	P × P	

But that is beyond the scope of this text. The important point, from the technical angle, is that in a game in which no tempo has been lost, an attacking thrust is likely to be met with either adequate defence, or strong counter-attack.

This leaves it a matter of taste whether to accept gambits or decline them.

On the same principle that one judges attacks, so one judges the placing of one's opponents (and one's own) pieces. A pawn advances to QB5 or KB5. This looks threatening by reason of its penetration into the defender's realm. But is it really good?

If tempo is being used, and no tempo has been lost by the other player, P—B5 can be bad play, unless some very serious restriction is caused by the advance. Normally one can expect that if a pawn arrives at QB5, the pawn that guards it from Q4 can be undermined. Similarly, if one arrives at KB5 its support at K4 can be undermined. Only if there is reason to believe that the advancer has justification for his advance because the other player has wasted time, or played bad moves, only then should shows of force cause anxiety.

To sum up, if rules of play are capable of being drafted, they are likely to be vague (though not useless) statements urging the player not to be irrelevant, not to waste time, not to let himself be left without scope in space. That advice only takes on meaning as experience increases. Being absorbed, it gives confidence, than which nothing in Chess is more desirable.

CHAPTER VIII

ON TAKING ADVANTAGE

Much of Chess is in the nature of petty larceny, to say nothing of catching bargains, and the picking up of unconsidered trifles. One element in technique is the familiarity with devices that achieve these processes neatly, if not surreptitiously.

The learner should know about masked batteries. Awareness of these should make him conscious of the dangers that attach to pieces which are not at the moment attacked but are only screened.

You have a Knight on your R4, on the line of your opponent's Queen at his Q1. He has a Knight on his KB3.

Are you aware that he may be able to capture your KP with his Knight, and that if you recapture with a pawn, he will take your Knight?

It was mentioned earlier that a Chess player likes to threaten two or more processes with one move. Even more than that, he likes to make moves that actually achieve two effects. The tactic mentioned—capturing with a screening piece—does this.

It may happen that the masking is not evident at first sight. You may have a Bishop at KKt5 when you play your Knight to R4. But suppose he plays P—R3, and you do not wish to exchange the Bishop for his Knight. You retreat the Bishop. Now Kt × P is playable.

This example illustrates what has been said earlier and emphasised, that technical features are intimately involved with tactical lines of play.

Technique may warn you against putting pieces on squares where an attack on them may be immediately disclosed. But more than one feature has to be borne in mind if the player is to anticipate exactly when the masked battery will develop.

Thus, suppose the opponent has a Knight on his Q5. Your King is at your Kt1, and your KBP and KP are at their fourth. Your opponent, with Q—QKt3, may be able to attack your QKtP, and threaten to exploit the masked battery that he has created against your King. You may, or may not, have moves to cope with this: B—K3 or Kt—QR4 (though the latter will not prevent a double check). The important lesson of such an occurrence is that you were not sufficiently aware of what your opponent could do with his Queen. Technique enables you to name what he has done to you. Tactical insight (assisted by technical experience) serves to avoid it.

The tactical aspect of Chess is amusingly illustrated by the following piece of play:

1 P—K4	P—K4	4 Kt—B3	Kt—B3
2 Kt—KB3	Kt—QB3	5 P—Q3	0—0
3 B—B4	B—B4		

White now wishes to do something more aggressive than B—Kt5 (met by B—K2).

6 Kt—KR4

He has moved his Knight under a masked battery.

6	Kt × P	7 Kt × Kt	Q × Kt

Black has won a pawn. But, alas,

8 B—KKt5

and Black has lost his Queen: it is 'dominated'. Evidently technique was not enough—or there was an insufficiency of it. The answer is that technique tells you how to do things, rather than what to do. Further, a certain 'technical sense' should warn Black that his Kt × P is a move that develops White's forces. If he has that feeling he may concentrate his attention on the moves that can follow his move; and if he is perceptive, may see B—Kt5. Thirdly, technique suggests that, White being fairly well developed, his moving of the Knight is warranted, and should not be compromising. A logical, natural, move should (of course) not be made merely because of its logic or naturalness. But, in a majority of cases, such moves are sound. The only criticism of Kt—KR4 is that its obvious sequel, Kt—KB5, is not particularly effective; and it gives Black tempo for Kt—K2 or Kt—Q5.

Note that if the Black pawn were at R3 instead of R2, Kt—KR4 would be wrong because the Black Queen could not be trapped.

What applies to the unmasking of batteries applies to all manœuvres with which the Chess player does two operations with one move. Forks, by pawns or pieces, are in point. Awareness of forking powers makes possible demonstrations quite early in the game—whenever a guarded square is occupied, or a guarded piece taken, because the opponent's capture, or recapture, can be countered with a fork.

Not all such manœuvres are good. They are good, generally, for the player who has already gained some slight advantage. But even very early they can be useful.

Thus, in the early opening:

| 1 P—K4 | P—K4 | 3 B—B4 | Kt—KB3 |
| 2 Kt—KB3 | Kt—QB3 | 4 Kt—QB3 | |

Black can play 4 .... Kt × P; because if 5 Kt × Kt, P—Q4 regains the piece. Interesting here is the fact that White cannot usefully exploit his 'desperado' Bishop by 5 B × P ch because after 5 .... K × B; 6 Kt × Kt, P—Q4; 7 QKt—Kt5 ch, K—Kt1 (or K1), Black is left better developed, and with Bishop for Knight, while White's QKt is not well placed.

However,

| 5 Kt × Kt | P—Q4 |

leaves White with a free move: Black has to use a move in order to regain his material. So White can play a variety of useful moves if he has any. He has, in fact, B—Kt5, or Q—K2 or B × P, which regain his pawn; or, more aggressively,

6 P—Q4

If then,

| 6 .... | P × Kt | 7 Kt—Kt5 |

is very good.
If

| 6 .... | P × B | 7 P—Q5 |

upsets Black's development.
If

| 6 .... | P × P |

he can allow the pawn to go lost, and play B—Kt3 followed by Kt—Kt5, or can castle with an aggressive development.

The lesson of this, again, is that the merit of the exploitation of technical possibilities is always to be assessed tactically and strategically. A little sacrifice, made because it looks clever, and in the knowledge that the material can be regained, may, in fact, constitute inferior play. One should look for these things in order to assist a developing attack, or in order to equalise; not in order to demonstrate that one can see a move or two ahead.

Nevertheless, at all stages, be aware of the possibility of useful petty larcenies, little snatchings of advantage.

Just as one sees that a move is made possible by a fork to follow, so many móves are made possible by other threats that can follow.

Thus, in the position in Diagram 181, Black cannot counter the attack on his pawn with 1 .... R—QKt1, because after 2 R × P, R × P; 3 R—B8 ch forces promotion.

181

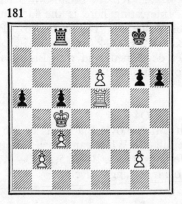

A similar effect would be obtained if a series of exchanges were to end with the White Rook on an open file, pawn at K6, Black King at KKt1, and a defending Rook which, in order to equalise, has to leave the back rank. This is the kind of small technical point, which, tactically perceived, enables one player to steal material from, or steal a march on, an unwary opponent. Such awareness, of course, is equally useful in defence.

The player should be aware of technical advantages. No exhaustive list can be drawn up, but a good approach is this. Think of the kind of position from which you can quickly seize material, or carry out a vigorous operation.

Many are obvious. Thus, if you find yourself with your Rook established on the seventh line, you will probably be able to seize pawns rapidly; or, with the aid of the other Rook develop a mating attack, doubling the Rooks on the rank. A Rook on the seventh or eighth can also pin, and reduce in power, important pieces, like Bishops and Knights. Even the threat of an advance to seventh or eighth may tie an opponent's Rook to its second or first rank.

This is why Chess players attach importance to open files, and why they are fond of doubling Rooks on open files.

All this is subject to the overriding consideration which is the total position. If your opponent is organising his own mating operations, your open file may not help you.

However, big central advantages usually prevent an opponent's mobilisation. Moreover, these advantages, being acquired, tend to be lasting, and can be assessed with little difficulty. One can double Rooks, usually without having to work through complexities. If it is available, usually one can seize an open file with an easy conscience. It is in dealing with open files and backward pawns, recognised as relatively good and relatively bad respectively, that the technician decides easily, while the tactician, thinking hard, usually has to occupy his time coping with the technical point.

Diagram 182 illustrates adequately at once some technical elements and a tactical involvement.

182

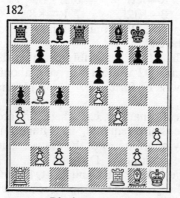

Black to move

White has just played B (from Q3)—Kt5. If it were now White's move, R—Q1 would gain obvious technical advantage. However, it is Black's move.

How to defend the open file, which for one moment is in his possession? 1 .... P—QKt3 comes to mind, but the answer is 2 B—B6, forcing R—Kt1.

Then 3 QR—Q1 makes B—Kt2 impossible for the moment. Quite sound, and evidently best, is

1 ....   B—Q2
That saves the file. Black, however, speculates: can he do better?

1 ....   R—Q7
Is this a bad move?

2 QR—Q1   R × BP   3 R—Q8
Now 3 .... R × P is met by B × P. But what is threatened?
Is it 4 B—Q7? As it happens, No! Not because of R—Q7 (R × B
meets that), but because of B × B followed, if R × R, by B—B3,
and White is heavily attacked.

Let Black play

3 ....   P—Kt3   4 B—B6
Now, not the clever-looking 4 .... B—Kt2 (inviting 5 R × R,
B × B, and receiving 5 R × B ch (*zwischenzug*), followed by B × B),
but

4 ....   R—Kt1   6 B × B!   R × B
5 KR—Q1   B—Kt2!   7 R—K8
and, as often happens, Black must stand helpless while the other
Rook comes to the eighth.

The lesson of that study is possibly this: that the technician who,
as Black, played B—Q2 without worrying about the tactical pro-
mise, was either wise or fortunate. Good players are not satisfied
by rule of thumb.

In other technical situations, e.g. where pins are concerned, great
tactical exactitude is also required. It is important to see, not only
the formal quality of a move, but the answer to it.

In point is the position in Diagram 183. The pawn at e4 is
pinned. So moves like P—B4 and P—Q4 seem right for Black.
Why is neither of these good? Simply because it does not threaten
anything. Black's P × P will be met by R × P. White can use the tempo
profitably, with a move which is not the easiest to see, 2 K—R1.

That suggests Black's best move, 1 .... Q—Q5. This, incidentally,
is a blockader. But it is not made for that purpose. Black is not
afraid of the play:

1 ....   P—B4   3 R × R   Q × R
2 P—Q4   Q × P   4 P × P
                                because, then, R—K8 wins.
The purpose of Q—Q5 is that it attacks something; incidentally
maintains a pin, and creates a 'half-pin' (i.e. each of the Rooks is
free—but both are not free).

Black to move

In answer to 1 .... Q—Q5; 2 KR—B3 and KR—K2 would both
be met by R × KP because the QP is pinned. Best seems Q—K2.
Then P—B4 and P—Q4 are destructive. The lesson of this is that
the formal characteristic of a situation can be a hint of advantage,
but not a guide to its exploitation. That must be seen, and accur-
ately seen.

A good pair of general statements are the following:

1. Anything that gives you safety is technically valuable.

2. Anything that gives you freedom and scope is technically
valuable.

In the light of those paramount purposes, a player learns to
value pieces and places with accuracy. Not the formal values,
but the functional, are the essence of Chess.

A Knight established on B5, or any good central square, Q5,
K5, Q6, K6, B4, even K3, can control so much space that its
settlement there seems intrinsically desirable. But a Knight on
QB5 is of little avail if operations are on the KKt file. In assessing
the value of the square, think in two ways. Think of the endgame.
For that purpose, the central square is usually valuable. But think
of it also in terms of the current middle-game.

Even more important is the assessment of pieces. We know
that a Rook is of greater value than a Knight or Bishop, but its
value as a factor in winning the game may be best realised if it is
sold cheap in order to improve a position.

Diagram 184 shows such a position. But the earlier play (by
the author) is of some technical interest. (Q.G.D. in effect.)

| 1 Kt—KB3 | P—Q4 | 3 P—Q4 | Kt—B3 |
| 2 P—B4 | P—QB3 | 4 Kt—B3 | P—K3 |

Black's fourth is 'technically' inferior in a very slight degree because it gives less than maximum development and allows White an economy.

184   Abrahams—Scarlett

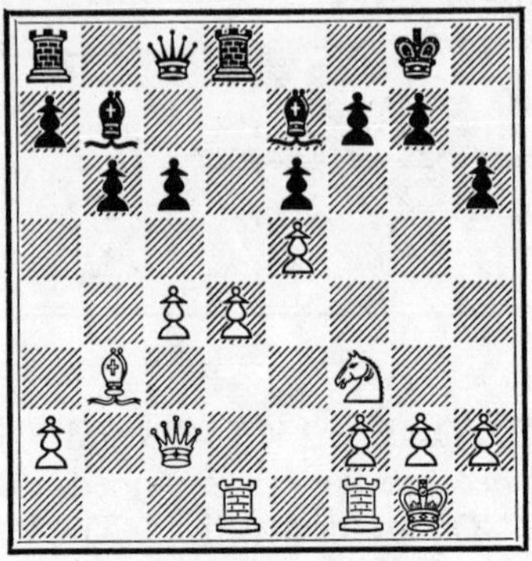

White to move

| 5 B—Kt5 | B—K2 | 7 Q—B2 |
| 6 P—K3 | QKt—Q2 | |

This is the economy. Normally, in Q.G.D., White has to play R—QB1, before Q—B2, because otherwise Black has the 'sharp' reply P (from QB2)—B4. This is not necessarily a turning of the tables. Here, however, White 'gets away' with a Queen and Rook development in two moves which could have taken longer.

| 7 .... | 0—0 | 8 R—Q1 | R—K1 |

A move which is reasonable if Black later plays Kt—B1, but which, if he does not do that, is less useful. It turns out 'wasted' because Black's other moves do not cohere with it.

| 9 B—Q3 | P—KR3 |

Not useful because it drives the Bishop to a good square.

| 10 B—B4 | P × P |

Not pointless; but the position has taken a shape in which Black would be better advised to hold the centre for the time being.

| 11 B × BP | Kt—Kt3 | 13 B—K5 | Kt × Kt |
| 12 B—QKt3 | QKt—Q4 | | |

Black's last three moves consumed time—for what? He made three moves with a piece in order to exchange a relatively unmoved piece, and in so doing gave White at least one good developing move.

14 P × Kt
(taking towards the centre)

14 ....   P—QKt3
An effort to achieve some development, but at a time, and in a direction, both unfavourable. Necessary is something vigorous, like P—QB4 (15 P × P, Q—R4; 16 B—Q6, Kt—Q2).

15 0—0
White has time for luxuries now.

| 15 .... | B—Kt2 | 17 B × Kt | B × B |
| 16 P—K4 | Q—B1 | 18 P—K5 | |

Achieved without waste of time because Black has pushed White's pieces in all the right directions.

| 18 .... | B—K2 | 19 P—B4 | R—Q1 |

(P—QB4 had to be played here though it is ineffective.)

Now we have the position in Diagram 184, achieved by White because he has been allowed plenty of time-space for his development.

20 P—B5
Technically a blockade; tactically more than that.

| 20 .... | P × P | 22 R—Q6 |
| 21 P × P | Q—B2 | |

This illustrates the earlier observation that the value of a piece is subordinate to the main purpose of the game, which is the destruction of the opponent's defences.

The rest of the play is fairly obvious.

22 ....   B × R
(Not desirable; but what can Black do? If R—Q2, White has time for Kt—Q2 and Kt—K4.)

23 KP × B
(Technically BP × B seems right—but White is concerned with squares immediately required.)

| 23 .... | Q—Q2 | 25 P—B4 | B—B1 |
| 24 Kt—K5 | Q—K1 | | |

(Arithmetically a loss of all the time used in its development.)

| 26 P—B5 | B—Q2 | 27 P—B6 |

(Note how nothing has been able to stop this pawn.)

| 27 .... | P—Kt4 | 29 R—R3 | QR—Kt1 |
| 28 R—B3 | Q—B1 | 30 Kt—Kt4 | Resigns.[1] |

The next illustration emphasises what has been already said: that technical advantages are tactically acquired. Technique advises the player on general methods of play and indicates what configurations are normally useful. The tactician finds ways of seizing technical advantages and keeping them. Diagram 185 illustrates this.

185   Abrahams (White)

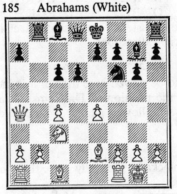

Black to move

White has played

10 Q—R4
Black replies

10 ....   Q—B2
and White seizes advantage with

[1] A flattering critic (the late Mr. du Mont) spoke of my handling of the pawns as 'reminiscent of Dr. Alekhine's technique'. I only quote this because I am interested in that word 'technique', and I think that Mr. du Mont has used it wrongly. The processes are tactical. He was, possibly, thinking of 'style', which is 'something else again'.

11 P—B5

Technically, if White can play P × QP followed by R—Q1 and B—B4, he has great pressure on his opponent's position and scope for development while his opponent is restricted. Tactically, the point is that

11 ....   P × P

is met by

12 P—K5

and Black cannot capture because of B—B4. If, instead,

12 ....   Kt—Q2   13 P—KB4

gives White control and scope—which will not last for ever, but are worth a pawn!

A companion piece comes from another game between the same opponents (the author, White).

1 P—Q4	Kt—KB3	7 Kt—KB3	R—K1
2 P—QB4	P—KKt3	8 B—K2	P—B3
3 Kt—QB3	B—Kt2	9 0—0	Q—B2?
4 B—B4	0—0	10 P—B5	P—Kt3
5 P—K3	P—Q3	11 P × QP	P × P
6 P—KR3	QKt—Q2	12 R—B1	

(now a lateral pin is added to the diagonal pin)

12	P—QR3	17 Kt—Kt5	P—KR3
13 P—QKt4	B—B1	18 P—Kt6	Q—Q2
14 P—Kt5	P—B4	19 Kt × P	Q × Kt
15 Q—Kt3	Kt—Kt1	20 Q × Q ch	K × Q
16 P × BP	KtP × P	21 B—B3	

and the Rook is lost, and later the game.

This play is interesting also as a demonstration of how pressure can create weaknesses in the defence, and give open lines to the attacker as the defender tries to cope with threats.

Good Chess frequently takes the form of creating in an opponent one or more weaknesses, and exploiting them, fast or slowly, according to the nature of the weakness.

In general, a good test of technical advantage is that it prevents the opponent from doing what he would like to do in the way of action. When restriction sets in, then, usually, tactical possibilities become available to the attacker.

He may be defending his Q2 with a Bishop at his QB3 against a Rook incursion. So a hostile Bishop presents itself at its K4 to capture or be captured and the defences are broken provided that the attack suffices for complete destruction.

Here we find weak squares; but they are only weak because the attack happens to be on them. The technical provision against them is full development and control of the board. There is no formula for this.

An important distinction, to be drawn between technical and tactical Chess, is that the latter involves, for the victim, a greater degree of surprise.

On occasion a technique will warn the player of the kind of danger that exists. Thus Black in the position in Diagram 186 should not be greatly surprised by White's 1 R × P. If he captures, then 2 Q × P demonstrates to him the meaning of open lines. But this is not the whole story. In the game in question (by Auerbach, in a simultaneous exhibition), Black played 1 .... P—QKt4. There followed 2 QR—KB1, P × B. And now White mates in three with

3 R × P ch	K × R	5 Q × P mate.
4 R—B7 ch	K × R	

That operation was harder to see.

186   187

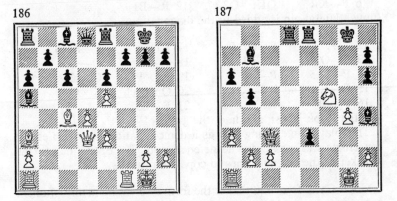

Similarly, it would require a very good player, in the position of White in Diagram 187, to see precisely how Black could turn the tables on him.

1	B—B7 ch	2 K—B1

And now what?

| 2 .... | R—Q8 ch! | 4 K × B | P × R (=Kt) ch |
| 3 R × R | P—K7 ch | and captures the Queen. |

No laws about unblockaded pawns and empty squares are adequate to prepare a player against such moves as these. Such moves must be seen. Nevertheless, learning or experience can familiarise a player with some strange possibilities, and that experience makes the mind sensitive to the atmosphere of tactics and ready for storms on the unharvested sea.

The element of surprise, the shock that possesses a player when something happens that he has not anticipated, is cheerfully accepted by players in bad positions. But players who lose in good positions frequently refer to surprises sprung by their opponents as 'swindles', and this term may seem consistent with my proposition that much of Chess is petty larceny. But, in practice, the word 'swindle' is over-used, is, indeed, abused. If the player with the better position makes a mistake, that is no fault of the other, even if the exploitation is 'shocking' in the sense of 'surprising'. Thus the author's opponent in the position in Diagram 188 only had his own greed to blame when he played K × P (instead of K—B7) and was stricken aghast by Q—Q4 ch.

188

189

White to move

Again, the opponent, who in the position in Diagram 189 replied to 1 R—Kt6 with R—B2 ch, was not 'swindled' when, in answer to K—K5, he played the psychologically easy R—B8. This was an error, because R—B6 ch wins for White.

Of traps and pitfalls, let it be said that unseen dangers are variations that should have been seen. Therefore there is no point in distinguishing, as some American experts do, between traps, of one's own creation, and pitfalls (prepared by the opponent). Let us experiment. My opponent's King is at h8; he has pawns at e6, f5, g7, h7 and other pieces. I have Rook on h1 (open file), Knight on h4, Bishop on b3, Queen on c2. I cleverly play Q × P (f5), expecting P × Q, allowing Kt—Kt6 mate. But, instead, using a piece I had ignored, he captures my Bishop, giving check.

Now can I usefully distinguish between two aspects of my conduct?

1. I dug a pit for him: if he captured the Queen he would be mated.

2. I dug a pit for myself.

The distinction is academic. The only useful term of abuse is one that could be applied to a player who makes the less than best move in the belief that his opponent will make a bad reply. This is rare among good players. An element of psychology is present when one declines a simplification in order to give oneself combative chances against an unimaginative opponent. But no one makes moves to that end that can be clearly refuted to his knowledge. Only in bad positions do good players 'swindle'. Then they play the move that is most likely to give the opponent an opportunity of error. But if he does not make the required mistake, then they are worse off. However, as one postulates that the game is in a bad way, nothing is lost.

The position in Diagram 190 is one in which White stands better. Black's best move is hard to find, and is, possibly, P—B3. However, Black played 1 .... P—Kt5, hoping for an error. White

190

Black to move

can capture the KtP or play Q—Q7. But he is tempted to 2 Q × BP.
There followed

| 2 .... | R—K7 ch | 4 P × R | R—B1 |
| 3 K—B1 | R(7) × Kt | wins the Queen. | |

To have seen that was meritorious, but justifies the play only
because sounder moves would have lost.

For the rest, the board abounds with opportunities for error;
unexpected configurations are constantly manifesting themselves.
Even in World Championship Chess points are missed. Here is
the position from the 17th game, played 1960, between Tal (White)
and Botvinnik (Black):

2r5,kpqr1pp1,pR2pktp1,2P5,3P1P2,Q5Kt1,6PP,1R4K1.

At move 37 Black played Q × KBP. Observe that if White had
a pawn at c4 this could not be done because of R × KtP ch, R × R,
Q × RP ch, with a mate to follow. However, this is not available
here, but White's attack is strong.

| 38 Kt—K2 | Q—K5 | 39 Q—QKt3 |

and this is more than a multiplication of force against the Queen's
Knight's pawn. But Black misses the point.

| 39 .... | Q—Q4 | 40 R × RP ch wins. |

Because if P × R,

| 41 Q—Kt6 ch | K—R1 | 43 Q × R(c8) mate. |
| 42 Q × RP ch | R—R2 | |

This is a complex that Black would normally have seen without
effort.

The student should try to make himself aware of all the geometric eccentricities of the board. These appear at all stages. Not
the least of instructive and amusing sequences is the following from
the Lopez.

To become aware of the mate that occurs in it, is to obtain a
better knowledge of the board.

1 P—K4	P—K4	4 B—R4	Kt—B3
2 Kt—KB3	Kt—QB3	5 0—0	Kt × P
3 B—Kt5	P—QR3	6 R—K1	

(A great deal of learning has established that P—Q4 leads to
a more enduring initiative.)

6 ....   Kt—B4

(6 .... P—Q4; 7 P—Q4, P × P; 8 Kt × P, B—Q3 constitutes the
Riga Defence, of which an amusing sequence is: 9 Kt × Kt, B × P ch;
10 K—R1, Q—R5; 11 R × Kt ch, P × R; 12 Q—Q8 ch, Q × Q;
13 Kt × Q dis ch, K × Kt; 14 K × B, P—B4; 15 B—Kt5, mate.
There is one amusing piece of Chess board geometry!)
    To revert to the main line, after

6	Kt—B4	10 Kt—Q5	0—0
7 Kt × P	Kt × Kt	11 Kt × B ch	K—R1
8 R × Kt ch	B—K2	12 Q—R5	
9 Kt—B3	Kt × B (?)	with the threat of	

| 13 Q × P ch | K × Q | 14 R—R4 mate. |

From the other end of the game observe what is latent in the
position reached by Tal against Botvinnik in the 8th game of the
return World Championship match (1961). 1kr1b3, 1p3pbp,
2P1p2p, 1P1pP3, 3Kt2r1, 5Kt2, 2R2PPP, 3R2K1. White, to move,
has to remember that in some variations his own back row is de-
nuded of defence, and he has not had time to 'make a hole for his
King'. 27 R—R1, B × KP; 28 Kt × B, R × Kt; 29 Kt—Q7 ch. Why
is the reply 'resigns'?
    If 29 .... B × Kt; 30 P × B, R—Q1; 31 R—B8 ch, R × R; 32 P × R
(= Q) ch, K × Q, Black is alive. If, instead, 31 R—R8 ch, K × R;
32 R—B8 ch, K—R2, Black is threatening mate. The answer is
that White can combine features of both these operations. 31 R—
B8 ch, R × R; 32 R—R8 ch, K × R; 33 P × R (= Q) ch, and wins the
Black Rook next move. That, not very difficult, play implies clarity
as to the order of moves as well as awareness of the sacrificial
resources.
    From the very beginning powers are latent. Suppose you have
played 1 Kt—KB3, Kt—KB3; 2 P—Q4, P—Q4, and you decide
that you want to control c5. You play 3 P—QR3, which is met
by the innocuous looking 3 .... P—K3. Can you now play
4 P—QKt4? If you do, the reply is 4 .... P—QR4, and you
become unhappily aware that the move you have forced your opponent to make is destructive. You cannot guard the KtP with
B—Q2 because Black's move has, inter alia, pinned your QRP.
    On the other side of the board, players are sometimes made un-
happy because when (having castled King's side) they try to drive
a Knight or Bishop from its KKt5 with P—R3, there comes

P—KR4 and, if the piece be captured, P × P brings a Rook into terrible activity. Sometimes the sacrifice fails, but the possibility is to be borne in mind. And so the moves of the heavier pieces are subtle as well as strong. You have let your opponent's Rook wander up the QR file because your Rook can attack his isolated KRP from your KR4. Have you noticed that his Rook can defend from behind your Rook at its R7, guarded by a Bishop? Similarly Bishop or Queen attacks, from say d4 on to b2, are thwarted by the entrance of a Bishop or Queen at e5 guarding the attacked piece or pawn from behind the attacker.

Do you fully appreciate pins? A sad example I can give is of a misfortune that befell a player much esteemed by me. He had Rooks on a1 and b1 and his Queen on b6, attacked by the opponent's Queen, but defended by the Rook on b1. What then upset White was R c1 ch by the opponent. A piece was inserted at f1. (The Rook is tied to the defence of the Queen.) Then Q × Q revealed the hideous fact that the Rook at b1 was 'pinned' against the Rook at a1. So R × Q led to the loss of a Rook: a very unusual pin, this. But technique thrives on the absorption of the unusual.

One final piece of advice. Don't be an automaton. I mean, do not automatically capture: more difficult—do not automatically re-capture. Suppose you are entering an ending with a pawn at h4. He has pawns at g7 and h6. His last move was a pawn capture. Before you decide that the recapture is 'now or never', make a strong analytic effort. It looks as if P—h5 has a much higher 'priority'.

At all events, if you think on those lines, you have moved from the very elementary technique which is the direct attacking and defending of pieces and pawns to the subtle valuation of the total position.

In conclusion, it is not the purpose of this book to expound all the devices, usual and unusual, that are exploited in play. It is hoped that a reader appreciating what is herein set out will, in the future, be less easily taken by surprise, less frequently left without resource.

INDEX OF THEMES

A CATALOGUE OF SELECTED DOVER BOOKS
IN ALL FIELDS OF INTEREST

A CATALOGUE OF SELECTED DOVER BOOKS
IN ALL FIELDS OF INTEREST

AMERICA'S OLD MASTERS, James T. Flexner. Four men emerged unexpectedly from provincial 18th century America to leadership in European art: Benjamin West, J. S. Copley, C. R. Peale, Gilbert Stuart. Brilliant coverage of lives and contributions. Revised, 1967 edition. 69 plates. 365pp. of text.
21806-6 Paperbound $3.00

FIRST FLOWERS OF OUR WILDERNESS: AMERICAN PAINTING, THE COLONIAL PERIOD, James T. Flexner. Painters, and regional painting traditions from earliest Colonial times up to the emergence of Copley, West and Peale Sr., Foster, Gustavus Hesselius, Feke, John Smibert and many anonymous painters in the primitive manner. Engaging presentation, with 162 illustrations. xxii + 368pp.
22180-6 Paperbound $3.50

THE LIGHT OF DISTANT SKIES: AMERICAN PAINTING, 1760-1835, James T. Flexner. The great generation of early American painters goes to Europe to learn and to teach: West, Copley, Gilbert Stuart and others. Allston, Trumbull, Morse; also contemporary American painters—primitives, derivatives, academics—who remained in America. 102 illustrations. xiii + 306pp.
22179-2 Paperbound $3.50

A HISTORY OF THE RISE AND PROGRESS OF THE ARTS OF DESIGN IN THE UNITED STATES, William Dunlap. Much the richest mine of information on early American painters, sculptors, architects, engravers, miniaturists, etc. The only source of information for scores of artists, the major primary source for many others. Unabridged reprint of rare original 1834 edition, with new introduction by James T. Flexner, and 394 new illustrations. Edited by Rita Weiss. 6⅝ x 9⅝.
21695-0, 21696-9, 21697-7 Three volumes, Paperbound $15.00

EPOCHS OF CHINESE AND JAPANESE ART, Ernest F. Fenollosa. From primitive Chinese art to the 20th century, thorough history, explanation of every important art period and form, including Japanese woodcuts; main stress on China and Japan, but Tibet, Korea also included. Still unexcelled for its detailed, rich coverage of cultural background, aesthetic elements, diffusion studies, particularly of the historical period. 2nd, 1913 edition. 242 illustrations. lii + 439pp. of text.
20364-6, 20365-4 Two volumes, Paperbound $6.00

THE GENTLE ART OF MAKING ENEMIES, James A. M. Whistler. Greatest wit of his day deflates Oscar Wilde, Ruskin, Swinburne; strikes back at inane critics, exhibitions, art journalism; aesthetics of impressionist revolution in most striking form. Highly readable classic by great painter. Reproduction of edition designed by Whistler. Introduction by Alfred Werner. xxxvi + 334pp.
21875-9 Paperbound $3.00

VISUAL ILLUSIONS: THEIR CAUSES, CHARACTERISTICS, AND APPLICATIONS, Matthew Luckiesh. Thorough description and discussion of optical illusion, geometric and perspective, particularly; size and shape distortions, illusions of color, of motion; natural illusions; use of illusion in art and magic, industry, etc. Most useful today with op art, also for classical art. Scores of effects illustrated. Introduction by William H. Ittleson. 100 illustrations. xxi + 252pp.

21530-X Paperbound $2.00

A HANDBOOK OF ANATOMY FOR ART STUDENTS, Arthur Thomson. Thorough, virtually exhaustive coverage of skeletal structure, musculature, etc. Full text, supplemented by anatomical diagrams and drawings and by photographs of undraped figures. Unique in its comparison of male and female forms, pointing out differences of contour, texture, form. 211 figures, 40 drawings, 86 photographs. xx + 459pp. 5⅜ x 8⅜.

21163-0 Paperbound $3.50

150 MASTERPIECES OF DRAWING, Selected by Anthony Toney. Full page reproductions of drawings from the early 16th to the end of the 18th century, all beautifully reproduced: Rembrandt, Michelangelo, Dürer, Fragonard, Urs, Graf, Wouwerman, many others. First-rate browsing book, model book for artists. xviii + 150pp. 8⅜ x 11¼.

21032-4 Paperbound' $3.50

THE LATER WORK OF AUBREY BEARDSLEY, Aubrey Beardsley. Exotic, erotic, ironic masterpieces in full maturity: Comedy Ballet, Venus and Tannhauser, Pierrot, Lysistrata, Rape of the Lock, Savoy material, Ali Baba, Volpone, etc. This material revolutionized the art world, and is still powerful, fresh, brilliant. With *The Early Work,* all Beardsley's finest work. 174 plates, 2 in color. xiv + 176pp. 8⅛ x 11.

21817-1 Paperbound $3.75

DRAWINGS OF REMBRANDT, Rembrandt van Rijn. Complete reproduction of fabulously rare edition by Lippmann and Hofstede de Groot, completely reedited, updated, improved by Prof. Seymour Slive, Fogg Museum. Portraits, Biblical sketches, landscapes, Oriental types, nudes, episodes from classical mythology—All Rembrandt's fertile genius. Also selection of drawings by his pupils and followers. "Stunning volumes," *Saturday Review.* 550 illustrations. lxxviii + 552pp. 9⅛ x 12¼.

21485-0, 21486-9 Two volumes, Paperbound $10.00

THE DISASTERS OF WAR, Francisco Goya. One of the masterpieces of Western civilization—83 etchings that record Goya's shattering, bitter reaction to the Napoleonic war that swept through Spain after the insurrection of 1808 and to war in general. Reprint of the first edition, with three additional plates from Boston's Museum of Fine Arts. All plates facsimile size. Introduction by Philip Hofer, Fogg Museum. v + 97pp. 9⅜ x 8¼.

21872-4 Paperbound $2.50

GRAPHIC WORKS OF ODILON REDON. Largest collection of Redon's graphic works ever assembled: 172 lithographs, 28 etchings and engravings, 9 drawings. These include some of his most famous works. All the plates from *Odilon Redon: oeuvre graphique complet,* plus additional plates. New introduction and caption translations by Alfred Werner. 209 illustrations. xxvii + 209pp. 9⅛ x 12¼.

21966-8 Paperbound $5.00

DESIGN BY ACCIDENT; A BOOK OF "ACCIDENTAL EFFECTS" FOR ARTISTS AND DESIGNERS, James F. O'Brien. Create your own unique, striking, imaginative effects by "controlled accident" interaction of materials: paints and lacquers, oil and water based paints, splatter, crackling materials, shatter, similar items. Everything you do will be different; first book on this limitless art, so useful to both fine artist and commercial artist. Full instructions. 192 plates showing "accidents," 8 in color. viii + 215pp. 8⅜ x 11¼. 21942-9 Paperbound $3.75

THE BOOK OF SIGNS, Rudolf Koch. Famed German type designer draws 493 beautiful symbols: religious, mystical, alchemical, imperial, property marks, runes, etc. Remarkable fusion of traditional and modern. Good for suggestions of timelessness, smartness, modernity. Text. vi + 104pp. 6⅛ x 9¼. 20162-7 Paperbound $1.25

HISTORY OF INDIAN AND INDONESIAN ART, Ananda K. Coomaraswamy. An unabridged republication of one of the finest books by a great scholar in Eastern art. Rich in descriptive material, history, social backgrounds; Sunga reliefs, Rajput paintings, Gupta temples, Burmese frescoes, textiles, jewelry, sculpture, etc. 400 photos. viii + 423pp. 6⅜ x 9¾. 21436-2 Paperbound $5.00

PRIMITIVE ART, Franz Boas. America's foremost anthropologist surveys textiles, ceramics, woodcarving, basketry, metalwork, etc.; patterns, technology, creation of symbols, style origins. All areas of world, but very full on Northwest Coast Indians. More than 350 illustrations of baskets, boxes, totem poles, weapons, etc. 378 pp. 20025-6 Paperbound $3.00

THE GENTLEMAN AND CABINET MAKER'S DIRECTOR, Thomas Chippendale. Full reprint (third edition, 1762) of most influential furniture book of all time, by master cabinetmaker. 200 plates, illustrating chairs, sofas, mirrors, tables, cabinets, plus 24 photographs of surviving pieces. Biographical introduction by N. Bienenstock. vi + 249pp. 9⅞ x 12¾. 21601-2 Paperbound $4.00

AMERICAN ANTIQUE FURNITURE, Edgar G. Miller, Jr. The basic coverage of all American furniture before 1840. Individual chapters cover type of furniture—clocks, tables, sideboards, etc.—chronologically, with inexhaustible wealth of data. More than 2100 photographs, all identified, commented on. Essential to all early American collectors. Introduction by H. E. Keyes. vi + 1106pp. 7⅞ x 10¾. 21599-7, 21600-4 Two volumes, Paperbound $11.00

PENNSYLVANIA DUTCH AMERICAN FOLK ART, Henry J. Kauffman. 279 photos, 28 drawings of tulipware, Fraktur script, painted tinware, toys, flowered furniture, quilts, samplers, hex signs, house interiors, etc. Full descriptive text. Excellent for tourist, rewarding for designer, collector. Map. 146pp. 7⅞ x 10¾. 21205-X Paperbound $2.50

EARLY NEW ENGLAND GRAVESTONE RUBBINGS, Edmund V. Gillon, Jr. 43 photographs, 226 carefully reproduced rubbings show heavily symbolic, sometimes macabre early gravestones, up to early 19th century. Remarkable early American primitive art, occasionally strikingly beautiful; always powerful. Text. xxvi + 207pp. 8⅜ x 11¼. 21380-3 Paperbound $3.50

ALPHABETS AND ORNAMENTS, Ernst Lehner. Well-known pictorial source for decorative alphabets, script examples, cartouches, frames, decorative title pages, calligraphic initials, borders, similar material. 14th to 19th century, mostly European. Useful in almost any graphic arts designing, varied styles. 750 illustrations. 256pp. 7 x 10.
21905-4 Paperbound $4.00

PAINTING: A CREATIVE APPROACH, Norman Colquhoun. For the beginner simple guide provides an instructive approach to painting: major stumbling blocks for beginner; overcoming them, technical points; paints and pigments; oil painting; watercolor and other media and color. New section on "plastic" paints. Glossary. Formerly *Paint Your Own Pictures*. 221pp.
22000-1 Paperbound $1.75

THE ENJOYMENT AND USE OF COLOR, Walter Sargent. Explanation of the relations between colors themselves and between colors in nature and art, including hundreds of little-known facts about color values, intensities, effects of high and low illumination, complementary colors. Many practical hints for painters, references to great masters. 7 color plates, 29 illustrations. x + 274pp.
20944-X Paperbound $2.75

THE NOTEBOOKS OF LEONARDO DA VINCI, compiled and edited by Jean Paul Richter. 1566 extracts from original manuscripts reveal the full range of Leonardo's versatile genius: all his writings on painting, sculpture, architecture, anatomy, astronomy, geography, topography, physiology, mining, music, etc., in both Italian and English, with 186 plates of manuscript pages and more than 500 additional drawings. Includes studies for the Last Supper, the lost Sforza monument, and other works. Total of xlvii + 866pp. 7⅞ x 10¾.
22572-0, 22573-9 Two volumes, Paperbound $11.00

MONTGOMERY WARD CATALOGUE OF 1895. Tea gowns, yards of flannel and pillow-case lace, stereoscopes, books of gospel hymns, the New Improved Singer Sewing Machine, side saddles, milk skimmers, straight-edged razors, high-button shoes, spittoons, and on and on . . . listing some 25,000 items, practically all illustrated. Essential to the shoppers of the 1890's, it is our truest record of the spirit of the period. Unaltered reprint of Issue No. 57, Spring and Summer 1895. Introduction by Boris Emmet. Innumerable illustrations. xiii + 624pp. 8½ x 11⅝.
22377-9 Paperbound $6.95

THE CRYSTAL PALACE EXHIBITION ILLUSTRATED CATALOGUE (LONDON, 1851). One of the wonders of the modern world—the Crystal Palace Exhibition in which all the nations of the civilized world exhibited their achievements in the arts and sciences—presented in an equally important illustrated catalogue. More than 1700 items pictured with accompanying text—ceramics, textiles, cast-iron work, carpets, pianos, sleds, razors, wall-papers, billiard tables, beehives, silverware and hundreds of other artifacts—represent the focal point of Victorian culture in the Western World. Probably the largest collection of Victorian decorative art ever assembled— indispensable for antiquarians and designers. Unabridged republication of the Art-Journal Catalogue of the Great Exhibition of 1851, with all terminal essays. New introduction by John Gloag, F.S.A. xxxiv + 426pp. 9 x 12.
22503-8 Paperbound $5.00

A HISTORY OF COSTUME, Carl Köhler. Definitive history, based on surviving pieces of clothing primarily, and paintings, statues, etc. secondarily. Highly readable text, supplemented by 594 illustrations of costumes of the ancient Mediterranean peoples, Greece and Rome, the Teutonic prehistoric period; costumes of the Middle Ages, Renaissance, Baroque, 18th and 19th centuries. Clear, measured patterns are provided for many clothing articles. Approach is practical throughout. Enlarged by Emma von Sichart. 464pp. 21030-8 Paperbound $3.50

ORIENTAL RUGS, ANTIQUE AND MODERN, Walter A. Hawley. A complete and authoritative treatise on the Oriental rug—where they are made, by whom and how, designs and symbols, characteristics in detail of the six major groups, how to distinguish them and how to buy them. Detailed technical data is provided on periods, weaves, warps, wefts, textures, sides, ends and knots, although no technical background is required for an understanding. 11 color plates, 80 halftones, 4 maps. vi + 320pp. 6⅛ x 9⅛. 22366-3 Paperbound $5.00

TEN BOOKS ON ARCHITECTURE, Vitruvius. By any standards the most important book on architecture ever written. Early Roman discussion of aesthetics of building, construction methods, orders, sites, and every other aspect of architecture has inspired, instructed architecture for about 2,000 years. Stands behind Palladio, Michelangelo, Bramante, Wren, countless others. Definitive Morris H. Morgan translation. 68 illustrations. xii + 331pp. 20645-9 Paperbound $3.00

THE FOUR BOOKS OF ARCHITECTURE, Andrea Palladio. Translated into every major Western European language in the two centuries following its publication in 1570, this has been one of the most influential books in the history of architecture. Complete reprint of the 1738 Isaac Ware edition. New introduction by Adolf Placzek, Columbia Univ. 216 plates. xxii + 110pp. of text. 9½ x 12¾. 21308-0 Clothbound $12.50

STICKS AND STONES: A STUDY OF AMERICAN ARCHITECTURE AND CIVILIZATION, Lewis Mumford.One of the great classics of American cultural history. American architecture from the medieval-inspired earliest forms to the early 20th century; evolution of structure and style, and reciprocal influences on environment. 21 photographic illustrations. 238pp. 20202-X Paperbound $2.00

THE AMERICAN BUILDER'S COMPANION, Asher Benjamin. The most widely used early 19th century architectural style and source book, for colonial up into Greek Revival periods. Extensive development of geometry of carpentering, construction of sashes, frames, doors, stairs; plans and elevations of domestic and other buildings. Hundreds of thousands of houses were built according to this book, now invaluable to historians, architects, restorers, etc. 1827 edition. 59 plates. 114pp. 7⅞ x 10¾. 22236-5 Paperbound $3.50

DUTCH HOUSES IN THE HUDSON VALLEY BEFORE 1776, Helen Wilkinson Reynolds. The standard survey of the Dutch colonial house and outbuildings, with constructional features, decoration, and local history associated with individual homesteads. Introduction by Franklin D. Roosevelt. Map. 150 illustrations. 469pp. 6⅝ x 9¼. 21469-9 Paperbound $5.00

THE ARCHITECTURE OF COUNTRY HOUSES, Andrew J. Downing. Together with Vaux's *Villas and Cottages* this is the basic book for Hudson River Gothic architecture of the middle Victorian period. Full, sound discussions of general aspects of housing, architecture, style, decoration, furnishing, together with scores of detailed house plans, illustrations of specific buildings, accompanied by full text. Perhaps the most influential single American architectural book. 1850 edition. Introduction by J. Stewart Johnson. 321 figures, 34 architectural designs. xvi + 560pp.
22003-6 Paperbound $4.00

LOST EXAMPLES OF COLONIAL ARCHITECTURE, John Mead Howells. Full-page photographs of buildings that have disappeared or been so altered as to be denatured, including many designed by major early American architects. 245 plates. xvii + 248pp. 7⅞ x 10¾.
21143-6 Paperbound $3.50

DOMESTIC ARCHITECTURE OF THE AMERICAN COLONIES AND OF THE EARLY REPUBLIC, Fiske Kimball. Foremost architect and restorer of Williamsburg and Monticello covers nearly 200 homes between 1620-1825. Architectural details, construction, style features, special fixtures, floor plans, etc. Generally considered finest work in its area. 219 illustrations of houses, doorways, windows, capital mantels. xx + 314pp. 7⅞ x 10¾.
21743-4 Paperbound $4.00

EARLY AMERICAN ROOMS: 1650-1858, edited by Russell Hawes Kettell. Tour of 12 rooms, each representative of a different era in American history and each furnished, decorated, designed and occupied in the style of the era. 72 plans and elevations, 8-page color section, etc., show fabrics, wall papers, arrangements, etc. Full descriptive text. xvii + 200pp. of text. 8⅜ x 11¼.
21633-0 Paperbound $5.00

THE FITZWILLIAM VIRGINAL BOOK, edited by J. Fuller Maitland and W. B. Squire. Full modern printing of famous early 17th-century ms. volume of 300 works by Morley, Byrd, Bull, Gibbons, etc. For piano or other modern keyboard instrument; easy to read format. xxxvi + 938pp. 8⅜ x 11.
21068-5, 21069-3 Two volumes, Paperbound $10.00

KEYBOARD MUSIC, Johann Sebastian Bach. Bach Gesellschaft edition. A rich selection of Bach's masterpieces for the harpsichord: the six English Suites, six French Suites, the six Partitas (Clavierübung part I), the Goldberg Variations (Clavierübung part IV), the fifteen Two-Part Inventions and the fifteen Three-Part Sinfonias. Clearly reproduced on large sheets with ample margins; eminently playable. vi + 312pp. 8⅛ x 11.
22360-4 Paperbound $5.00

THE MUSIC OF BACH: AN INTRODUCTION, Charles Sanford Terry. A fine, nontechnical introduction to Bach's music, both instrumental and vocal. Covers organ music, chamber music, passion music, other types. Analyzes themes, developments, innovations. x + 114pp.
21075-8 Paperbound $1.50

BEETHOVEN AND HIS NINE SYMPHONIES, Sir George Grove. Noted British musicologist provides best history, analysis, commentary on symphonies. Very thorough, rigorously accurate; necessary to both advanced student and amateur music lover. 436 musical passages. vii + 407 pp.
20334-4 Paperbound $2.75

JOHANN SEBASTIAN BACH, Philipp Spitta. One of the great classics of musicology, this definitive analysis of Bach's music (and life) has never been surpassed. Lucid, nontechnical analyses of hundreds of pieces (30 pages devoted to St. Matthew Passion, 26 to B Minor Mass). Also includes major analysis of 18th-century music. 450 musical examples. 40-page musical supplement. Total of xx + 1799pp.
(EUK) 22278-0, 22279-9 Two volumes, Clothbound $17.50

MOZART AND HIS PIANO CONCERTOS, Cuthbert Girdlestone. The only full-length study of an important area of Mozart's creativity. Provides detailed analyses of all 23 concertos, traces inspirational sources. 417 musical examples. Second edition. 509pp.
21271-8 Paperbound $3.50

THE PERFECT WAGNERITE: A COMMENTARY ON THE NIBLUNG'S RING, George Bernard Shaw. Brilliant and still relevant criticism in remarkable essays on Wagner's Ring cycle, Shaw's ideas on political and social ideology behind the plots, role of Leitmotifs, vocal requisites, etc. Prefaces. xxi + 136pp.
(USO) 21707-8 Paperbound $1.75

DON GIOVANNI, W. A. Mozart. Complete libretto, modern English translation; biographies of composer and librettist; accounts of early performances and critical reaction. Lavishly illustrated. All the material you need to understand and appreciate this great work. Dover Opera Guide and Libretto Series; translated and introduced by Ellen Bleiler. 92 illustrations. 209pp.
21134-7 Paperbound $2.00

BASIC ELECTRICITY, U. S. Bureau of Naval Personel. Originally a training course, best non-technical coverage of basic theory of electricity and its applications. Fundamental concepts, batteries, circuits, conductors and wiring techniques, AC and DC, inductance and capacitance, generators, motors, transformers, magnetic amplifiers, synchros, servomechanisms, etc. Also covers blue-prints, electrical diagrams, etc. Many questions, with answers. 349 illustrations. x + 448pp. 6½ x 9¼.
20973-3 Paperbound $3.50

REPRODUCTION OF SOUND, Edgar Villchur. Thorough coverage for laymen of high fidelity systems, reproducing systems in general, needles, amplifiers, preamps, loudspeakers, feedback, explaining physical background. "A rare talent for making technicalities vividly comprehensible," R. Darrell, *High Fidelity*. 69 figures. iv + 92pp.
21515-6 Paperbound $1.35

HEAR ME TALKIN' TO YA: THE STORY OF JAZZ AS TOLD BY THE MEN WHO MADE IT, Nat Shapiro and Nat Hentoff. Louis Armstrong, Fats Waller, Jo Jones, Clarence Williams, Billy Holiday, Duke Ellington, Jelly Roll Morton and dozens of other jazz greats tell how it was in Chicago's South Side, New Orleans, depression Harlem and the modern West Coast as jazz was born and grew. xvi + 429pp.
21726-4 Paperbound $3.00

FABLES OF AESOP, translated by Sir Roger L'Estrange. A reproduction of the very rare 1931 Paris edition; a selection of the most interesting fables, together with 50 imaginative drawings by Alexander Calder. v + 128pp. 6½x9¼.
21780-9 Paperbound $1.50

AGAINST THE GRAIN (A REBOURS), Joris K. Huysmans. Filled with weird images, evidences of a bizarre imagination, exotic experiments with hallucinatory drugs, rich tastes and smells and the diversions of its sybarite hero Duc Jean des Esseintes, this classic novel pushed 19th-century literary decadence to its limits. Full unabridged edition. Do not confuse this with abridged editions generally sold. Introduction by Havelock Ellis. xlix + 206pp. 22190-3 Paperbound $2.50

VARIORUM SHAKESPEARE: HAMLET. Edited by Horace H. Furness; a landmark of American scholarship. Exhaustive footnotes and appendices treat all doubtful words and phrases, as well as suggested critical emendations throughout the play's history. First volume contains editor's own text, collated with all Quartos and Folios. Second volume contains full first Quarto, translations of Shakespeare's sources (Belleforest, and Saxo Grammaticus), Der Bestrafte Brudermord, and many essays on critical and historical points of interest by major authorities of past and present. Includes details of staging and costuming over the years. By far the best edition available for serious students of Shakespeare. Total of xx + 905pp. 21004-9, 21005-7, 2 volumes, Paperbound $7.00

A LIFE OF WILLIAM SHAKESPEARE, Sir Sidney Lee. This is the standard life of Shakespeare, summarizing everything known about Shakespeare and his plays. Incredibly rich in material, broad in coverage, clear and judicious, it has served thousands as the best introduction to Shakespeare. 1931 edition. 9 plates. xxix + 792pp. 21967-4 Paperbound $4.50

MASTERS OF THE DRAMA, John Gassner. Most comprehensive history of the drama in print, covering every tradition from Greeks to modern Europe and America, including India, Far East, etc. Covers more than 800 dramatists, 2000 plays, with biographical material, plot summaries, theatre history, criticism, etc. "Best of its kind in English," *New Republic*. 77 illustrations. xxii + 890pp. 20100-7 Clothbound $10.00

THE EVOLUTION OF THE ENGLISH LANGUAGE, George McKnight. The growth of English, from the 14th century to the present. Unusual, non-technical account presents basic information in very interesting form: sound shifts, change in grammar and syntax, vocabulary growth, similar topics. Abundantly illustrated with quotations. Formerly *Modern English in the Making*. xii + 590pp. 21932-1 Paperbound $4.00

AN ETYMOLOGICAL DICTIONARY OF MODERN ENGLISH, Ernest Weekley. Fullest, richest work of its sort, by foremost British lexicographer. Detailed word histories, including many colloquial and archaic words; extensive quotations. Do not confuse this with the Concise Etymological Dictionary, which is much abridged. Total of xxvii + 830pp. 6½ x 9¼. 21873-2, 21874-0 Two volumes, Paperbound $7.90

FLATLAND: A ROMANCE OF MANY DIMENSIONS, E. A. Abbott. Classic of science-fiction explores ramifications of life in a two-dimensional world, and what happens when a three-dimensional being intrudes. Amusing reading, but also useful as introduction to thought about hyperspace. Introduction by Banesh Hoffmann. 16 illustrations. xx + 103pp. 20001-9 Paperbound $1.25

POEMS OF ANNE BRADSTREET, edited with an introduction by Robert Hutchinson. A new selection of poems by America's first poet and perhaps the first significant woman poet in the English language. 48 poems display her development in works of considerable variety—love poems, domestic poems, religious meditations, formal elegies, "quaternions," etc. Notes, bibliography. viii + 222pp.

22160-1 Paperbound $2.50

THREE GOTHIC NOVELS: THE CASTLE OF OTRANTO BY HORACE WALPOLE; VATHEK BY WILLIAM BECKFORD; THE VAMPYRE BY JOHN POLIDORI, WITH FRAGMENT OF A NOVEL BY LORD BYRON, edited by E. F. Bleiler. The first Gothic novel, by Walpole; the finest Oriental tale in English, by Beckford; powerful Romantic supernatural story in versions by Polidori and Byron. All extremely important in history of literature; all still exciting, packed with supernatural thrills, ghosts, haunted castles, magic, etc. xl + 291pp.

21232-7 Paperbound $2.50

THE BEST TALES OF HOFFMANN, E. T. A. Hoffmann. 10 of Hoffmann's most important stories, in modern re-editings of standard translations: Nutcracker and the King of Mice, Signor Formica, Automata, The Sandman, Rath Krespel, The Golden Flowerpot, Master Martin the Cooper, The Mines of Falun, The King's Betrothed, A New Year's Eve Adventure. 7 illustrations by Hoffmann. Edited by E. F. Bleiler. xxxix + 419pp. 21793-0 Paperbound $3.00

GHOST AND HORROR STORIES OF AMBROSE BIERCE, Ambrose Bierce. 23 strikingly modern stories of the horrors latent in the human mind: The Eyes of the Panther, The Damned Thing, An Occurrence at Owl Creek Bridge, An Inhabitant of Carcosa, etc., plus the dream-essay, Visions of the Night. Edited by E. F. Bleiler. xxii + 199pp. 20767-6 Paperbound $1.50

BEST GHOST STORIES OF J. S. LEFANU, J. Sheridan LeFanu. Finest stories by Victorian master often considered greatest supernatural writer of all. Carmilla, Green Tea, The Haunted Baronet, The Familiar, and 12 others. Most never before available in the U. S. A. Edited by E. F. Bleiler. 8 illustrations from Victorian publications. xvii + 467pp. 20415-4 Paperbound $3.00

MATHEMATICAL FOUNDATIONS OF INFORMATION THEORY, A. I. Khinchin. Comprehensive introduction to work of Shannon, McMillan, Feinstein and Khinchin, placing these investigations on a rigorous mathematical basis. Covers entropy concept in probability theory, uniqueness theorem, Shannon's inequality, ergodic sources, the E property, martingale concept, noise, Feinstein's fundamental lemma, Shanon's first and second theorems. Translated by R. A. Silverman and M. D. Friedman. iii + 120pp. 60434-9 Paperbound $2.00

SEVEN SCIENCE FICTION NOVELS, H. G. Wells. The standard collection of the great novels. Complete, unabridged. *First Men in the Moon, Island of Dr. Moreau, War of the Worlds, Food of the Gods, Invisible Man, Time Machine, In the Days of the Comet.* Not only science fiction fans, but every educated person owes it to himself to read these novels. 1015pp. (USO) 20264-X Clothbound $6.00

LAST AND FIRST MEN AND STAR MAKER, TWO SCIENCE FICTION NOVELS, Olaf Stapledon. Greatest future histories in science fiction. In the first, human intelligence is the "hero," through strange paths of evolution, interplanetary invasions, incredible technologies, near extinctions and reemergences. Star Maker describes the quest of a band of star rovers for intelligence itself, through time and space: weird inhuman civilizations, crustacean minds, symbiotic worlds, etc. Complete, unabridged. v + 438pp. (USO) 21962-3 Paperbound $2.50

THREE PROPHETIC NOVELS, H. G. WELLS. Stages of a consistently planned future for mankind. *When the Sleeper Wakes,* and *A Story of the Days to Come,* anticipate *Brave New World* and *1984,* in the 21st Century; *The Time Machine,* only complete version in print, shows farther future and the end of mankind. All show Wells's greatest gifts as storyteller and novelist. Edited by E. F. Bleiler. x + 335pp. (USO) 20605-X Paperbound $2.50

THE DEVIL'S DICTIONARY, Ambrose Bierce. America's own Oscar Wilde—Ambrose Bierce—offers his barbed iconoclastic wisdom in over 1,000 definitions hailed by H. L. Mencken as "some of the most gorgeous witticisms in the English language." 145pp. 20487-1 Paperbound $1.25

MAX AND MORITZ, Wilhelm Busch. Great children's classic, father of comic strip, of two bad boys, Max and Moritz. Also Ker and Plunk (Plisch und Plumm), Cat and Mouse, Deceitful Henry, Ice-Peter, The Boy and the Pipe, and five other pieces. Original German, with English translation. Edited by H. Arthur Klein; translations by various hands and H. Arthur Klein. vi + 216pp. 20181-3 Paperbound $2.00

PIGS IS PIGS AND OTHER FAVORITES, Ellis Parker Butler. The title story is one of the best humor short stories, as Mike Flannery obfuscates biology and English. Also included, That Pup of Murchison's, The Great American Pie Company, and Perkins of Portland. 14 illustrations. v + 109pp. 21532-6 Paperbound $1.25

THE PETERKIN PAPERS, Lucretia P. Hale. It takes genius to be as stupidly mad as the Peterkins, as they decide to become wise, celebrate the "Fourth," keep a cow, and otherwise strain the resources of the Lady from Philadelphia. Basic book of American humor. 153 illustrations. 219pp. 20794-3 Paperbound $2.00

PERRAULT'S FAIRY TALES, translated by A. E. Johnson and S. R. Littlewood, with 34 full-page illustrations by Gustave Doré. All the original Perrault stories—Cinderella, Sleeping Beauty, Bluebeard, Little Red Riding Hood, Puss in Boots, Tom Thumb, etc.—with their witty verse morals and the magnificent illustrations of Doré. One of the five or six great books of European fairy tales. viii + 117pp. 8⅛ x 11. 22311-6 Paperbound $2.00

OLD HUNGARIAN FAIRY TALES, Baroness Orczy. Favorites translated and adapted by author of the *Scarlet Pimpernel.* Eight fairy tales include "The Suitors of Princess Fire-Fly," "The Twin Hunchbacks," "Mr. Cuttlefish's Love Story," and "The Enchanted Cat." This little volume of magic and adventure will captivate children as it has for generations. 90 drawings by Montagu Barstow. 96pp. (USO) 22293-4 Paperbound $1.95

THE RED FAIRY BOOK, Andrew Lang. Lang's color fairy books have long been children's favorites. This volume includes Rapunzel, Jack and the Bean-stalk and 35 other stories, familiar and unfamiliar. 4 plates, 93 illustrations x + 367pp.
21673-X Paperbound $2.50

THE BLUE FAIRY BOOK, Andrew Lang. Lang's tales come from all countries and all times. Here are 37 tales from Grimm, the Arabian Nights, Greek Mythology, and other fascinating sources. 8 plates, 130 illustrations. xi + 390pp.
21437-0 Paperbound $2.75

HOUSEHOLD STORIES BY THE BROTHERS GRIMM. Classic English-language edition of the well-known tales — Rumpelstiltskin, Snow White, Hansel and Gretel, The Twelve Brothers, Faithful John, Rapunzel, Tom Thumb (52 stories in all). Translated into simple, straightforward English by Lucy Crane. Ornamented with headpieces, vignettes, elaborate decorative initials and a dozen full-page illustrations by Walter Crane. x + 269pp.
21080-4 Paperbound **$2.00**

THE MERRY ADVENTURES OF ROBIN HOOD, Howard Pyle. The finest modern versions of the traditional ballads and tales about the great English outlaw. Howard Pyle's complete prose version, with every word, every illustration of the first edition. Do not confuse this facsimile of the original (1883) with modern editions that change text or illustrations. 23 plates plus many page decorations. xxii + 296pp.
22043-5 Paperbound $2.75

THE STORY OF KING ARTHUR AND HIS KNIGHTS, Howard Pyle. The finest children's version of the life of King Arthur; brilliantly retold by Pyle, with 48 of his most imaginative illustrations. xviii + 313pp. 6⅛ x 9¼.
21445-1 Paperbound $2.50

THE WONDERFUL WIZARD OF OZ, L. Frank Baum. America's finest children's book in facsimile of first edition with all Denslow illustrations in full color. The edition a child should have. Introduction by Martin Gardner. 23 color plates, scores of drawings. iv + 267pp.
20691-2 Paperbound **$2.50**

THE MARVELOUS LAND OF OZ, L. Frank Baum. The second Oz book, every bit as imaginative as the Wizard. The hero is a boy named Tip, but the Scarecrow and the Tin Woodman are back, as is the Oz magic. 16 color plates, 120 drawings by John R. Neill. 287pp.
20692-0 Paperbound $2.50

THE MAGICAL MONARCH OF MO, L. Frank Baum. Remarkable adventures in a land even stranger than Oz. The best of Baum's books not in the Oz series. 15 color plates and dozens of drawings by Frank Verbeck. xviii + 237pp.
21892-9 Paperbound $2.25

THE BAD CHILD'S BOOK OF BEASTS, MORE BEASTS FOR WORSE CHILDREN, A MORAL ALPHABET, Hilaire Belloc. Three complete humor classics in one volume. Be kind to the frog, and do not call him names . . . and 28 other whimsical animals. Familiar favorites and some not so well known. Illustrated by Basil Blackwell. 156pp.
(USO) 20749-8 Paperbound $1.50

EAST O' THE SUN AND WEST O' THE MOON, George W. Dasent. Considered the best of all translations of these Norwegian folk tales, this collection has been enjoyed by generations of children (and folklorists too). Includes True and Untrue, Why the Sea is Salt, East O' the Sun and West O' the Moon, Why the Bear is Stumpy-Tailed, Boots and the Troll, The Cock and the Hen, Rich Peter the Pedlar, and 52 more. The only edition with all 59 tales. 77 illustrations by Erik Werenskiold and Theodor Kittelsen. xv + 418pp.   22521-6 Paperbound $3.50

GOOPS AND HOW TO BE THEM, Gelett Burgess. Classic of tongue-in-cheek humor, masquerading as etiquette book. 87 verses, twice as many cartoons, show mischievous Goops as they demonstrate to children virtues of table manners, neatness, courtesy, etc. Favorite for generations. viii + 88pp. 6½ x 9¼.
                    22233-0 Paperbound $1.50

ALICE'S ADVENTURES UNDER GROUND, Lewis Carroll. The first version, quite different from the final *Alice in Wonderland,* printed out by Carroll himself with his own illustrations. Complete facsimile of the "million dollar" manuscript Carroll gave to Alice Liddell in 1864. Introduction by Martin Gardner. viii + 96pp. Title and dedication pages in color.   21482-6 Paperbound $1.25

THE BROWNIES, THEIR BOOK, Palmer Cox. Small as mice, cunning as foxes, exuberant and full of mischief, the Brownies go to the zoo, toy shop, seashore, circus, etc., in 24 verse adventures and 266 illustrations. Long a favorite, since their first appearance in St. Nicholas Magazine. xi + 144pp. 6⅝ x 9¼.
                    21265-3 Paperbound $1.75

SONGS OF CHILDHOOD, Walter De La Mare. Published (under the pseudonym Walter Ramal) when De La Mare was only 29, this charming collection has long been a favorite children's book. A facsimile of the first edition in paper, the 47 poems capture the simplicity of the nursery rhyme and the ballad, including such lyrics as I Met Eve, Tartary, The Silver Penny. vii + 106pp. (USO) 21972-0 Paperbound
                    $2.00

THE COMPLETE NONSENSE OF EDWARD LEAR, Edward Lear. The finest 19th-century humorist-cartoonist in full: all nonsense limericks, zany alphabets, Owl and Pussycat, songs, nonsense botany, and more than 500 illustrations by Lear himself. Edited by Holbrook Jackson. xxix + 287pp.   (USO) 20167-8 Paperbound $2.00

BILLY WHISKERS: THE AUTOBIOGRAPHY OF A GOAT, Frances Trego Montgomery. A favorite of children since the early 20th century, here are the escapades of that rambunctious, irresistible and mischievous goat—Billy Whiskers. Much in the spirit of *Peck's Bad Boy,* this is a book that children never tire of reading or hearing. All the original familiar illustrations by W. H. Fry are included: 6 color plates, 18 black and white drawings. 159pp.   22345-0 Paperbound $2.00

MOTHER GOOSE MELODIES. Faithful republication of the fabulously rare Munroe and Francis "copyright 1833" Boston edition—the most important Mother Goose collection, usually referred to as the "original." Familiar rhymes plus many rare ones, with wonderful old woodcut illustrations. Edited by E. F. Bleiler. 128pp. 4½ x 6⅜.   22577-1 Paperbound $1.00

TWO LITTLE SAVAGES; BEING THE ADVENTURES OF TWO BOYS WHO LIVED AS INDIANS AND WHAT THEY LEARNED, Ernest Thompson Seton. Great classic of nature and boyhood provides a vast range of woodlore in most palatable form, a genuinely entertaining story. Two farm boys build a teepee in woods and live in it for a month, working out Indian solutions to living problems, star lore, birds and animals, plants, etc. 293 illustrations. vii + 286pp.

20985-7 Paperbound $2.50

PETER PIPER'S PRACTICAL PRINCIPLES OF PLAIN & PERFECT PRONUNCIATION. Alliterative jingles and tongue-twisters of surprising charm, that made their first appearance in America about 1830. Republished in full with the spirited woodcut illustrations from this earliest American edition. 32pp. $4\frac{1}{2}$ x $6\frac{3}{8}$.

22560-7 Paperbound $1.00

SCIENCE EXPERIMENTS AND AMUSEMENTS FOR CHILDREN, Charles Vivian. 73 easy experiments, requiring only materials found at home or easily available, such as candles, coins, steel wool, etc.; illustrate basic phenomena like vacuum, simple chemical reaction, etc. All safe. Modern, well-planned. Formerly *Science Games for Children*. 102 photos, numerous drawings. 96pp. $6\frac{1}{8}$ x $9\frac{1}{4}$.

21856-2 Paperbound $1.25

AN INTRODUCTION TO CHESS MOVES AND TACTICS SIMPLY EXPLAINED, Leonard Barden. Informal intermediate introduction, quite strong in explaining reasons for moves. Covers basic material, tactics, important openings, traps, positional play in middle game, end game. Attempts to isolate patterns and recurrent configurations. Formerly *Chess*. 58 figures. 102pp. (USO) 21210-6 Paperbound $1.25

LASKER'S MANUAL OF CHESS, Dr. Emanuel Lasker. Lasker was not only one of the five great World Champions, he was also one of the ablest expositors, theorists, and analysts. In many ways, his Manual, permeated with his philosophy of battle, filled with keen insights, is one of the greatest works ever written on chess. Filled with analyzed games by the great players. A single-volume library that will profit almost any chess player, beginner or master. 308 diagrams. xli x 349pp.

20640-8 Paperbound $2.75

THE MASTER BOOK OF MATHEMATICAL RECREATIONS, Fred Schuh. In opinion of many the finest work ever prepared on mathematical puzzles, stunts, recreations; exhaustively thorough explanations of mathematics involved, analysis of effects, citation of puzzles and games. Mathematics involved is elementary. Translated by F. Göbel. 194 figures. xxiv + 430pp. 22134-2 Paperbound $3.50

MATHEMATICS, MAGIC AND MYSTERY, Martin Gardner. Puzzle editor for Scientific American explains mathematics behind various mystifying tricks: card tricks, stage "mind reading," coin and match tricks, counting out games, geometric dissections, etc. Probability sets, theory of numbers clearly explained. Also provides more than 400 tricks, guaranteed to work, that you can do. 135 illustrations. xii + 176pp.

20335-2 Paperbound $1.75

MATHEMATICAL PUZZLES FOR BEGINNERS AND ENTHUSIASTS, Geoffrey Mott-Smith. 189 puzzles from easy to difficult—involving arithmetic, logic, algebra, properties of digits, probability, etc.—for enjoyment and mental stimulus. Explanation of mathematical principles behind the puzzles. 135 illustrations. viii + 248pp.
20198-8 Paperbound $1.75

PAPER FOLDING FOR BEGINNERS, William D. Murray and Francis J. Rigney. Easiest book on the market, clearest instructions on making interesting, beautiful origami. Sail boats, cups, roosters, frogs that move legs, bonbon boxes, standing birds, etc. 40 projects; more than 275 diagrams and photographs. 94pp.
20713-7 Paperbound $1.00

TRICKS AND GAMES ON THE POOL TABLE, Fred Herrmann. 79 tricks and games—some solitaires, some for two or more players, some competitive games—to entertain you between formal games. Mystifying shots and throws, unusual caroms, tricks involving such props as cork, coins, a hat, etc. Formerly *Fun on the Pool Table.* 77 figures. 95pp.
21814-7 Paperbound $1.25

HAND SHADOWS TO BE THROWN UPON THE WALL: A SERIES OF NOVEL AND AMUSING FIGURES FORMED BY THE HAND, Henry Bursill. Delightful picturebook from great-grandfather's day shows how to make 18 different hand shadows: a bird that flies, duck that quacks, dog that wags his tail, camel, goose, deer, boy, turtle, etc. Only book of its sort. vi + 33pp. 6½ x 9¼.
21779-5 Paperbound $1.00

WHITTLING AND WOODCARVING, E. J. Tangerman. 18th printing of best book on market. "If you can cut a potato you can carve" toys and puzzles, chains, chessmen, caricatures, masks, frames, woodcut blocks, surface patterns, much more. Information on tools, woods, techniques. Also goes into serious wood sculpture from Middle Ages to present, East and West. 464 photos, figures. x + 293pp.
20965-2 Paperbound $2.00

HISTORY OF PHILOSOPHY, Julián Marias. Possibly the clearest, most easily followed, best planned, most useful one-volume history of philosophy on the market; neither skimpy nor overfull. Full details on system of every major philosopher and dozens of less important thinkers from pre-Socratics up to Existentialism and later. Strong on many European figures usually omitted. Has gone through dozens of editions in Europe. 1966 edition, translated by Stanley Appelbaum and Clarence Strowbridge. xviii + 505pp.
21739-6 Paperbound $3.50

YOGA: A SCIENTIFIC EVALUATION, Kovoor T. Behanan. Scientific but non-technical study of physiological results of yoga exercises; done under auspices of Yale U. Relations to Indian thought, to psychoanalysis, etc. 16 photos. xxiii + 270pp.
20505-3 Paperbound $2.50

Prices subject to change without notice.
Available at your book dealer or write for free catalogue to Dept. GI, Dover Publications, Inc., 180 Varick St., N. Y., N. Y. 10014. Dover publishes more than 150 books each year on science, elementary and advanced mathematics, biology, music, art, literary history, social sciences and other areas.